Springer Series in Language and Communication 23

Editor: W. J. M. Levelt

Springer Series in Language and Communication

Editor: W. J. M. Levelt

Roger Säljö (Ed.)

The Written World

Studies in Literate Thought
and Action

Springer-Verlag
Berlin Heidelberg New York
London Paris Tokyo

Professor Dr. ROGER SÄLJÖ
Linköping University
Department of Communication Studies
581 83 Linköping, Sweden

Series Editor
Professor Dr. WILLEM J. M. LEVELT
Max-Planck-Institut für Psycholinguistik
Wundtlaan 1
6525 XD Nijmegen, The Netherlands

With 7 Figures

ISBN 3-540-18145-8 Springer-Verlag Berlin Heidelberg New York
ISBN 0-387-18145-8 Springer-Verlag New York Berlin Heidelberg

Library of Congress Cataloging-in-Publication Data. The Written world : studies in literate thought and action / Roger Säljö, ed. p. cm.–(Springer series in language and communication ; 23). Bibliography: p. Includes indexes. ISBN 0-387-18145-8 (U.S.) 1. Written communication. 2. Literacy. I. Säljö, Roger, 1948-. II. Series. P211.W745 1988 001.54'3–dc 19 88-4942 CIP

© Springer-Verlag Berlin Heidelberg 1988
Printed in Germany

The use of registered names, trademarks, etc. in this publication does not imply, even in the absence of a specific statement, that such names are exempt from the relevant protective laws and regulations and therefore free for general use.

Product Liability: The publishers can give no guarantee for information about drug dosage and application thereof contained in this book. In every individual case the respective user must check its accuracy by consulting other pharmaceutical literature.

Media conversion and printing: Druckhaus Beltz, Hemsbach/Bergstr.
Bookbinding: Konrad Triltsch, Graphischer Betrieb, Würzburg
2126/3130-543210 – Printed on acid-free paper

Preface

The chapters of this volume were originally contributions presented at a seminar entitled "The Written Code and Conceptions of Reality" held on the island of Sydkoster in August, 1985. The seminar was financed by a grant to the editor from The Swedish Council for Research in the Humanities and Social Sciences.

The word-processing of manuscripts was carried out by Christine Aranda, Maria Axelson, Marianne Axelson and Lotta Strand, who carried the major burden. Their help in this project, as well as in many other common concerns, is deeply appreciated. The preparation of a book that is a collective enterprise is, in some respects, greatly facilitated by modern word-processing. When it comes to putting together the final product, however, the limitations of technologies are easily recognized as a result of the complications that arise from the variation in systems used by contributors. Lotta Strand was responsible for the coordination necessary for completing the final version of the manuscript. Without her patient efforts and skills in this new type of literacy, word-processing technology would have been an obstacle rather than an asset.

Excellent bibliographic assistance was provided by Christina Brage, Lennart Eriksson and Inger Karlsson of the library at the Departments of Theme Studies of the University Library of Linköping. Linguistic advice on the chapters written by contributors who were not wise enough to be born with English as their mother tongue was given by Alex de Courcy.

The preparation and publication of this book has been made possible through financial assistance from The Swedish Council for Research in the Humanities and Social Sciences.

Considerable support and encouragement to the editor have been consistently provided by Lena, Björn and Karin.

ROGER SÄLJÖ

Contents

List of Contributors

Aronsson, Karin, Department of Communication Studies,
Linköping University, S-581 83 Linköping, Sweden

Francis, Hazel, Department of Child Development and Educational
Psychology, University of London, 24–27 Woburn Square,
London WC 1H 0AA, Great Britain

Hounsell, Dai, Centre for Teaching, Learning & Assessment,
57 George Square, Edinburgh EH8 9JU, Scotland

Larsen, Steen Folke, Department of Psychology, University of
Aarhus, Asylvej 4, DK-8240 Risskov, Denmark

Lian, Arild, Department of Psychology, University of Oslo,
Boks 1094, Blindern, Oslo 3, Norway

Linell, Per, Department of Communication Studies, Linköping
University, S-581 83 Linköping, Sweden

Olson, David R., Ontario Institute for Studies in Education,
252, Bloor Street W, Toronto M5S IV6, Ontario, Canada

Pramling, Ingrid, Department of Education, University of Göteborg,
Box 1010, S-431 26 Mölndal, Sweden

Rommetveit, Ragnar, Department of Psychology, University of
Oslo, Boks 1094, Blindern, Oslo 3, Norway

Säljö, Roger, Department of Communication Studies, Linköping
University, S-581 83 Linköping, Sweden

Street, Brian V., School of Social Sciences, The University of Sussex,
Arts Building, Falmer, Brighton BN1 9QN, Great Britain

van Rossum, Erik Jan, The Hotel School Hague,
Brusselselaan 2, NL-258 AH The Hague, The Netherlands

Introduction

Roger Säljö

All linguistic structuring of the world involves abstraction. Reality "reflected in sign is not merely reflected but *refracted*", as Vološinov (1973, p. 23) puts it. In this process of refraction perspectives on reality are shaped by systematic human attempts to make the world intelligible and to manipulate it in the service of needs experienced. Communicative growth thus involves more than the acquisition of a language with fixed meanings, it is also the adoption of perspectives on reality inherent to the linguistic community where socialisation takes place and the ability to utilize these perspectives in novel situations.

While spoken language has been with us long enough to be conceived of as an integral aspect of what defines us as human, other means of communicating that have acquired prominence in society are more recent. Today, when communication is very much at the centre of the social and political agenda, the possibilities, problems and even dangers inherent in modern electronic mediation of messages and pictures receive considerable attention. The consequences of this development for human interaction, and even for our images of ourselves, appear as recurring topics of discussion among laymen, politicans and experts in various fields.

In this perspective, it may seem far fetched to many to regard such commonplace activities as reading and writing as technology based. Relating to written discourse has become such a deeply interiorised and natural activity in life that it escapes our conscious attention. Indeed, this is the way in which much research into orality and literacy has proceeded. "Language study in all but recent decades", Ong (1982, p. 8) argues, "has focused on written texts rather than orality" and "oral creations have tended to be regarded generally as variants of written production or, if not this, as beneath serious scholarly attention". In a broader ideological context, written language has been an essential ingredient of implicit Western ethnocentrism. It has been seen as a prerequisite for civilisation, and many scholars have assumed that "any civilised culture worth the name has to be a literate culture" (Havelock, 1973, p. 332). If we continue the parallel with present-day developments in electronics and their consequences for human communication, writing seems to place itself half-way between spoken language and the wonders of modern technology. It is clearly a human invention that relies for its use on the availability of both intellectual tools such as an alphabet of some kind and artefacts such as instruments for writing and man-made materials on which the writing can be easily done. In this sense, written language is parallel to the computer in that it is linked with specific competencies on the part of the person utilising it and in its dependence on a number of artefacts. Yet, it seems to have been a part of Western communicative practices long enough to have become transparent and perceived as a natural and neutral alternative of conveying messages that does not refract reality in any specific way, to use the expression suggested by Vološinov.

It is obvious in many ways that written language is not "a mother tongue" (Olson, 1977, p. 86) of the human species. Learning to master written language is, in many cases, an arduous process that presupposes conscious learning efforts of a kind that differ from the activities involved in acquiring a first language. In the annals of mankind, writing is a relatively recent practice with a history of about five millennia, the exact dating depending on the definition preferred (cf. Graff, 1987). For many centuries, reading and writing were practices that were important only in certain specific sectors of society and of little concern to the everyday life of the majority of the population. Even in our time, the use of writing for some groups in what is commonly conceived as literate societies is a marginal activity limited to a rather narrow class of communicative situations (Heath, 1983). Well into the medieval period, not only were the concrete artefacts of writing not widely available, but the language situation in many parts of the Western world was such that there was no strong, common, spoken language that could serve as the base for writing.

The successive infiltration of written language into various sectors of Western societies can be accounted for through dynamic interactions of technological innovations and changes in social organisation. If the Greek alphabet, with its limited number of signs that could be easily acquired, provided an important base for a more general literacy, other significant milestones in the spread of literacy can be represented by such diverse phenomena as the printing press, the Reformation and the changes in practices in commercial, legal and administrative systems. When writing established itself as a dominant form of communication, this process implied a change in our conception of and attitudes towards oral language as well. As Stock (1983) points out, the use of the written word in a growing number of social contexts meant that "oral discourse effectively began to function within a universe of communication governed by texts" (p. 3), and many of the standards established for language use derive from the written version, as will be discussed in the chapters to follow.

Our collective literate biases of today are obvious in wide circles. In the regularly reappearing discussions of alleged increases in illiteracy – often used as a euphemism for an assumed lowering of standards in education as a whole – a movement back to traditional reading, writing and spelling exercises has been perceived as a remedy. This seems, for instance, to have been the message of the 'back-to-basics' movement in the USA during the 1970s. As has been pointed out by Resnick and Resnick (1977), looking "backward for solutions (to literacy problems) ... can succeed only when social conditions and educational goals remain relatively stable" (p. 370), and a good argument can be made for the case that criteria of what counts as a literate person have been, and still are, changing rapidly. However, our constructions of literacy to a large extent lead us to view reading and writing as involving essentially technical skills, and the cultural practices and biases inherent in literate activities go unnoticed.

Literate Conceptions and Conceptions of Literacy

To people living in a constant interchange with texts, a written statement is seen as a mere counterpart to the spoken word. Indeed, as Ong (1982) points out, thinking about a word without imagining its written form is difficult. Writing gives a concrete, thing-like appearance to the elusive spoken word, and this reification of the word has had a profound impact on our conception of language and on our conceptions of research into language and communication. In his contribution to this volume, Ragnar Rommetveit analyses 'the myth of literal meaning' and the influence of this myth on epistemologies dominating the study of human communication. Written language, through its objectivation of the linguistic form as such, has been an important underpinning for our current conceptions of language and communication by reducing issues of human intersubjectivity and joint communicative concerns in social interaction to an image of communication in terms of a transfer of decontextualised pieces of information from sender to receiver. However, the trivialisation of human communication inherent in the myth of the existence of literal meanings in language is not a myth in a conventional sense; it is also a social reality and an ideology in which people live their life and in terms of which they judge themselves and others.

The line of reasoning taken by Ragnar Rommetveit is continued in the two succeeding chapters. Per Linell analyses the 'written language bias' of the very discipline of linguistics itself and of the folk models of language and communication in Western, 'highly' literate societies. Following Reddy's (1979) dictum that "the stories English speakers tell about communication are largely determined by semantic structures of language itself" (p. 285), Linell ventures to show that wide-spread notions both inside and outside scientific accounts of human communication owe their legacy to written language. In linguistics, the written version of language has had profound influences not only on the type of data that linguists prefer to analyse as prototypes of language, but also on the analytic tools through which such data are analysed. This circular dependence on writing has determined the present conception of language and communication in linguistics.

In discussing recent literature on orality and literacy, Brian V. Street argues that the recent trend of allegedly deserting the traditional distinction of a 'great divide' in favour of regarding orality and literacy more in terms of a continuum is more apparent than real. Drawing on a distinction between an 'ideological' and an 'autonomous' model of literacy, Street sets out to illustrate that attempts to achieve a comprehensive understanding of literacy must go beyond a narrow focussing on technical aspects of the means of communication itself. Written language is not what makes a difference, but rather the larger matrix of communicative practices in which reading and writing are embedded.

Our use of the written word is thus not merely an aspect of our culture in a neutral sense; such practices are linked to power structures in a society and to the dominance of certain forms of communication. Also in recent literature, where the existence of a 'great divide' between oral and literate societies is explicitly denied, assumptions of differences of a similar nature between written and spoken language forms reappear, although in disguise. Street scrutinises statements typically found to the effect that 'cohesion' is typical of written texts while oral communication relies on 'paralinguistic' features, or that meaning is more 'autonomous' and explicit in writing than in spoken discourse. All such attempts at generalised accounts of differences in forms of communication *per se* are bound to fail and are explainable only through the traditional academic division of labour between linguists and social scientists of various branches, where the former prefer to keep to a narrow understanding of social context.

Karin Aronsson raises the issues of how language awareness develops or, alternatively expressed, how language becomes visible. Just as bilingualism may lead to an increased awareness of language, it is reasonable to assume that literate practices may contribute to an awareness of language as form. Taking the language situation of Ethiopia as a point of departure, Aronsson discusses the characteristics and communicative consequences of multilingualism and multiliteracy. She shares with Street the concern for de-emphasising the role of literacy as such and the necessity of focussing on literate practices for understanding the cognitive consequences, yet argues that written language may be seen as having clear implications for language awareness.

In the age of information technology, new forms of mediating information become important. The question asked by Steen Folke Larsen is in what sense computer literacy is related to literacy. Just as spoken language is ideally suitable for communicating in face-to-face encounters, written language made possible communication across physical and social distance as well as over time. Writing implied the development of awareness of conceptual issues in the sense that the reliance on a more exclusive linguistic form of communication called for the development of more generalised and standardised forms of expression that could function in the less personalised communicative circumstances under which reading takes place. Computer technology, in turn, if seen as a new means of mediating messages, focusses on another level, namely that of mastering procedures. Programming languages as symbolic systems, so Larsen argues, contain and describe procedures that operate on the world.

Replacing the concept of computer literacy with procedural literacy, Larsen suggests not only that programming as a human activity relies on an extensive knowledge of the procedures involved in handling certain types of problems, but also that the use of such languages for word-processing and other ends will lead to an increased awareness of the procedures involved in solving specific problems as well as in life in general.

The birth of modern, empirical research into human cognition can be dated back a hundred years to the publication of Hermann Ebbinghaus' epoch-making study *Über das Gedächtnis* (1885). Inspired by the success of the rational experimental procedures of the hard sciences, Ebbinghaus designed an approach to research into memory congenial with the *Zeitgeist* of his era. The invention of the nonsense syllable was a brilliant solution to the problem of controlling the confounding influences of previous experiences on memory and was to have a profound impact on empirical research into this human faculty for the coming century. What was learnt and remembered could be effectively separated from the person's previous knowledge. The perspective adopted by Ebbinghaus, by virtue of its focussing on the memory as a repro-ductive faculty is, according to Arild Lian, a typically literate one. Ebbing-haus' insistence on a sharp distinction between the original (the text) and its reproduction from memory as the very activity of remembering is understand-able as a consequence of the role of the written record in society. In his chapter, Lian takes a long-term perspective on the development of our con-ception of memory, and he analyses the problem of what is biological and what is cultural about our capacities for remembering. To understand memory, it is important to analyse the organisation of society and the uses of memory that become prominent in various types of labour and other activities. Writing, for instance, does not – as is commonly argued – merely extend memory, it gives memory a new role in society, and it gives prominence to a new set of cognitive activities that have more to do with the ability of being selective and directed towards understanding complex discourses than simply storing them in their original form.

Literate Practices and Human Cognitive Repertoires

Within a social-constructivist conception of human cognition, it is reasonable to assume that the impact of the written word on cultural practices in society at large should also be mirrored in patterns of cognitive development. Exposure to and use of written texts in a wide class of situations should lead to the growth of intellectual tools that are appropriate for handling this medium of commu-nication. In the literature, one of the most suggestive accounts of changes in modes of thought and 'categorical thinking' related to literacy has been given by Luria (1976) in his studies of villagers in central Asian parts of the Soviet Union during the early 1930s. With intellectual inspiration from the works of

Vygotsky, Luria and his collaborators followed the consequences of the collectivisation of agriculture and the introduction of new forms of organisation of social life for the peasants' ways of construing reality. The changes taking place involved an increase in the villagers' responsibilities for making decisions related to production and administration of local resources as well as participation in literacy courses. Comparing how the peasants responded to various tasks such as classification tasks and syllogisms before and after their involvement in new activities that also included reading and writing, Luria found that the preferred mode of responding mirrored a change from organising objects in the world according to their practical co-appearance and use to regarding them in terms of more abstract concepts. Prior to their exposure to education and other aspects of modernisation, respondents asked to point out objects that do or do not belong in a group such as 'hammer-saw-log-hatchet' would typically not use the abstract concept of 'tool' as the basic principle of organisation (thus stating that the log is the odd object). Rather, they would perceive the dominant similarity to be based on the co-appearance of the objects in practical situations. The hatchet was thus considered the odd object, since it was not used in the same practical activity as the others. Similarly, the villagers' modes of responding to syllogisms and their understanding of the logic underlying syllogistic reasoning was dramatically affected by their new experiences.

Although Luria did not attempt to separate the specific effects of reading and writing on thinking, but rather saw these activities as embedded in the wider pattern of change that took place in the lives of these people, it is obvious that the written word is a powerful determinant of the changes in cognition described. While the previous form of thought was "based on an individual's practical experience", the "core of 'conceptual' or 'categorical' thinking is the shared experience of society conveyed by its linguistic system" where "words become the principal tool for abstraction and generalisation" (Luria, 1976, p. 52).

This development towards more abstract modes of thought is greatly influenced by the dominance of the written word as a basis for codifying phenomena. David Olson, in his chapter, analyses the historical impact of literacy on conceptual development, arguing that literacy was important in creating a distinction between what is 'given' and our interpretations of these 'givens'. Literacy thus introduced the need for hermeneutics, and the awareness of the difference between objective reality and our perceptions and interpretations of this reality became fundamental in many contexts such as science, law and religion. Through a number of empirical studies of the ontogenetic development of children's mastery of the distinction between what is given (or said) and what is inferred, Olson and his co-workers demonstrate how literacy seems to be a prerequisite for – or at least considerably facilitates – the understanding of these kinds of conceptual distinctions. The studies thus yield evidence of the adaption of children to a theory of interpretation that has its roots in literate practices and that at the same time is fundamental to ways of structuring reality dominant in many "provinces of meaning" (Berger & Luck-mann, 1967) in society.

To most people, the notion of literacy is closely tied to the skills in dealing with the written word acquired in school. Learning to read and write is conceived of as one of the essential ingredients of schooling, and this linking of schooling and literacy is also a fundamental reason why schools are often made responsible for the assumed crises in literacy skills (Heath, 1980). In historical terms, this view of literacy is not the true story, since wide-spread literacy was achieved in many societies well before the introduction of formal schooling. As has been shown by Johansson (1977), the Protestant movement became the ideological underpinning for a broad literacy campaign in Sweden as early as in the 17th century. Teaching took place in the home and was organised and supervised by the local parish clergy and their assistants. However, the social construction of literacy has changed from earlier periods, in which a "*pluralistic* idea about literacy as a composite of different skills related to reading and writing for many different purposes and sections of a society's population" was the norm to "a twentieth-century notion of a single, standardized *schooled literacy*." (Cook-Gumperz, 1986, p. 22). One can thus argue that schooled literacy is a particular form of literacy geared towards the needs of a particular social institution that views activities of reading and writing as ends in themselves rather than as means to fulfil other projects. Hazel Francis discusses literacy and children's conceptions of such activities in relation to schooling. Schools may thus provide a new and opaque context for reading and writing in which the motives for such activities are not easily recognised. The result is often that the child's relationship to writing is restricted to performing a particular type of task central to the pedagogy of formal institutions. Where this occurs, the child may fail to develop an increasing awareness of the various ways in which writing is used in human communication. In the formal setting, the 'text' thus becomes central rather than the authentic communicative situation in terms of which writing makes sense outside school. This tradition does not merely imply a certain relationship to the particular tasks of reading and writing, but becomes central to the child's conceptions of learning and knowledge acquisition in general.

The metaphorics of children's conceptions of knowledge and learning is the focus of the chapter by Ingrid Pramling. To learn, children must develop an understanding of appropriate perspectives and roles in a wide class of communicative encounters. In an interview study of a large group of pre-school and first- and second-grade children, Pramling depicts the development of children's metacognitive language and, as a consequence, of their orientations towards the learning activities in which they engage. The study reveals a development from a personalised conception of knowledge and learning, in which one is assumed to acquire knowledge from a person who is expert at a particular skill, to a more depersonalised conception, in which information acquired through books and media comes to be perceived as the major source of knowledge. This latter conception gains prominence as a result of children's

experiences of schooling. Pramling then discusses how institutionalised learning in school-like situations, through its decontextualised nature, seems to
reinforce this distinction between learning in various settings, thus preparing
the child for a career as student.

Although reading and writing – as pointed out in several of the chapters –
are often understood as more or less technical skills, they are often involved in
social practices that are governed by implicit as well as explicit rules. The
nature of such rules and actors' identification of them in one specific setting
form the topic of the study by Dai Hounsell on undergraduates' essay writing.
In a sense, the research reported can be described as an ethnography of essay
writing and a study of the conceptions held by teachers and students with
respect to what it means to write an essay. What is illustrated is that the
outcome of the students' endeavours does not in any simplistic manner reflect
their general ability to write essays, but rather their familiarity with the particular type of discourse that qualifies as instances of academic text. Variations
in success may therefore reflect differing interpretations of this culturally
highly loaded form of discourse, a variation that may go unnoticed by students
as well as teachers. On the basis of his empirical data from the fields of
psychology and history, Hounsell argues that even within the context of aca-
demia, the assumptions as to what constitutes a coherent and logically convincing essay differ as a function of the nature and traditions of various disciplines. Cracking the implicit code of writing within these disciplines may be
the most significant learning experience at university, although the road to
achieving insights of this kind is generally not understood in this way by the
actors.

Variations in interpretation of written discourse also constitute the focus of
the chapter by Roger Säljö, although in this case, it is the reader rather than
the writer who is scrutinised. The point of departure here is how people learn
from reading in the sense of how they extract meaning from written passages.
The empirical results on interpretation of texts presented are at odds with
current attempts to account for discourse processing in terms of structural
characteristics of the text at a general level and/or in terms of the propositional
content of statements/sentences. Säljö shows how readers arrive at clearly
differing, although perfectly reasonable, versions of what constitutes the
author's meaning or the 'gist' of the expository text used. Understanding is
thus a genuinely creative activity, and the reader's contribution is a vital part of
the communicative chain. The difference between readers is analysed in terms
of – to use the language of Gestalt psychology – the figure-ground relationships
that they perceive in the text read. Säljö's chapter also shows how efforts to
make the text meaningful result in variations in interpretations among a group
of readers with differing degrees of expertise.

The starting point for the chapter written by Erik Jan van Rossum is the
assumption that students' activities, when reading texts with the intention of
learning, mirror their interpretations of what it means to learn from written
discourse. Van Rossum argues that a reproductive approach to written dis-

course – seeing the task of learning as essentially one of being able give back texts verbatim – appears to be contingent on a specific implicit personal conception of what it means to understand texts. The author then accounts for the various meanings that students ascribe to the process of understanding texts, and he argues that the proclivity to conceive the reading of texts as an active, meaning-generating and problem-solving type of task may not be natural to many students.

In conclusion, a common background of the chapters that make up this volume is the interest in how practices associated with writing have shaped our conceptions of reality and taught us to see the world with a literate world-view. Since science and research as human activities have themselves been conditioned by this literate heritage, an important aim of our undertaking is one of unlearning some of the taken-for-granted perspectives that have been provided by such an outlook on the world. Following the distinction used by David Olson in his chapter, the result of such an endeavour may, at best, be a richer and more sensitive 'interpretation' of what we can reasonably consider as 'given' about human communication.

References

Berger, P., & Luckmann, T. (1967). *The social construction of reality*. New York: Doubleday Anchor.

Cook-Gumperz, J. (1986). Literacy and schooling: an unchanging equation? In J. Cook-Gumperz (Ed.), *The social construction of literacy* (pp. 16–44). Cambridge: Cambridge University Press.

Ebbinghaus, H. (1885). *Über das Gedächtnis* [On memory]. Leipzig: Duncker.

Graff, H.J. (1987). *The legacies of literacy*. Bloomington: Indiana University Press.

Havelock, E.A. (1973). Prologue to Greek literacy. In *Lectures in memory of Louise Taft Semple, second series, 1966–1970*. Cincinnati: University of Oklahoma Press for the University of Cincinnati Press.

Heath, S.B. (1980). The functions and uses of literacy. *Journal of Communication, 30,* 123–133.

Heath, S.B. (1983). *Ways with words*. Cambridge: Cambridge University Press.

Johansson, E. (1977). *The history of literacy in Sweden*. Umeå: University of Umeå.

Luria, A.N. (1976). *Cognitive development. Its cultural and social foundations*. Cambridge, Mass.: Harvard University Press.

Olson, D.R. (1977). The languages of instruction: On the literate bias of schooling. In R.C. Andersson, R.J. Spiro, & W.E. Montague (Eds.), *Schooling and the acquisition of knowledge* (pp. 65–89).Hillsdale, N.J.: Erlbaum.

Ong, W.J. (1982). *Orality and literacy. The technologizing of the word*. London: Methuen.

Reddy, M.J. (1979). The conduit metaphor – A case of frame conflict in our language about language. In A. Ortony (Ed.), *Metaphor and thought* (pp. 284–324). Cambridge: Cambridge University Press.

Resnick, D.P., & Resnick, L.B. (1977). The nature of literacy: An historical explo-
ration. *Harvard Educational Review, 47,* 370–385.
Stock, B. (1973). *The implications of literacy.* Princeton, N.J.: Princeton University
Press.
Vološinov, V.N. (1973). *Marxism and the philosophy of language.* (L. Matejka and I. R.
Titunik, Trans.). New York: Seminar Press. (Original work published 1930)

Part 1
Literate Conceptions and Conceptions of Literacy

CHAPTER 1

On Literacy and the Myth of Literal Meaning

Ragnar Rommetveit

Introduction

Issues concerning literalness of meaning range all the way from folk linguistics to axiomatic features of formalized semantic theory. Acceptance of "literal" as a primitive, undefined term in delineation of an autonomous field of "pure" semantics may hence be in part due to the intuitive appeal of pervading pretheoretical notions such as, for instance (Goffman, 1976, p. 303), "...the common sense notion ... that the word *in isolation* will have a general basic, or most down-to-earth meaning ...". Such presuppositions seem to form part of the myth of literal meaning in our highly literate societies.

Myths emerge out of human wondering about questions beyond available commonsense and scientific accounts, as tentative answers to riddles of a vaguely apprehended ontological nature. Myths of creation such as the Hebrew *Genesis* and the Norse *Elder Edda*, for instance, are seductively simple accounts of how the One became the Many. The myth of literal meaning addresses the basic semantic riddle of how the Many may become the One. It tries to explain how language can bring about a spiritual union of the Many, how one state of intersubjectivity or "shared meaning" is attained by linguistic means in encounters between different subjective worlds. Issues concerning literalness belong hence – when defined so broadly – to that part of semantics which according to Pylyshyn (1980, p. 159), "...remains largely shrouded in mystery".

Lay notions of the kind described by Goffman (1976), however, suggest a seductivley simple answer to the riddle: mutual understanding must rest upon some underlying common code of basic meanings (Grundbedeutungen, see Allwood, 1981, p. 183) of words and expressions, i.e. on invariant features and/or correlates of the linguistic medium *as such* rather than, for example, contextual or social-interactional features of language use. A crucial feature of the myth of literal meaning, as I conceive of it, is thus a pervading constraint upon our wondering about linguistically mediated intersubjectivity. This constraint is by no means a matter of folk linguistics only, but part and parcel of our dominant paradigms of linguistic thought and perhaps most cogently revealed as definite "written language biases" within semantics (Olson, 1977; Linell, 1982).

Any plausible historical account of such current scientific elaborations of the myth of literal meaning has to deal with the development of writing, the impact of literacy on oral language in general, and the significance of (certain types of) written texts as a point of departure in the seminal work of the founders of Western linguistics. Vološinov argued more than half a century ago that the stronghold of the "abstract objectivism" of Descartes and Saussure is largely due to the fact that "...the first philologists and the first linguists were always and everywhere priests" and that "...European linguistic thought formed and matured over concern with the cadavers of written language" (see Vološinov, 1973, p. 41, 71 and 74). Similar claims, though far less polemically formulated, are raised by Olson (1977) in his early essay on transformational-generative linguistics as a model for the structure of autonomous written prose and by Linell (1982) in his survey of written language biases in linguistics.

Versions of the myth of literal meaning which have gained academic respectability have been under attack, not only from philosophers of language, from representatives of model theoretical semantics, but – more recently – even from rebels within the field of artificial intelligence (AI) research. Wittgensteins's *Philosophical Investigations*, for instance, may indeed be read as a gigantic effort to free us from the devastating constraint imposed upon our wondering about language by the "abstract objectivism" referred to by Vološinov. His target is according to Baker and Hacker (1980, p. 163) "...nothing less than the illusion which has dominated European philosophy, that language has foundations in simple concepts".

Similar but less radically critical comments on mainstream analytical philosophy of language are also voiced by Barwise and Perry (1983) in their recent works on situation semantics. Their major complaint about traditional model theory is that it has taken "non-efficient expressions" and so-called eternal sentences as paradigms for linguistic meaning. These are sentences which are supposed to make the same claim about the world no matter who says them and when, i.e. sentences whose meanings can be unequivocally assessed without any concern about discourse situations and contexts of use. The stipulation of literal meaning within traditional model theoretical semantics seems thus to rest upon the assumption that the world can be exhaustively analysed in terms of context-free data or atomic facts.

This is, according to Dreyfus (1979, p. 205), also the deepest assumption underlying current research within AI research and the very reason why AI seems doomed to fail in its attempts at capturing the essentials of human cognition and use of natural language. Flores and Winograd, surveying the field of cognitive science from within, arrive at the same general conclusion. The semantic theory adopted by AI, they argue, is essentially a theory of literal meaning transformed into a model of internal representations of atomic facts. What is fundamentally wrong with the myth of literal meaning is hence, in computerized versions of it, cogently exposed as a total incapacity to capture certain basic prerequisites for linguistically mediated intersubjectivity. These have to do with the perspectivity inherent in human cognition, the dependency of linguistic meaning upon tacitly taken-for-granted background conditions, and its embeddedness in communicative social interaction (see Flores & Winograd, 1983, p. 16, pp. 25–29, and p. 51; Winograd, 1985, p. 99).

The point of departure for my reflections on written language biases within various branches of semantics is a position from which embeddedness of linguistic meaning in social interaction acquires a particular saliency. Such an outlook, of course, implies a definite bias against general paradigms aiming at explanatory accounts of human intersubjectivity exclusively or primarily in terms of invariant features of the linguistic medium as such. The myth of literal meaning, however, cannot be discarded as a mere illusion within such a social-cognitive perspective. Myths are not only "stories told" but also "realities lived" (Malinowski, 1984), i.e. they are *social* realities and of considerable theoretical interest as such. And the myth of literal meaning, I shall argue, is in our highly literate societies a *reality lived* by enlightened laymen under subtle influence from *stories told* by prominent scholars of semantics.

On Components of Plausibility, Truth and Illusion in the Modern Myth of Literal Meaning

The lay notion that a word or sentence in isolation will have some "...general, basic, or most down-to-earth meaning" is truly mythical in the sense that it is rooted in faith rather than knowledge. The faith on which it is founded, however, is a "lived reality" in the form of a pervading and profound confidence in the possibility of mutual understanding. Hence, it may, possibly in future axiomatization of pragmatics, be expressed as a basic postulate of efficient verbal communication: human intersubjectivity has to be taken for granted in order to be attained (Rommetveit, 1974, p. 56).

Such a postulate, moreover, implies *assumed similarity* on the part of individual human beings engaged in successful verbal communication *with respect to individuation of the talked-about world into aspects and entities*. And those shared and invariant aspects and entities, it seems, must somehow be mirrored in invariant features of ordinary language. How could we otherwise establish convergence of attention and/or intention onto the things we talk about?

Our commonsense confidence in the possibility of mutual understanding is thus grounded in a profound and profoundly plausible attitude of naive realism, i.e. in the "natural attitude" (Schutz, 1945, p. 534) that "...the world is from the outset not the private world of the single individual, but an intersubjective world, common to all of us, in which we have not a theoretical but an eminently practical interest". Such a naive realism is in ordinary conversation repeatedly and thoroughly confirmed in convergence of attention onto particular material objects within a shared perceptual field. And since convergence of attention is achieved by verbal means, we reason, words and expressions must somehow *refer to* or mediate *mental representations of* invariant aspects and entities of an external world "common to all of us". What evades reflective consciousness in such extrapolations, however, is the dependency of successful reference upon subtle social and contextual features. In ordinary human communication reference is achieved within an immediately exerienced yet constantly changing life world made up of self-evident background assumptions and naively mastered skills. This constantly changing life world is, according to philosophers belonging to the phenomenological tradition of Husserl and Heidegger, transcendental and by definition inaccessible to the reflective consciousness of conversation partners. It is, if I have understood Hildyard and Olson (1982) correctly, the world of "the casual meaning of oral discourse" and, according to Habermas (1981, I, p. 449) an immediately meaningful world which "...*den Kommunikationsteilnehmern im Rücken bleibt*" (literally: "remains behind the communicationpartners", i.e. remains inaccessible). It is no wonder, therefore, that it has proved utterly inattractive and impenetrable as a prospective object of enquiry to analytic philosophers and experimental psycholinguists.

What remains inaccessible to conversation partners while actively engaged in communication, however, is not necessarily unintelligible to a non-participant observer who speaks their language and whose repertory of potential perspectives on the talked-about state of affairs stem from a common experiential base. Mutual understanding in casual oral discourse, for instance, may to such an observer become intelligible in terms of a joint commitment on the part of conversation partners to a temporarily shared social reality rather than invariant (literal) meanings of words and expressions. One and the same relatively simple state of affairs such as Mr. Smith's mowing of the lawn may thus be properly and truthfully referred to by the expressions *working* or *not working*, depending upon what constitutes the joint, immediate, and "eminently practical interest" of the participants in the conversation. They may be concerned with Mr. Smith's laziness and focus on his actual conduct relative to salient alternatives such as staying inactive in his bed or, alternatively, wonder whether he is on the job or free to go fishing with them (Rommetveit, 1983a, p. 100). And, as Dreyfus (1979, p. 205) maintains, "...*being concerned in a certain way or having a certain purpose is not something separate from our awareness of our situation*".

My sustained interest in potentially invariant and orderly features of such proper and efficient ordinary language use stems from a strong suspicion that "casual meaning" may not be so casual after all. Perspectivity seems to be an ubiquitous ingredient of human cognition, and mutual understanding is accordingly contingent upon joint commitment with respect to perspective on talked-about states of affairs. Dyadic control of the temporarily shared life world of participants in a dialogue, moreover, can hardly become intelligible at all unless we venture to examine social-interactional features of verbal communication such as our intuitive mastery of dialogue roles. What happens the moment we expand our enquiries into linguistically mediated intersubjectivity in such directions, however, is that traditional boundaries between semantics and pragmatics break down.

Literal meaning was in some modern, prestigious and scientifically elaborated versions of the myth initially conceived of as *context free*. This is, in view of the perspectivity inherent in human cognition and communication, an illusion, yet an underlying assumption in speech act and psycholinguistic theory based upon the "conduit paradigm" of verbal communication (Rommetveit, 1983b). Within such approaches, casual, indirect, and metaphorical meaning is in principle to be accounted for in terms of contextually plausible chains of inference from some linguistically mediated and invariant base. This is also the general strategy adopted by Searle (1979) in his account of literal utterances, metaphorical utterance and indirect speech acts, even though he argues convincingly elsewhere (Searle, 1978) that literal meaning – contrary to the received opinion – is not contextfree at all. Even the literal meanings of words within semantic fields where optimists hope to capture semantic universals, he argues, are contingent upon certain background assumptions. What is literally meant by the preposition *on* in the utterance *the cat is on the mat*, for instance, is contingent upon pervasive (and, most of the time, veridical) assumptions about location of objects within a gravitational field.

Searle's discussion of literalness thus testifies to a certain ambivalence: literal meaning is conceived on the one hand as the invariant base from which contextually appropriate casual meaning is inferred, yet on the other hand as itself contingent upon assumptions which (Searle, 1978, p. 219) "...are not and in most cases could not also be completely represented...". Contextually appropriate truth about lawn mowing conveyed by either one of the expressions *working* and *not working*, for instance, may from such a position be hard to explain. One may postulate two lexical entries for the verb *working* corresponding to separate and equally literal entities, consider only one of the meanings as literal and the other as casual and parasitic upon it, or search for some invariant literal base underlying two different and equally casual meanings. The background assumptions pertaining to any imaginable literal and invariant meaning of *working*, however, may prove exceedingly difficult to identify. And multiplication of lexical entries, while possible, is hardly a very promising approach. It is neither likely to strengthen our faith in the psychological reality of literal meaning nor to increase our insight into the dependency of casual meaning upon *temporarily shared* background assumptions.

Searle's notion of context-bound literal meaning represents in a way a compromise between a commitment to formal truth-conditional semantics and a proper recognition of the situatedness and inherent perspectivity of human cognition. And it is interesting to notice that Frege, one of the founders of modern truth-conditional semantics, attempted to balance eternal truth and mortal perspectivity in a somewhat similar way. This is particularly evident in the passage of his *Funktion, Begriff, Bedeutung* (1969) where he invites us to conceive of sense as analogues to the real image (of the moon) inside a telescope. He writes (p. 45):

> Das Bild im Fernrohr ist zwar nur einseitig; es ist abhängig vom Standorte; aber ist doch objektiv, insofern es mehreren Beobachtern dienen kann. Es liesse sich allenfalls einrichten, dass gleichzeitig mehrere es benutzen. Von den Netzhautbildern würde jeder doch sein eigenes haben.[1]

Frege's choice of analogy is clearly in the spirit of the "abstract objectivism" of Descartes and Saussure, as is his subsequent reference (Frege, 1969, p. 55) to the logically perfect language as a *written* version (*"Begriffsschrift"*). His world of sense bears little resemblance to that intersubjective world in which we have "an eminently practical interest". But it is not devoid of perspectivity – and hence: of options with respect to perspective.

He concedes that the image, though objective, is nevertheless determined by the location and orientation of the telescope. The issue of responsibility for its location and orientation is thus implicity raised and via his analogy converted into the unresolved issue of normative components in Frege-inspired semantics. His notion of sense is therefore as ambiguous as Searle's notion of context-bound literal meaning. It may even be interpreted as a methodological prescription: scholars within the field of formal semantics should engage in normative idealization of linguistic meaning, i.e. in a search for the foundations of language in simple concepts.

Frege's impact upon modern semantics and various scientifically orientated versions of the myth of literal meaning can hardly be overestimated. The term "literal" is often used ambiguously, yet most of the time in such a way as to define the domain of proper and theoretical semantics in terms of Fregean sense. This is, for instance, the way Hausser (1983, p. 275) uses the term when he maintains: "Semantics deals with the truth- (or rather denotation-) conditional analysis of the literal meaning of natural language expressions". And pure semantics is, according to Katz a study of meaning based upon the assumption that "...meaningfulness depends exclusively on intrasentential sense relations...". Hence he is not at all concerned with *"sentence uses in actual speech"*, but with *"sentences in the language"* (see Katz, 1981, p. 219 and 222).

The expression "sentences in the language" entails the abstract notion of *"the system sentence"*, a theoretical construct "...whose principal function in the linguistic model of the language-system is to define the concept of grammaticality" (Lyons, 1977, p. 632). The analysis of "meaningfulness" in terms of intrasentential sense relations allows Katz, therefore, to detach his academic trade from problems of reference and tag it on to logic and formal syntactics.

---

1 Translation: The image in the telescope is biased; it is dependent on the location; it is, however, objective insofar as it is useful to several observers. If need be, it could be installed so that several people could use it at the same time. However, everybody would have his own retinal image.

And common to most current branches of pure Fregean semantics is a proclamation of emancipation from any commitment to account for the contam-
ination of linguistic sense in real-life verbal communication by shifting practical human interests and ideosyncracies due to mental imagery.

Such a proclamation is perfectly legitimate for a discipline honouring formal stringency more than substantial insight and – for that reason – apparently
completely detached from lay people's wondering about language. But even
such a discipline is institutionally embedded in society at large. Its normative
idealizations of linguistic meaning may hence in principle via influence on the
lexicographer and *his* impact upon public education enter modern folk linguistics in the form of partially self-fulfilling prophecies. This possibility will be
further explored when we return to the issues of literacy and components of
plausibility and truth within the modern myth of literal meaning.

Frege-inspired notions of literalness are particularly problematic when
encountered within psycho- and sociolinguistics, i.e. in theories of meaning
explicitly geared toward "psychological realities" and pragmatics of human
discourse. Searle's theory of speech acts, for instance, is based upon the
apparently innocent assumption that whatever can be meant can be said. This
"principle of expressibility", however, will (Searle, 1974, p. 20) "...enable us
to account for important features of Frege's theory of reference and sense..."
and "...has the consequence that cases...of...nonliteralness are not theoretically essential to linguistic communication". The recognition that even
literal meaning is contextbound, one would expect, might lead Searle to think
twice about such a consequence of the principle. But he finds nothing in his
more recently advanced thesis of the relativity of literal meaning which is
inconsistent with it. His novel notion of context bound literal meaning, he
maintains, forces him only to distinguish the special role of the context of
utterance in all cases of non-literalness from the role that background assumptions play in the interpretation of literal meaning (see Searle, 1978,
p. 221).

But what, then, is actually implied by the notion of literalness embedded in
Searle's principle of expressibility? Is it possibly a normative notion in disguise? If not, how will he describe more precisely the difference between
literal and casual meaning with respect to dependency upon perspective and
background assumptions? Is perhaps the context of utterance in cases of
non-literalness accessible to reflective consciousness and hence in principle
"computable" (Pylyshyn, 1980) whereas the context of utterance in cases of
literalness is not?

Such a tentative solution may seem plausible to softhearted cognitive scientists who want to define the borderline between rationally intelligible contextual features on the one hand and intuitively recognized background assumptions of a Heideggerian type on the other. It is neither plausible nor even
logically possible within Searle's model, however, because background assumptions of the literal meaning of any given linguistic expression according to
him are embedded in that very expression's context of utterance in all cases of

non-literal use. "Utterance meaning" – whether indirect, metaphorical, or
ironical – is in every case arrived at by "going through literal sentence meaning" (Searle, 1979, p. 122).

It is accordingly difficult to decide what is actually being expressed in
Searle's principle of expressibility when read in conjunction with his notion of
context-bound literal meaning. What is meant must be something beyond a
commitment to formal stringency and a recognition of context dependency as
some sort of a semantic universal. The claim that cases of non-literalness are
not theoretically essential, however, testifies to a remarkable lack of interest in
linguistically conducted negotiation concerning *temporarily* intersubjectively
valid background assumptions and perspectives. Such negotiation appears to
be a sine qua non of communication *in* and *about* an only partially known and
pluralistic social world, and even highly literate people engaged in it may at
times be in need of collectively endorsed standards of correctness and normative idealizations. The hidden arbiters they seek and lean on may upon
closer examination turn out to be priests, technicians, natural scientists, and
even scholars of semantics such as Searle. And hitherto concealed normative
components of his notions of literalness may indeed become visible to us if he
extends his case analysis of literal meaning and background assumptions from
on to other words such as *working*, *infant* and *human* (Rommetveit,
1983b).

This brings us back to the issues of literacy and literal meaning suggested by
Vološinov's polemic remark about the priesthood of the first philologists and
linguists (see p. 14). Ordinary people have probably always felt that what is
meant is at times, even though accurately enough expressed, beyond their
comprehension. This is true of all of us. But such experiences do not force us to
abandon our profound faith in an intersubjective world "common to all of us":
the real image of the talked-about entity inside Frege's metaphorical telescope
is one and the same, we feel, even if *we* are not in possession of the expertise
required in order to put the telescope in the appropriate position.

Such a commitment to some collectively endorsed and believed-in standard of correctness is indeed a very plausible component of the myth of literal
meaning lived by the enlightened layman. Literal meanings are somehow
embedded in the language he speaks and the culture to which he belongs in the
sense that what is meant by what is said very often appears to be contingent
upon background assumptions, standards of correctness and/or world knowledge transcending his immediate life world, individual semantic competence
and knowledge of the real world. And arbitration concerning potentially competing perspectives and background assumptions is in highly literate societies
also indeed institutionalized: "literally literal" meanings exist visibly, on paper, inside continually updated dictionaries and encyclopedias.

What is particulary deceptive about Frege's choice of the telescope analogy
is that it may lead linguists and layman alike to believe in standards of correctness based upon veridical world knowledge within domains of human
meaning where no such standards are available at all. And his impact upon

linguistics extends also to applied fields, far beyond formal semantics. The Fregean notion of sense, it seems, has even penetrated into lexicography in terms of particular features of a widely accepted format for explication of meaning. The meaning potential of polysemous words and expressions, for instance, is in academically respectable dictionaries remarkably often explicated in terms of separate *primary* and *secondary*, successively more "parasitic", meanings.

Such rank orderings seem to be both practical and – at least to cultural conformists – eminently plausible. They are nevertheless, in addition, of considerable theoretical interest to pluralistically orientated philosophers engaged in sceptical wondering (Naess, 1969) as well as to social scientists intrigued by self-fulfilling prophecies. And for obvious reasons: the rank ordering may reflect prevailing, though hidden ontological presuppositions concerning which one of multiple possible perspectives yields the "real image" of the world. The primary and literal meaning of a word written down in the dictionary at any time, moreover, is shortly afterwards publicly available as an officially endorsed answer to the ontologically innocent and insecure layman's question about the "general, basic, or most-down-to-earth" meaning of that word. Secondary meanings, on the other hand, are supposed to inform him about far less important things such as, for instance, connotations provided by "*Dichtkunst und Beredsamkeit*" ("poetry and eloquence") (Frege, 1969, p. 45).

If Frege went around today, knocking at the doors of ordinary people and asking them about meanings of expressions, he would in a way encounter his own monistic ghost in many doorways. This is also, by the way, essentially the predicament of linguists who currently study metalinguistic awareness. Part of the story Frege told us about reference and sense has been assimilated into folk linguistics and become embedded in the myth of literal meaning lived by enlightened and literate citizens. Such consequences of his work were hardly foreseen. Nor were they intended. And my entire story about the potential impact of *his* story is, of course, intelligible only against taken-for-granted and pervasive background conditions having to do with written language, literacy and schooling. Let us therefore turn to a few of the more general problems of literacy raised by Vološinov (1973), Bakhtin (1973/1984), Olson and coworkers (Olson, 1977; Hildyard & Olson, 1982; Geva & Olson, 1983; Olson & Torrance, 1985) and Linell (1982).

Reflections on Speech as Social Activity Versus Text as Publicly Available Product of Writing

Scholars in search of antidotes against prejudices of literacy in their own thinking about language may find it very rewarding to read the works of eminent representatives of Soviet psychology, philosophy of language and literary analysis from the early post-revolutionary period, such as Vygotsky, Vološinov and Bakhtin. They are all seriously concerned with language and thought, but from a humanistic and Marxist rather than Cartesian position, as "dialogical activity" embedded in social life.

Vološinov, for instance, maintains (1973, p. 93): "The organizing center of any utterance, of any experience, is not within but outside – in the social milieu surrounding the individual being". Bakhtin's profound insight into truly collective, yet at the same time dynamic, features of language is in part condensed into his general notion of "*intertextuality*". He writes (Bakhtin, 1984, p. 270):[2]

> The life of a word is contained in its transfer from one mouth to another, from one social collective to another, from one generation to another generation. In this process the word does not forget its own path and cannot completely free itself from the power of these concrete contexts into which it has entered.

The features of linguistic meaning he is primary intrigued by are hence such that they cannot be captured at all by focusing some imaginary telescope on external referents of expressions. The futility of such an approach is also clearly reflected in another key notion in Bakhtin's work. This is the notion of "*the loophole of consciousness and the word*", i.e. (Bakhtin, 1984, p. 313) "...the retention for oneself of the possibility for altering the ultimate, final meaning of one's words". Such a possibility is, according to Bakhtin, an essential feature of *language alive*. It is also a recurrent theme in Habermas' phenomenological analysis of the shifting shared *Lebenswelt* ("life world") of communication partners, in Levelt's and Marslen-Wilson's psycholinguistic studies of "on-line" language processing, and in Mukarovsky's literary analysis of poetry. Mukarovsky, for instance, writes (1976, p. 50):

> Every word in an utterance remains semantically 'open' up to the moment that the utterance ends. As long as the utterance flows, each of its words is accessible to additional shifts in its reference and to changes in meaning due to further context.

Such shifts are often – and, according to Vološinov and Bakhtin: perhaps always – a dyadic and "dialogical" affair. And they are not shifts of word meaning only. I may, for instance, start out *asserting* something on the tacit presupposition that my conversation partner will agree. In the middle of my utterance, however, I can already read in her face that this will not be the case, and the initially intended assertion is, by my intonation from that moment on, transformed in such a way as to end up as a *question*. The kind of context dependency Mukarovsky describes in a somewhat literary style, moreover, has been studied in detail in carefully conducted experiments on the listener's

---

2 Citations dated 1984 stem from M. Holquist's in-progress translation of an expanded version of Bakhtin's book. The latter is also available in German translation (*Probleme der Poetik Dostoevskys*. Munich: Carl Hanser Verlag, 1971).

comprehension and the speaker's organization of discourse. Interactional features, it turns out, also affect the way corrections are constructed by conversation partners in on-line repair of utterances (see Levelt, 1983, 1984; Levelt & Cutler, 1983; Marslen-Wilson & Komisarjevsky-Tyler, 1980).

Spoken language, whether we study it as social activity or in terms of individual processing, is in certain respects notoriously ephemeral and transient. The articulatory activity involved in it is shortlived, and speech sounds fade away immediately. Letters, on the other hand, are lasting products of activities of writing. And ephemeral, context-bound features of writing vanish once letters become constituents of finished written texts. Words are then considered largely or ideally as records (Linell, 1982, p. 153): what is meant by them is something somehow captured by the letters, in principle publicly available, beyond repair. It is by no means incidental, therefore, that stipulated "most-down-to-earth" meaning of words and expressions is coined "literal" by lay- as well as learned people within literate societies. As Vološinov (1973, p. 80) maintains: "The fiction of a word's realia promotes...the reification of its meaning".

The "word in isolation" Goffman refers to in his discussion of lay notions of literal meaning, it seems, is precisely the word as record, spatially identifiable as a graphic pattern within the finished, written text. The writing activity, of which it is a lasting trace, is to the reader a matter of the past, beyond human intervention, and its meaning can no longer be affected by the "loophole of consciousness" of the author. A basic difference between the word as record and the word alive has hence to do with general problems of human agency and ontic openness versus closure, i.e., with problems of the kind discussed by von Wright in his philosophy of agency and causation (von Wright, 1974).

The past is ontically closed in the sense that it cannot be interfered with, yet hardly ever known completely and for certain. The future, on the other hand, is both ontically and epistemically open. What is meant by a word with "a loophole" is thus necessarily only partially determined the moment it is heard. Whatever is being meant by a word as a written record, on the other hand, cannot any longer be altered by its author. Modifications and/or repairs due to queries from potential readers are "lost possibilities" (von Wright, 1974, p. 34). And ontic closure implies the *possibility* of epistemic closure as well: what the author meant can *in principle*, provided that it has been "accurately expressed" in written form, also become fully known. This follows from Searle's principle of expressibility (see Searle, 1974, p. 20).

What Vološinov refers to as "the fiction of a word's literal realia", it seems, is largely due to the peculiar combination of ontic closure and public availability of finished, written text. The perfect case of text-immanent and "literally literal" meaning is attained when, in addition, accuracy of expression is firmly assumed. This is the case of sacred texts as read by firm believers. The sentences making up such a text are to the reader indeed "eternal sentences". They are presumedly completely uncontaminated by practical concerns of mortal men – and being imbued by holy omniscience – convey truths that cannot be contested at all. What is meant by them must accordingly be something invariant and at the same time beyond the reader's knowledge and semantic competence.

The latter presupposition, however, is also part of the modern, enlightened man's predicament whenever he is reading certain types of secular "autonomous prose" (Olson, 1977) beyond what happens to be his own particular and restricted field of expertise. His basic attitude toward such texts may hence, historically, have religious roots. But those he leans on in his search for meaning beyond his own comprehension are in such cases, for example, teachers and authors of textbooks rather than priests. The aim of schooling is no longer exclusively nor primarily revelation of divine wisdom, but dissipation of rational, objective knowledge. Authors of textbooks mediate publicly endorsed and presumedly cumulative knowledge, and they explain what words and expressions mean the way good Frege-inspired lexicographers do. The promised land of modern public education is hence an intersubjectively valid, "objective" world. And it is in principle made accessible to the enlightened layman in the form of basic and pervasive background assumptions of literal meanings embedded in authoritative, textbook-type texts.

This is the world Hildyard and Olson (1982) are concerned with from an ontogenetic point of view. It is made available fragment by fragment, it seems, when children manage to "create contexts" from sentences and passages of written prose alone. It is also "the objective world" as Habermas conceives of it, historically, within his general theory of human rationality and communicative action. Habermas, however, is less concerned with its dependency upon literacy than with its possible roots in pre-literate notions about an objective order over and beyond the notoriously shifting "*Lebenswelt*" (see Habermas, 1981, II, p. 205). And his "*objektive Welt*" ("objective world") is neither merely a pragmatic postulate nor just a "natural attitude", but also a component of human rationality and prerequisite for assessment of truth in ordinary face-to-face discourse. He writes (1981, I, p. 149):

> Die Aktoren selbst sind es, die den Konsens suchen und an Wahrheit, Richtigkeit und Wahrhaftigkeit bemessen, also an fit und misfit zwischen der Sprechhandlung einerseits und den drei Welten, zu denen der Aktor mit seiner Äusserung Beziehungen aufnimmt, andererseits. Eine solche Beziehung besteht jeweils zwischen der Äusserung und
> - der objektiven Welt (als der Gesamtheit aller Entitäten, über die wahre Aussagen möglich sind);
> - der sozialen Welt (als der Gesamtheit aller legitim geregelten interpersonalen Beziehungen); und
> - der subjektiven Welt (als der Gesamtheit der privilegiert zugänglichen Erlebnisse des Sprechers).[3]

---

3 It is the actors themselves who look for mutual understanding and assess truth, accuracy and sincerity, that is, the fit and misfit of the speech act on the one hand, and, on the other, the three worlds with which the actor, by his utterance, enters into a relationship. Such a relationship exists between the utterance and

Habermas does not deal explicitly and in detail with issues of literacy and literal meaning. His stipulated objective, social and subjective worlds are derived from Bühler's theory of basic linguistic functions (Bühler, 1934), and the objective world corresponds to Bühler's abstract functional domain of purely cognitive, symbolic representation. To the extent that Habermas' general theory entails a version of the myth of literal meaning, it seems thus to be a version in which acceptance of divine authority within a monistic universe is being replaced by commitment to collective human reason. Mutual understanding is attained by adopting the perspective of the *rational* "generalized other", and the taken-for granted shared world of enlightened lay people is constantly being infiltrated by Popper's "world 3 of objective knowledge" (Popper, 1971). Relations of intertextuality (see p. 22) between written scientific texts and adult face-to-face discourse about matters of practical concern may be very remote and difficult to trace, but hardly anyone would deny that they exist.

Vygotsky (1962) dealt with such relations, but primarily from an ontogenetic point of view and in terms of transformation of initially "natural" into "scientific concepts". Both he and Bakhtin were indeed, despite their primary concern with language as social activity, intrigued by possible objective and invariant features of language underlying mutual understanding. Vygotsky's discussion of the impact of scientific concepts, for instance, may be interpreted as a concession that language may have "foundations in simple concepts" after all. And Bakhtin (1973, pp. 151–152) writes:

> Linguistics studies "language" and its specific logic in its *commonality* (*obshenost*) as that fact which makes dialogical discourse *possible*, but it consistently refrains from studying those dialogical relationships themselves ... Dialogical relationships are totally impossible without logical and concrete semantic relationships, but they are not reducible to them; they have their own specificity.

This passage from Bakhtin sounds as if he might very well endorse the kind of pure semantics of literal meaning proposed by Katz (see p. 18) as some sort of prerequisite or base for his own literary or "metalinguistic" analysis of dialogical relationships. Even Vygotsky and Bakhtin as well as Habermas, it seems, are thus somewhat and in certain respects constrained by the myth of literal meaning. They are all, though in different ways, seriously concerned with dynamic and interactional features of language alive. But options with respect to perspective and orderly negotiation of meaning are not the foci of attention and theoretical interest in their search for the foundations of lin-

---

- the objective world (the sum total of all the entities about which it is possible to make true assertions);
- the social world (the sum total of all the legitimately determined interpersonal relationships); and
- the subjective world (the sum total of all the experiences to which the speaker has privileged access).

guistically mediated intersubjectivity. Hence, let us now bring precisely such social-interactional features into focus in a case study of casual versus literal meaning.

On Bananas and Parts of Bananas

The case I have chosen for further explorations of casual versus literal meaning is an excerpt from the television series *Sesame Street*, first discussed by Newman (1982). It is presented by Olson and Torrance (1985, p. 16) as follows:

1. Earnie: "I'm going to divide this banana up so both of us can have some".
2. Earnie gives Bert the skin. "See, I took the inside and here's the outside part for you".

First-graders commenting upon this episode think that Earnie lied. By grade three, however, some children begin to notice that the sentence is both true and false. Olson and Torrance interpret this observation, together with similar findings from systematic studies of the development of metalinguistic awareness in children, as evidence of an increasing capacity to distinguish what is actually *said* from what is *meant*. Metalinguistic awareness thus implies a capacity to treat language as an object, i.e. to discover possible literal sentence meanings over and beyond what is intended and contextually appropriate in the particular discourse situation. Such literal sentence meanings, they maintain, constitute, prior to the emergence of metalinguistic awareness, transparent and implicit ingredients of casual meaning. And Olson and Torrance (1985, p. 11 and p. 13) describe certain characteristic features of children's development during school years as follows:

> there is a shift from attention to the beliefs and intentions of persons towards the meanings and structures of sentences; a shift from intended meanings to sentence meanings. This shift is marked by a significant change in the metalanguage. The metalinguistic verb *say* comes to be differentiated into the verbs *say* and *mean* .... the child uses sentence meanings to express or compute intended meanings, but...the sentence meaning remains implicit and, hence, transparent....What he or she begins to do primarily under the impact of literacy and schooling, is to become aware of, to make explicit, the sentence meaning.

Olson and Torrance illuminate issues of literacy and literal meaning from an ontogenetic point of view, by empirical evidence from studies of general cognitive development. A major theoretical contribution is their systematic, thorough and, in most respects, very convincing analysis of the interrelationships between literacy, schooling, metalinguistic awareness and mastery of literal sentence meaning. I shall in what follows, however, question their stipulation of functional, though pre-conscious or "transparent", literal meanings prior to the stage of metalinguistic awareness. And I shall side with kindergarten children and first-graders on the issue of whether Earnie lied and/or told the truth. Any plausible and psycholinguistically relevant version of truth-conditional semantics, I shall claim, should label him a liar.

Let us assume that Bert immediately and correctly understands Earnie's first utterance as *a promise*. This allows us to simplify matters considerably. The interesting semantic issue we encounter in the episode is then even more succinctly raised if Earnie simply says to Bert:

1. "I'll give you part of this banana".

But Burt feels cheated when he subsequently receives only the skin, and so would all of us have felt. Why? What is *meant* and *referred to* by the expression *part of this banana* within the frame of this slightly modified Earnie-and-Bert episode?

We may, following Habermas, analyse the episode in terms of fits and misfits between Earnie's speech act on the one hand and the objective world, Earnie's and Bert's sustained common social world and Earnie's subjective world, respectively, on the other. The objective world stipulated by Habermas is detached from the shifting and temporarily shared life world of conversation partners and hence clearly such that banana skins are proper parts of bananas. Since truth within Habermas' theory is a matter of correspondence between utterance and the objective world, moreover, we are forced to conclude that Earnie is telling *the truth*.

The contextually valid rules for interpersonal relations, however, are rules concerning sharing of bananas among friends and hence most likely such that the skin is a *socially incorrect* referent for Earnie's expression *part of this banana*. As for the sincerity ("*Wahrhaftigkeit*") of Earnie's speech act, more-over, it seems to depend upon whether he, at the moment he is making the promise, actually intends to give Bert only the skin. If he does, his speech is also *sincere*. And so will be the case even if he knows that Bert expects to receive some edible and tasty part.

A similar conclusion follows from Searle's version of Fregean semantics and, more specifically, from his principle of expressibility (see Searle, 1974, p. 20): if Earnie wants to cheat Bert, we must concede, he can hardly hit upon a more accurate expression than *part of this banana* for the intended referent, the skin. Accuracy of expression is within Searle's theory of speech acts a matter of correspondence between *speaker's* intention and her or his expression only. His principle of expressibilty does not deal with mutual commitment of conversation partners to a temporarily shared social world at all. And sincerity of speech acts is assessed by Habermas exclusively in terms of correspondence between speaker's intention and her or his utterance, not in terms of the speaker's commitment as an agent engaged in cooperative social activity.

Utterances whose truth and sincerity are assessed in such a way, however, are *from the point of view of the listener "eternal sentences"* in the sense that *their meaning is assessed independently of her or his legitimate demand upon the speaker by virtue of their complementary dialogue roles.* Poor Bert in our case, for instance, is granted no opportunity whatsoever to impose constraints upon what Earnie can legitimately mean by what he says to him. And Bert's feeling cheated is accordingly neither due to a lie nor insincerity on the part of Earnie, but to the violation of a social convention. What we initially conceived of as a potentially interesting semantic problem can thus on closer examination be discarded as a purely moral or ethically contaminated pragmatic issue. This seems indeed to be our conclusion if we adopt the position of either Habermas or Searle. And such a conclusion is hardly surprising to philosophers who are sceptical towards stipulated, monistic, objective worlds and critical of Fregean semantics.

However, bananas and parts of bananas can be examined from alternative philosophical positions. Putnam, being concerned with interest-relativity of explanation and human options with respect to perspective on the real world, considers the study of natural language meaning as a "moral science". His outlook is that of the sophisticated realist who (Putnam, 1978, p. 51)

> ... recognizes the existence of equivalent descriptions because it follows from his theory of the world that there are various descriptions, as it follows from a geographer's description of the earth there are alternative descriptions ...

A consistently pluralistic approach to semantic problems implies a rejection of the real-image-in-the-telescope type notion of sense as a pivotal notion in explanation of successful reference. Multiple different aspects of any given real object or state of affairs can in principle be brought into the focus of joint attention and/or intention of conversation partners on different occasions, depending upon from which one of multiple alternative positions it is being talked about (Rommetveit, 1979). Which particular aspect(s) of a banana is brought into the focus of joint attention the moment the expression a banana is uttered is accordingly not at all determined by the linguistic expression as such. A very important aspect of bananas, such as their *edibility*, moreover, is a genuinely transactional aspect: it resides neither in the bananas nor in the people eating them. Meaningful aspects of the real world are generated by people interacting with it and talking about it out of practical interest and concern. They constitute, according to the biologically founded epistemology of Maturana and Varela (1980) a separate "phenomenal domain" which enters human communication in the form of the "consensual domain" of linguistically mediated meaning.

Lyons (1977, p. 184) maintains that the major challenge within linguistic research on reference is to account for the way in which we use language to draw attention to what we are talking about. Convergence of attention onto the same material object, moreover, may be attained in many different ways. Successful reference of a word such as *banana*, for instance, is by no means contingent upon a matching of invariant "sense" or "most-down-to-earth meaning" against external referents. On the contrary. A noun such as *banana* is, according to the semantic theory developed by Kripke (1977), Putnam (1978) and Føllesdal (1983), a "genuine singular term" or "rigid designator", i.e *a term designating the same object in all possible worlds*. Its uniquely stable reference is, however, according to their causal (or historical) theory of reference, established and sustained by some sort of causal chain of communicative acts within the speech community.

Such a causal chain presupposes credibility and commitment to a shared world on the part of the agents involved in it. But the communicative episodes constituting its links may vary greatly. The reference of *banana*, for instance, may in a given case be "fixed" once and for all by means of an incidental and apparently misleading attributive definite description. Imagine an English-speaking visitor from outer space who neither knows bananas nor the word *banana*. He may, in principle, become "chained" and committed to the stable, collectively established reference of the word by a gesture of pointing in conjunction with the utterance: *"That inedible thing over there is a banana"*. Possible incidental features of the episode such as, for example, that *the particular banana referred to happens to be spoiled* or, alternatively, that *his conversation partner does not like bananas at all*, will not bar him from identifying bananas correctly ever afterwards nor from discovering that they are most of the time both edible and tasty.

Conversation partners' mutual commitment to a temporarily shared social world is a basic prerequisite for linguistically mediated intersubjectivity. This is perhaps most cogently revealed in cases in which a demonstrative *that* will refer to entirely different things depending upon the joint and mutually taken-for-granted focus of attention the moment the word is uttered. Consider, for instance, the following situation. I am sitting together with a friend. On the table between us there are a pot with tea in it and several cups, only some of which are clean.

1. My friend: "Jim tries to get me fired from the job by spreading false rumours about me".
2. I: "That is dirty".

Consider, next, two different conditions of dyadic coordination of attention at the moment of my utterance. The first is a condition of mutual gaze. The two of us are in sustained eye contact throughout the chat, and my *that* refers hence anaphorically and unequivocally to *the indecent behaviour of Jim* my friend has drawn my attention to. The other condition is as follows: my friend has at the moment of my utterance the teapot in his hand and is on the verge of pouring tea in one of the cups on the table. I am watching this, *he is aware of my watching it, and I know that he is*. My *that* is in that case deictically and unequivocally referring to *the dirty cup in front of him*. This follows from our intuitive mastery of dialogue roles. My privilege as a speaker to decide what is meant and/or referred to by what I say to my conversation partner at any stage of our discourse is constrained in an orderly fashion by our mutual commitment to the temporarily shared world at that stage.

This is also clearly a basic assumption within Hintikka's game theoretical approach to semantics. Hintikka and Kulas (1982, p. 392) maintain: "Anaphoric *the*-phrases... rely on the temporary semantic situation in a game...". And the temporary semantic situation does not include fully determined individuals only, but even jointly attended-to *possibilities*. Consider, for instance, the utterance:

If John buys a car or a motorcycle, he will take good care of the vehicle.

The two possibilities (car or motorcycle) brought into joint focus of attention are by mutual commitment preserved in the reference of the expression *the vehicle* at the end of the utterance (see Hintikka and Kulas, 1982, p. 393).

The constraints upon what can be legitimately meant by what is said imposed by such mutual commitment are considerably more difficult to pin down, even though perhaps even more crucial, when we turn to the issue of which *aspects* of talked-about objects and entities are brought into joint focus attention. This is the issue Dreyfus (1979) is struggling with, I believe, when he argues (see p. 16) that conversation partners being concerned in a certain way or having a certain purpose is not something separate from their awareness of their situation. It is also, I think, what Flores and Winograd have in mind when they provokingly maintain (Flores & Winograd, 1983, p. 51): "Words themselves do not have meaning, but are given meaning by a listening for commitments in a background of shared understanding". Let us now return to the slightly modified *Sesame Street* episode, therefore, and examine parts of bananas in terms of potential aspects of talked-about whole bananas.

The expression *this banana* is no doubt used deictically and efficiently by Earnie in order to focus Bert's attention on a particular banana. Which aspects of that banana are thereby intersubjectively attended to, however, is not a matter for Earnie alone to decide. What can be *meant* and *truthfully asserted* by his expression *part of this banana* is constrained in an orderly fashion by their discourse situation and mutually taken-for-granted concern. If Earnie and Bert were talking about a particular banana while jointly concerned with it in a botanics class, for instance, the skin might thus very likely be a contextually relevant and properly talked-about part of it. But a banana *to study* in a botanics class is in semantically significant respects different from a banana *to eat* and/or to be *shared by friends*. And what constitutes proper parts of bananas cannot be determined independently of mortal men's joint concern with them and *their reasons for dividing them up*. This follows necessarily, I am afraid, once we concede that we do not (yet) know the ultimate, objective world and have hence to abandon the notion of any literal, basic, invariant and "most-down-to-earth" meaning of *banana*.

The *edibility* of the banana Earnie refers to in his friendly chat with Bert is clearly by mutual commitment part of their temporarily shared world. Earnie's giving Bert the skin is therefore as anomalous as, for example, Mrs. Smith's use of the expression *working* to refer to her husband's lawn mowing in response to a pal of his who, both of them take it for granted, is concerned with whether Mr. Smith is on the job or free to go fishing. And a similar case of anomaly would be my use of *that* to refer to the dirty conduct of Jim if the cup in front of my friend is jointly attended to by him and me at the moment of utterance. All are cases of *semantic* anomaly. Earnie's reference to the skin by the expression *part of this banana*, Mrs. Smith's reference to Mr. Smith's leisure time activity in the garden by the word *working*, and my reference to Jim's indecent conduct by the demonstrative *that*, I shall argue, violate a universal constraint upon linguistically mediated intersubjectivity having to do with mutual commitment to a temporarily shared and intersubjectively valid world.

Any ethically acceptable and psycho- and sociolinguistically plausible version of truth-conditional semantics has to live with and within this predicament. The study of meaning within natural language is thus in a very significant respect a "moral science": it leads us into absurdities unless we take into account mortal men's partial world knowledge, options with respect to perspective, and *mutual commitment to temporarily shared perspectives*. The issue of "rightness of categorization" (Goodman, 1978) must be settled prior to assessment of truth or falsity of what is meant, i.e. we have to identify the intersubjectively valid position from which something is being talked about and asserted before we can decide upon the procedures to be used to verify or falsify whatever is being asserted by what is said. The assumption underlying my somewhat pedantically elaborated "dialogical truth tables" (Rommetveit, 1979; 1984) is thus that there is a fundamental difference between *eternal* and *situated truth*. The latter is necessarily bound by mutual commitment and dyadic, dialogical control of what can be meant by what is said. This implies, in a way, a reversal of the traditional evaluation of casualness of so-called casual literal sentence meaning in ordinary, everyday discourse: literal sentence meanings are indeed from the point of view of *joint epistemic responsibility on the part of conversation partners* notoriously "casual" because they are by definition not constrained at all by mutual commitment in the discourse situation.

It is precisely at this point, however, that literacy, schooling, textbook-type written texts and Fregean semantics come soothingly to the aid of ontologically innocent lay people in need of a monistic "real world", apparently at least as early as at Grade three of elementary school. Literal sentence meanings, we are seduced to believe, stem from a far more pervasive and profoundly objective world than that of, for example, students of botanics engaged in dividing up fruits for the purpose of learning about fruit anatomy. The essences of entities within this stipulated ultimate reality are apparently such, moreover, that even eminently practical aspects such a edibility of objects are secondary and parasitic upon them. This, in short, seems to be the general kind of presupposition underlying third-graders concession that Earnie is *also* telling the truth: a standard of correctness for certain uses of *banana* anchored in textbooks of botanics is endorsed as its literal meaning and illegitimately applied to a real-life conversation between two kids concerned with bananas as edible, tasty and attractive objects.

This reversed outlook on literal sentence meaning is fully congruent with the reflections of Olson and Torrance (1985, p. 23) on literacy and schooling as the avenues to possible language-mediated worlds beyond the domain of context-bound everyday discourse, including the worlds of science, fiction, and science fiction. Their findings from developmental studies provide us with very convincing evidence concerning the way in which children in our literate societies come to treat language as an object. Their tentative map of (Olson & Torrance, 1985, p. 22) "... the route through which literacy (in our society) has its effect on cognition ..." is also fully congruent with experimental evidence of children's growing capacity to comprehend what is conveyed by the utterance as such when pictorially presented contexts seduce them to falsely focus upon purely contextually mediated features (Rommetveit, 1985).

What I question, however, is their apparent theoretical anchorage in Searle's intentional semantics and the conception of language-mediated real and/or imaginary worlds as the domain of his stipulated basic, yet context-bound literal meaning. Such a philosophical anchorage is even more clearly indicated by Hildyard and Olson (1982) in their essay on the structure and meaning of prose text. My major reservation concerning the general theory developed by Olson and coworkers can therefore be condensed into three provokingly formulated questions. What, more precisely and in socio- and psycholinguistic terms, is the (literal) sentence meaning from which casual meaning is "computed" – by Bert, for instance, and in general: *by all children before they master language as an object*? How is the stipulated "computation" of casual meaning related to mutual commitments of conversation partners with respect to temporarily yet intersubjectively valid perspective on the talked-about state of affairs? Is perhaps, after all, the very notion of (literal) sentence meaning as a "transparent" base for computation of casual meaning due to a residual of unwarranted mythical faith in literal meaning?

A pervading Utopian feature of the "abstract objectivism" of Western semantics ever since Descartes and Saussure has been a search for at least *formally acceptable* Archimedian points in assessment of linguistically mediated meaning. Winograd (1985, p. 91) comments upon the background for and outcome of this search as follows:

> In order to separate the study of semantics from problems of ontology and epistemology, it is necessary to explicate the meaning of linguistic objects in terms of something non-linguistic – something whose nature is taken for granted within the semantic theory, rather than being analyzed as part of it .... The genius of analytic philosophy has been its ability to make this kind of separation, and therefore create domains in which formal problems can be posed and solutions found.

Most of the time psycho- and sociolinguists have joined the trade of semantics with a remarkable willingness to accept even mythically stipulated entities as part of its foundation, provided that such entities are formally defined and free them from adopting hermeneutic methods or, at least, from openly confessing that they do. But such methods seem to be necessary, even though clearly insufficient in themselves, in any systematic and adequate account of casual meaning bound by mutual commitment in particular discourse situations. We cannot as researchers make sense of nor analyse the Earnie-and-Bert episode theoretically in a satisfactory way unless we somehow draw upon and systematically exploit tacit background knowledge based on our own transactions with bananas, experiences from similar situations in which friends have been sharing food, etc. Systematic exploitation of such knowledge is part and parcel of our understanding of other human beings as in some respects rational and similar to ourselves. And, as Toulmin (1970, p. 20) maintains: "...taking up the ‚rational' point of view involves considering a man's action, not *from the outside* ... but *from within the context* of the action itself..."

A major aim of *situation semantics* as it is being developed by Barwise and Perry (1983) is to preserve the assets of Fregean model theoretical semantics while modifying it radically so as to be able to account for what is meant by what is said *from within the context of the discourse situation*. Attention is thereby shifted from the conditions under which a statement is true to the conditions under which a statement "carries information" and what information it carries under those conditions. Options with respect to perspective on perceived and talked-about situations are dealt with by Barwise and Perry in terms of notions such as "visual alternatives", "visual options", and "ways of knowing". Linguistic meanings of expressions are conceived of as conventional constraints on utterances. The constraints are conditional, however, i.e. contingent upon certain background conditions (B) of types of discourse situations. And (Barwise, 1985, p. 38) "... as long as all situations that arise are of type B, then there is no reason that one will ever be aware of the dependence on B".

It remains to be seen whether the conceptual tools of situation semantics can be further developed so as to capture mutual commitment with respect to perspective of the kind illustrated by the *Sesame Street* case and Mrs. Smith's perfectly appropriate reference to her husband's lawn mowing by the expressions *working* and *not working* in two different discourse situations. Seeing the skin as part of the banana, we may perhaps argue, is not a visual alternative to either Earnie or Bert because such possibility is incompatible with what each of them firmly knows and takes for granted that his conversation partner knows about the situation.

The notion of linguistic meaning of an expression as a conditional constraint, moreover, resembles that of 'drafts of contracts' constrained by "metacontracts" of verbal communication (Rommetveit, 1974). It allows for the possibility that mutually taken-for-granted background assumptions may determine in an orderly way which components of an expression's meaning potential will be contextually appropriate. That bananas are something to eat, for instance, may very likely be considered such a background assumption embedded in the Earnie-and-Bert episode as a discourse situation.

A somewhat hermeneutically twisted version of situation semantics may hence possibly yield the conclusion concerning bananas and parts of bananas that the skin of Earnie's banana is neither a visual alternative nor a proper referent for the expression *part of this banana* in that particular discourse situation. And the verdict that Earnie is simply lying and not simultaneously telling the truth will in that case indicate that situation semantics is a "moral science", i.e. an attempt at capturing significant features of linguistically mediated meaning within a formalized conceptual framework devoid of hidden normative components and mythical faith in literal meaning.

Epilogue on Texts and Anti-texts

I do not want to conclude a discussion of literacy and the myth of literal meaning by expressing a naive and fragile hope that we may be saved from the academic evils of the myth by novel, pragmatically orientated versions of formal semantics. Winograd, among others, is utterly sceptical towards such a possibility (see Winograd, 1985). And what has been read about it above was indeed written "under erasure", to use one of Derrida's favourite terms (Derrida, 1974).

But writing under erasure is, if I have understood Derrida correctly, writing "anti-text". It is a truly revolutionary and anarchist strategy, aimed at total destruction of all those textbook-type literal meanings which not only enable Earnie to cheat Bert but jointly constitute the ontological prison of conventionally enlightened modern men. Such writing represents a fanatic protest against the ontic closure of the written text, a deliberately planned evasive manoeuvre, and is therefore clearly an illegitimate strategy within the genre of (presumedly) scientific prose. Hence, let me in my concluding reflections return to the issue of oral language alive versus written text, but add some comments (*not* under erasure!) on *writing* and *reading* as *social activities*. And I hope my readers will forgive me for starting out from a purely personal, subjective angle.

I have after a period of active empirical research for several years been reading extensively within the field of philosophy of language, formal semantics, cognitive science, psycho- and sociolinguistics and literary analysis. My reading, I must admit, has to a considerable extent been a *reading under erasure* in the sense that I have felt free to erase what was literally meant within the context provided by the author and interpret her or him against background assumptions she or he hardly held. My reading activity has for that reason, I am convinced, been replete with potentially fruitful misunderstandings.

Every attempt to *write* about the issues I was persistently concerned with while reading within this wide and diffusely defined interdisciplinary domain, however, has until now proved utterly futile. I have myself been paralysed, in a way, by fully realizing the ontic closure of the finished written text. This is particularly painful when the complexity of the topic is such that every word you tentatively ponder in order to write down is a word with a loophole, i.e. when, the very moment you hit upon it, you become fully aware of its ambiguity, how readers who do not share your background assumptions will necessarily misunderstand you, how what you want to express is only partially and imperfectly captured by that word.

My present phobia against writing, I think, is somehow profoundly related to my somewhat morbid and personal concern with the myth of literal meaning. I may perhaps, and to an extent I would not like to admit, myself have been enslaved by the myth ever since I entered the academic world. This enslavement had in my earlier and more optimistic days a magic effect which made me euphorically go on writing. What happened, I suppose, was that I attributed entirely unwarranted features of credibility and truth to my own feeble and not-fully-thought-through ideas the moment I "saw" them materialized in print, in principle preserved for eternity. This magically derived mood, however, has faded away. I have instead felt more and more stunned by realizing that whatever goes to print is beyond the scope of my modification and repair. Potential readers may freely modify and even erase it without any more mercy than I show when reading texts of authors I do not know.

My dilemma may hence perhaps be summarized as follows: I wish that what I write were written in a universally valid code, so explicitly and with such accuracy of expression that what is meant by it were, in principle, unequivocally and literally available to anyone. Something deep down inside me – the intellectualized lust for power, Derrida might say – thus wants the myth of literal meaning to come true in my own prose. But I know with absolute certainty from my life in a pluralistic and only fragmentarily known world that such a desire is futile and, indeed, absurd. And among the many consolatory features of the imperfect world I live in are the possibilities that novel insight may emerge from ambiguities and that fruitful misunderstandings may arise when texts are read within a perspective different from that of its author.

My reflections on texts and anti-texts represent an attempt to depersonalize this dilemma and hopefully raise it to a level of general theoretical interest by interpreting it as a reflection of a tension between opposed forces within our vast and varied heritage of written words. The wish for the myth of literal meaning to come true and the enjoyment of the ambiguity of human meaning, I shall argue, are in a way institutionalized in very different genres of written texts and correspondingly different ideologies of writing. Precision at the cost of semantic closure within an impoverished monistic world seems thus to be the predicament of scientific prose; ambiguity and interdeterminacy rewarded in terms of openness towards multiple "world versions" (Goodman, 1978) that of the genre of fiction writing Bakhtin, Derrida and others are particularly concerned with.

Consensus with respect to what is referred to and meant by what is written is a prerequisite for cumulative effects of individual contributions to scientific knowledge by authors living far apart. The procedures employed in a laboratory experiment, for instance, have to be accurately reported. They are not at all written down with the purpose of eliciting a manifold of potentially interesting interpretations on the part of readers who may want to replicate the study. Theoretical notions should, ideally, be equally unequivocally conveyed in formal, expository prose in order for colleagues to be able either to refute them or to accept and build further upon them. Whatever is being meant by such notions, moreover, is ontically closed in the sense that its truth or falsity can only be assessed within the particular world version endorsed by competent researchers within that particular, restricted domain of enquiry. An expression such as *father of* within the science of human genetics is thus stripped of any reference to, for example, such aspects as social kinship role.

Scientists within fields in which telescopes and microscopes come to the aid of their naked eyes can hence *live* a truly Fregean version of the myth of literal meaning while writing down their insight for eternity. Such a strategy, it seems, is not only essential to progress, but also to scientific credibility and academic respect. Ontic closure in the sense of words without any loopholes, literal meanings of expressions, and a conduit paradigm of verbal communication thus constitute from a pragmatic point of view eminently appropriate ideals for scientific writing as collective activity geared towards cumulative and consensual knowledge within restricted and world-version-closed domains. And what Popper and Habermas try to capture by the notions of "world 3 of objective knowledge" and "*die objektive Welt*", respectively, seems to be something like the sum total of updated world versions generated by institutionalized science.

The ideal-type written product of science as such a social activity are *autonomous texts* in Olson's sense. The resultant – ideally: fully text-immanent literal meaning – may, according to Olson, however, entail an intriguing component of self-fulfilling prophecy. Thus Olson (1977, p. 275) remarks: "Whether or not all meaning can be made explicit in the text is perhaps less critical than the belief that it can..." And the plausibility and theoretical significance of such a conjecture, I suspect, will be particularly cogently revealed when we turn from an analysis of pragmatic aspects of scientific writing as viewed from within that activity, to systematic investigations of relations of intertextuality between written scientific prose, dictionaries and encyclopedias, mass media texts, textbooks, discussions in schoolrooms, and everday discourse among enlightened laymen.

The *text*, in relation to which certain genres of modern fictional writing may be considered instances of *anti-text*, is language – written or oral – within which stipulated literal meanings provide a base for unwarranted faith in intersubjectivity or in an objective world by virtue of the intriguing self-fulfilling prophecy entailed within them. It is, vaguely defined, that intersection of intertextually related domains ranging all the way from authoritative scientific prose and holy scriptures to everyday oral discourse in which language users are seduced to take for granted that their human world – like finished written texts – is ontically closed and can be known by scientists in terms of atomic facts and/or by priests with access to God's wisdom. The domain of text in this particular sense is accordingly also a domain in which meaning is (Harman, 1974, p. 110) "... partly a matter of what is firmly accepted", yet *not reflected upon in terms of man-made standards of correctness.*

Endorsement of literal meaning is hence, according to the proponents of the ideology of writing underlying anti-texts, *religious faith* (in *science* and/or *God* and/or *law and order* and/or *the generalized other*) *in disguise.* It is by no means incidental, therefore, that Derrida draws heavily upon philosophers such as Heidegger and Nietzsche in his "grammatology". Another ideologist of anti-text writing, Julia Kristeva, elaborates upon Bakhtin's basic distinction between realist versus "polyphonic" novels in terms of monological versus dialogical discourse. She maintains (1978, p. 70 and pp. 76–77):

> A literary semantics must be developed on the basis of *poetic logic* where the concept of the *power of the continuum* would embody the 0–2 interval.... Within this "power of the continuum" from 0 to a specifically poetic double, the linguistic, psychic and social prohibition is 1 (God, Law, Definition).... With Bakhtin, who assimilates narrative discourse into epic discourse, narrative is a prohibition, a *monologism*, a sub-ordination to code 1, to God.... The dialogue is smothered by a *prohibition*, a censorship, such that this discourse refuses to turn back upon itself, to enter into dialogue with itself.... The narrator's absolute point of view ... coincides with the wholeness of a god or a community.

Anti-texts, on the other hand, are genuinely dialogical and self-referential in the sense that graphic patterns are written and read on the assumption that they are not to be dealt with as ontically closed products of writing, but as *traces of words with loopholes.* What is meant by them will therefore always entail a residual of indeterminacy, they remain semantically open to modification, and novel loopholes may be added when they are read by people with different background assumptions and enter into novel intertextual relations.

Ambiguity and self-reference, however, constitute characteristic features of poetic language in general (Eco, 1977, p. 262) and do not necessarily imply an *anarchistic* protest against conventionally endorsed literal meaning in the sense that what is meant *by the words by which the protest is mediated* is entirely devoid of either "God", "Law" or "Definition", i.e. detached from any collectively endorsed standard of correctness whatsoever. The most intrinsic purpose of poetic neologism is, according to Mukarovsky (1976, p. 42), "... to oppose the automatization of the act of designation". Emancipation from the prosaic, impoverished and monistic world mediated and sustained by literal meaning, however, may possibly be most safely and efficiently achieved by exploiting some linguistic conventions in order to violate others. A poet may thus cause deautomatization of designation by an unconventional syntagmatic construction, for instance, but on the firm and valid presupposition that *her or his reader is imprisoned within what is conventionally meant by the constituent words.* An illustrative case is Dylan Thomas's expression "a grief ago" (see Rommetveit, 1974, p. 21).

Derrida's chief concern is, according to his translator (Chakravorty Spivak, in Derrida, 1974, p. lxxxiv) "...to problematize the name and proper (literal) meaning, the proper in general". This is being done, it seems, in a far less destructive way by philosophers engaged in the elaboration of a causal theory of reference as an alternative to Fregean semantics (see p. 29). Preachers of the ideology of anti-text writing are self-destructive in their ardent fight against the myth of literal meaning because they do not fully appreciate the components of plausibility and truth entailed within it. They do not only fight the kind of literal meanings introduced by priests, sustained by unwarranted ontic trust in science, and reinforced by Fregean semantics, but also reject collectively endorsed standards of correctness of a kind which appears to be essential even in a poetically conducted warfare against social conventions. Such standards of correctness in conjunction with orderly negotiation of what is meant based upon mutual commitment to a temporarily shared world, I venture to claim, are prerequisites for linguistically mediated intersubjectivity between writer and reader as well as between speaker and listener.

Acknowledgement. I want to express my sincere gratitude to James V. Wertsch for inspired guidance to the works of Vygotsky, Vološinov and Bakhtin and for stimulating discussions of some of the main issues dealt with in this paper.

References

Allwood, J. (1981). On the distinction between semantics and pragmatics. In W. Klein & W. Levelt (Eds.), *Crossing the boundaries in linguistics.* Dordrecht: Reidel.

Baker, G. P., & Hacker, P. M. S. (1980). *Wittgenstein. Meaning and understanding.* Oxford: Blackwell.

Bakhtin, M. (1973). *Problems of Dostoevsky's poetics.* Ann Arbor: Ardis.

Barwise, J. (1985). *The situation in logic: Part 2. Conditionals and conditional information.* Mimeo; Stanford University.

Barwise, J. & Perry, J. (1983). *Situations and attitudes.* Cambridge, MA: M.I.T. Press

Bühler, K. (1934). *Sprachtheorie.* Jena: Fischer.

Derrida, J. (1974). *Of grammatology.* Baltimore: John Hopkins University Press.

Dreyfus, H. L. (1979). *What computers can't do. The limits of artificial intelligence.* New York: Harper.

Eco, U. (1977). *A theory of semantics.* London: McMillan.

Flores, C. F., & Winograd, T. (1983). *Understanding computers and cognition: A new foundation for design.* Mimeo, Stanford University.

Frege, G. (1969). *Funktion, Begriff, Bedeutung. Fünf logische Studien.* Göttingen: Vandenhoeck & Ruprecht.

Føllesdal, D. (1983). Situation semantics and the "slingshot" argument. *Erkenntnis,*

Geva, E., & Olson, D. (1983). Children's story telling. *First Language*, *4*, 85–109.

Goffman, E. (1976). Replies and responses. *Language in Society, 5*, 257–313.

Goodman, N. (1978). *Ways of worldmaking*. Hassocks: Harvester Press.

Habermas, J. (1981). *Theorie des kommunikativen Handelns*, I & II. Frankfurt: Suhrkamp Verlag.

Harman, G. (1974). *Thought*. New Jersey: Princeton University Press.

Hausser, R. R. (1983). On vagueness. *Journal of Semantics*, *2*, 273–302.

Hildyard, A., & Olson, D. R. (1982). On the structure and meaning of prose text. In W. Otto & S. White (Eds.), *Reading Expository Material* (pp. 155–184). New York: Academic Press.

Hintikka, J., & Kulas, J. (1982). Russell vindicated: Towards a general theory of definite descriptions. *Journal of Semantics, 1*, 387–397.

Katz, J. J. (1981). Literal meaning and logical theory. *Journal of Philosophy, 78*, 203–233.

Kripke, S. (1977). Identity and necessity. In S. P. Schwartz (Ed.), *Naming, necessity, and natural kinds* (pp. 66–101). Ithaca: Cornell University Press.

Kristeva, J. (1978). *Desire in language. A semiotic approach to literature and art*. New York: Columbia University Press.

Levelt, W. J. M. (1983). The speaker's organization of discourse. In S. Hattori & K. Inoue (Eds.), *Proceedings of the XIIIth International Congress of Linguists* (pp. 278–279). Tokyo: Proceedings Publishing Committee.

Levelt, W. J. M. (1984). Spontaneous self-repairs in speech: Processes and representations. Mimeo, Max Planck Institute for Psycholinguistics, Nijmegen.

Levelt, W. J. M., & Cutler, A. (1983). Prosodic marking in speech repair. *Journal of Semantics, 2*, 205–217.

Linell, P. (1982). *The written language bias in linguistics*. Linköping University, Studies in Communication 2.

Lyons, J. (1977). *Semantics*. Cambridge University Press.

Malinowski, B. (1984). *"Magic, science and religion" and other essays*. Glencoe: Free Press.

Marslen-Wilson, W., & Komisarjevsky-Tyler, L. (1980). The temporal structure of spoken language understanding. *Cognition, 8*, 1–17.

Maturana, H. P., & Varela, F. J. (1980). *Autopoiesis and cognition. The realization of the living*. Dordrecht: Reidel.

Mukarovsky, J. (1976). *On poetic language*. Lisse: Peter de Ridder.

Naess, A. (1969). *Hvilken verden er den virkelige?* [Which world is the real one?] Oslo: Universitetsforlaget.

Newman, D. (1982). Perspective taking versus content in understanding lies. *The Quarterly Newsletter of the Laboratory of Comparative Human Cognition, 4*, 26–29.

Olson, D. R. (1977). From utterance to text: The bias of language in speech and writing. *Harvard Educational Review, 47*, 257–281.

Olson, D. R., & Torrance, N. G. (1985). Literacy and cognitive development: A conceptual transformation in the early school years. Mimeo. To appear in S. Meadows (Ed.), *Issues in childhood cognitive development*. London: Methuen & Co.

Popper, K. R. (1971). *Objective knowledge. An evolutionary approach*. Oxford: Clarendon Press.

Putnam, H. (1978). *Meaning and the moral sciences*. London: Routledge & Kegan Paul.

Pylyshyn, Z. W. (1980). Computation and cognition: Issues in the foundations of cognitive science. *The Behavioral and Brain Sciences, 3,* 111–169.

Rommetveit, R. (1974). *On message structure. A framework for the study of language and communication,* London: Wiley.

Rommetveit, R. (1979). On "meanings" of acts and what is meant by what is said in a pluralistic social world. In M. Brenner (Ed.), *The Structure of Action* (pp. 108–149). Oxford: Blackwell & Mott.

Rommetveit, R. (1983a). Prospective social psychological contributions to a truly interdisciplinary understanding of ordinary language. *Journal of Language and Social Psychology, 2,* 89–104.

Rommetveit, R. (1983b). In search of a truly interdisciplinary semantics. A sermon on hopes of salvation from hereditary sins. *Journal of Semantics, 2,* 1–28.

Rommetveit, R. (1984). The role of language in the creation and transmission of social representations. In R. M. Farr & S. Moscovici (Eds.), *Social representations* (pp. 331–359). Paris and Cambridge: Maison des Sciences de l'Homme and Cambridge University Press.

Rommetveit R. (1985). Language acquisition as increasing linguistic structuring of experience and symbolic behavior control. In J. V. Wertsch (Ed.), *Culture, communication and cognition: Vygotskian perspectives* (pp. 183–204). New York: Cambridge University Press.

Schutz, A. (1945). On multiple realities. *Philosophy and Phenomenological Research, 5,* 533–576.

Searle, J. R. (1974). *On speech acts.* Cambridge: Cambridge University Press.

Searle, J. R. (1978). Literal meaning. *Erkenntnis, 13,* 207–224.

Searle, J. R. (1979). Metaphor. In A. Ortony (Ed.), *Metaphor and thought* (pp. 92–123). Cambridge: Cambridge University Press.

Toulmin, S. (1970). Reasons and causes. In R. Borger & F. Cioffi (Eds.), *Explanation in the behavioral sciences* (pp. 1–26). Cambridge: Cambridge University Press.

Vološinov, V. N. (1973). *Marxism and the philosophy of language.* New York: Seminar Press.

Vygotsky, L. S. (1962). *Thought and language,* New York: Wiley.

Winograd, T. (1985). Moving the semantic fulcrum. *Linguistics and Philosophy, 8,* 91–104.

von Wright, G. H. (1974). *Causality and determinism.* New York: Columbia University Press.

CHAPTER 2
The Impact of Literacy on the Conception of Language: The Case of Linguistics

Per Linell

Introduction

In recent years, we have witnessed a rapid increase in the number of books and papers dealing with differences between speech and writing, or between orality and literacy, and with the alleged social and psychological consequences of these differences (for references, see e.g. Street, 1988). Very broadly stated, we could say that after a long period of ignoring or belittling differences between speech and writing (the latter was considered basically as a trivial recording or representation of the former), media theorists as well as linguists, psychologists and anthropologists (e.g. McLuhan, Ong, Goody, Olson) started to claim that differences between speech and writing were fundamental and very important, causing far-reaching differences between oral and literate cultures. Later on, in the last few years, we have seen the antithesis of this, scholars claiming that there are many different kinds of literate and oral cultures and that relatively few, if any, properties of these cultures could be derived from the media as such (e.g. Street, 1984, 1988). It seems probable that many scholars who are conversant with the full complexity of the issues involved will opt for a synthesis; most, if not all, differences are thoroughly culture-specific and dependent on technologies, social organizations, and cultural traditions which cannot be understood as simple effects of the use of different media (speech vs. writing), and yet many of these differences are not accidental, given some of the inherent features of universal or prototypical uses of speech and writing. For example, there are bound to be some consequences of the fact that speech is multimodal (i.e., not only oral-acoustic but accompanied by various nonvocal signals) and temporally distributed, whereas writing is unimodal (visual) and spatially organized; or the fact that conversation in face-to-face encounters is highly interactional and the exchange of written messages usually much less interactional (the communication process often being unidirectional).

However, I will not discuss this issue any further here; I will simply draw attention to some of the most obvious points where the conceptions of language and communication (in the language sciences and to some extent in society at large) are strongly influenced by our long traditions of regarding certain types of written language as (the only) proper language and analysing mainly this kind of language.

The Consequences of Literacy

The term "literacy" can be used in several different ways and both at an individual level and at a collective level. For our present purposes, the latter level is more relevant. One may talk about a literate community or society if a substantial proportion of the members of the community or society is capable of reading and writing, and, in general, sharing and actively participating in a culture where writing and written language play a major role. Obviously, such a definition covers several types of "literacies" (cf. Street, 1988), each characterized by the cultural and social practices ("contexts" in Street's comprehensive sense) within which written texts and signs are used. I have chosen to set aside problems of variation here and merely assert that our Western post-industrial societies are highly literate in the general sense adopted here, and that the language sciences from which I will draw my examples are deeply embedded within these societies. It is also quite obvious that in at least some limited sectors of the Western cultures and societies, literacy has existed for hundreds of years, even a couple of millennia, and that here linguistics has had a major function in establishing, maintaining, and developing written subcultures.

There is hardly any doubt that literacy has had a major impact on the individual lives and collective achievements of people throughout history. In literature, a very broad and divergent spectrum of cognitive and social consequences has been attributed to literacy and the uses of written language. In this paper, I will focus on one specific domain, i.e., views on language itself; properties attributed to language and communication, relations between speech and writing, between language and culture, form and content, thought and communication, etc. Primarily, I will refer to present-day theories and models in linguistics and neighbouring sciences (such as philosophy of language, psychology of language, theory of literature, etc), but some of their theoretical preferences have a very long tradition in the history of linguistic ideas. Once contingent on various practical and political goals of linguistics (the maintenance and development of written language varieties used, for example, in administration, legislation, education, foreign language translation, religious contexts, etc.), they are now usually justified (at least by the linguists) on rather different ("theoretical") grounds.

The Conduit Metaphor of Communication

It seems appropriate to begin with the extremely pervasive model of linguistic communication which portrays the communication process as the conveyance of a message, or, in other words, some kind of "transportation" of a certain fixed meaning or "content" from the speaker to the listener, a transmission of information, or a transfer of thoughts and feelings, as if these latter phenomena were independent of or prior to the various "coding" processes involved at different stages. Reddy (1979) introduced the term "conduit metaphor" for this way of construing linguistic communication:

> (1) Language functions like a conduit, transferring thoughts bodily from one person to another; (2) in writing and speaking, people insert their thoughts and feelings in the words; (3) words accomplish the transfer by containing the thoughts or feelings and conveying them to others; and (4) in listening or reading, people extract the thoughts and feelings once again from the words.(p. 290)

There are a number of other designations for this type of model, e.g., "translation theory of speech communication" (e.g. Harris, 1981) or "pipeline model of communication" (Ong, 1982, p. 176), and a lot of common terms and everyday expressions are connected with it. Words, sentences, and texts are seen as containers loaded with content, i.e., meaning; words are "meaning-full" (see Reddy, op. cit., for many examples). Terms like "sender" and "receiver" (or "recipient") are commonplace and may invite a way of looking upon speakers and listeners as simply "sending" and "receiving" packages with ready-made contents.

The "translation theory" has a long history. It has been put forward by, among others, Locke in *An Essay Concerning Human Understanding* (cf. Parkinson, 1977; Harris, 1981, pp. 86–88). Locke assumed communication to be a matter of transferring thoughts from one person's mind to another's. Saussure (1916/1964) accepted the same kind of theory (*circuit de la parole*), and later the theory acquired some new inspiration from Shannon and Weaver's classical model of technical information transfer. It recurs in almost every modern introduction to linguistics or speech communication (cf. e.g., Fig. 1). In generative grammar, psycholinguistics, information-processing theories of cognitive psychology, etc., it appears disguised in slightly different terms, often with more abstract labels (Fig. 2).

The translation model is a thoroughly misleading and inadequate model of interpersonal communication, particularly as regards face-to-face interaction. It is, however, less inaccurate when applied to communication by means of written texts. In this latter case, production and comprehension activities are more easily separated, writers operate more or less independently of readers, and the whole process is often unidirectional in nature; i.e. one person first writes a letter or a book, then sends it away to an addressee/recipient (or a group of recipients), who will then read it. The written text has to be relatively explicit and relatively autonomous in various ways.

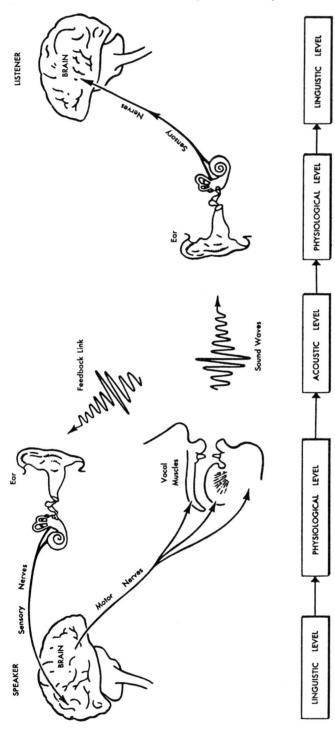

Fig. 1. The Speech Chain: the different forms in which a spoken message exists in its progress from the mind of the speaker to the mind of the listener. (From Denes & Pinson, 1963)

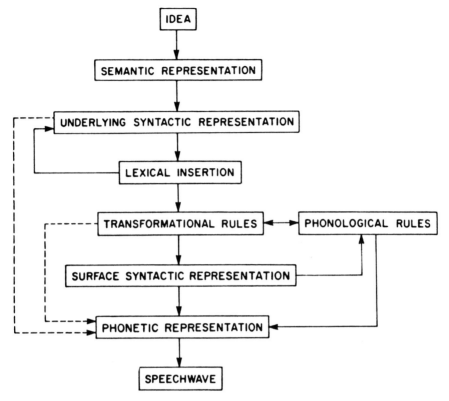

Fig. 2. A possible information-flow model of speech production. *Dotted lines* represent controversial routes of information-flow to which some of this paper is addressed. Note that the information carried by these dotted lines could, alternatively, be transmitted via the *solid lines*. In addition, the placement of Semantic Representation is not meant to imply that *all* semantic processing is conducted at this level. In fact, there is linguistic rationale for the notion that some semantic interpretation is applied after the computation of a surface structure. (Figure and text from Cooper, 1980)

Although the reader too must rely on various expectations and background knowledge, he is often strongly guided by the text in his interpretive activities. However, contrary to what the conduit metaphor may seduce us into believing, the actual situated interpretations relevant to speakers and listeners, and to writers and readers, are never equal to the linguistic meaning associated with the linguistic expressions used in the discourse or text. Any interpretation goes beyond the linguistic meaning (which is in itself vague and allusive, next section), and rests upon knowledge of the world and a (more or less) shared commitment to a particular perspective on the subject matter (cf. Rommetveit, 1988).

Furthermore, the conduit metaphor provides a distorted picture of the

creativity and interactivity involved in speaking and listening. Spoken interaction is not a matter of sequencing a number of distinct unidirectional processes. It is misleading to think that the whole process basically involves one
person (A) first getting an idea, then coding it in words (speaking), then
another person (B) perceiving and comprehending this utterance, then B
getting some new ideas, coding them, i.e. producing a second utterance, then
A receiving this, etc. What is going on is something rather different. There is,
at least in the case of impromptu speech, no complete linguistic meaning and
no fully developed, intended interpretation in the mind of the speaker before
he has found his words and thus compiled his utterance. Many aspects of
meaning are the result of the verbalization process itself, and often enough the
speaker himself discovers possible interpretations after having produced his
utterance. In fact, speakers speak not only in order to be understood, but also
in order to understand what they themselves say and think. Thus, the speaker
is also a recipient, and there is some parallel between the speaker's predicament and the listener's; they both proceed from pre-understanding to understanding.

   A related point, which is also completely missed by the conduit metaphor,
is the fact that so much of the dialogue and its constituents is the outcome of a
collective achievement by the interlocutors. While speaking, the speaker normally reacts to the feedback provided by his interactants in the form of various
non-verbal signals, so-called backchannel talk, perhaps attempts at taking
over the floor. Empirical data have shown that speakers' plans for what will be
said later on in the same utterance are quite short-ranged and subject to
constant modification. The listeners' behaviour often influences the contin-
uation and completion of the speaker's utterances. Sometimes, the listener's
interventions involve filling in words or completing the speaker's sentences,
and in some cases the whole dialogue temporarily turns into a verbal duet.

The Notion of Literal Meaning

Another popular and time-honoured idea, much cherished in linguistics as
well as in our literate culture at large, is the view that there are fixed meanings
or interpretations inherent in or associated with the linguistic signs as such, i.e.
words, sentences and even texts are believed to have certain context-independent "linguistic meanings" in them. Sometimes, these semantic entities are
called "literal meanings" (note the term which suggests that what is fixed and
given is present in the "written letter"). The assumption of literal meanings
pertains to several linguistic levels. I will briefly mention two (see also Rommetveit, 1988).

   The standard view is that word meanings are definite, fixed and stable, e.g.
a set of invariant semantic features. These meanings are ready-made, existing
"out there" in the language as a system, and as such they are available for use

by speakers and listeners (or writers and readers). Vološinov (1930/1973) argues that this conventional view on word meaning derives from the traditional work by linguists and philologists on written texts in foreign languages which has necessitated the construction of dictionaries with their standard definitions presupposing that lexical meanings can be given in terms of a fixed configuration of semantic features (or a fixed combination of *other* words).

If we were to build a theory of word meaning on observations of what words mean in actual use in spoken interaction, it would probably be more natural to look upon the meaning of a given word as something which is "dynamic, only partially determined" and "open and susceptible to contextual modifications" "in communication when what is initially intersubjectively shared becomes expanded and/or modified" (Rommetveit & Blakar, 1978, p. 354). The lexical meaning of the word must then be looked upon as something very abstract, a *potential* of eliciting, in interaction with various situational factors, certain semantic operations in the mind of the language user who will end up with some kind of understanding in the specific contexts. But there are no fixed "literal" meanings which are invariably activated when utterances containing certain specific words are processed, no invariant features constituting the subject matter every time a particular word is used. In each single case different things are, or may be, made known and understood.

Another part of the theory of literal meaning has to do with meanings or interpretations of specific communicative acts, discourses or texts. Here, the theory says that there are basically two kinds of communicative acts, one in which the situational interpretation, i.e. what is or should be made known and understood, is simply and precisely equal to the linguistic ("literal") meaning of the words (configuration of words) used, and one more complex type in which the understanding involves something more; the speaker does not mean (or is not understood to mean) "exactly what he says", and hence we must compute some kind of "non-literal" or "figurative" interpretation (such as indirect requests, metaphors, jokes, irony, sarcasm, and many other implicatures). This theory, which builds upon a possible discrepancy between "what is given in the words" and "what is reinterpreted into them, or assigned to them", is clearly part of our common literate culture and has, in fact, been attributed precisely to the development of writing and printing (Olson, 1987). In modern linguistic pragmatics, it forms the basis of the distinction between direct and indirect speech acts (e.g. Searle, 1969).

Even if communicative acts clearly vary along dimensions of directness and explicitness, there seem to be no cases where understanding amounts "just" to retrieving or constructing a literal meaning and where the speaker only relies on language in his attempt to have the listener understand something. There are always aspects of communication which go beyond what follows from the linguistic expressions as such; various kinds of background knowledge have to be used, reference to situation-specific elements (so-called indexical features) is very often necessary, the "why of communication" (Ducrot, 1972) (why is this said and here, now?) is always more or less relevant and cannot be directly or exhaustively derived from the linguistic expressions as such. As Rommetveit (1988) argues, what is meant, truthfully asserted, and mutually taken for granted in each discourse situation is profoundly context bound. In real life, we are constantly engaged in attempts at interpreting and understanding parts of the world around us, and these sense-making activities are performed within a "wide context" (cf. Street, 1988) involving sedimented and culturally shared conceptualizations as well as our personal knowledge of the world (large parts of which have never been verbalized, cf. Polanyi, 1978). There is now a fairly unanimous agreement (see several contributions to this volume) that very little of these sense-making practices can be explicated in terms of literal word and sentence meanings, with their decontextualization, item orientation and secludedness.

On the other hand, there are some specific situations in our literate culture, where the use of written messages comes close to some kind of context independency and autonomy. The most extreme examples can probably be found in the use and interpretation of mathematical and logical symbols. In addition, there are quite different contexts, where texts are used under the tacit convention that the user should not read his own subjective ideas into them. (Accordingly, *this*, i.e. these conventions, belongs to the background knowledge needed for anyone to behave properly in *these* situations.) Examples range from the exegesis of religious texts (Luther's idea that the meaning of the Holy Scripture was there in "God's pure words") to the habit among contemporary linguists to analyze (written) sentences in abstracto, thereby figuring out what their "semantic representations" might be.

Language as a Structured Set of Abstract Objects

Human language can be studied within many different frames of conceptualization. Accordingly, the approaches of different disciplines are quite divergent. Within linguistics, however, we find a traditional preference for an abstract, decontextualized way of looking upon language. In modern linguistics a dichotomy is often made between the *structure* and the *use* of language. Although both perspectives are usually regarded as perfectly legitimate, there is no doubt that the structural perspective is considered to be the one appropriate for linguistics proper. That is, linguists study "structure" rather than "use", "system" rather than "behaviour" (or actual texts), "abstract resources" rather than "signals" or "actions" (in which the abstract resources are put to use). Other well-known term pairs are "langue" vs "parole" (Saussure), "competence" vs "performance" (Chomsky) and "language" vs "speech" (or "discourse").

It would not be unfair to say that the dominant attitude within linguistics has been to ignore the differences between the linguistic systems underlying speech and writing. It has been assumed that (within each linguistic community) there is one single system (in Saussurean terms: *la langue*) underlying all kinds of (correct) manifestations of the linguistic system. (By linguistic system we could then mean (in lay terms) either a "language", e.g. English, or a "dialect", e.g. Cockney). However, it is also true that linguists have, despite the arguments for the primacy of spoken language, based their descriptions and theories of this underlying monolithic linguistic system upon considerations of (certain kinds of) written language. In fact, terms like "speech" and "parole" have been reserved for the use of language in context, something which has been, as we just noted, of secondary interest to linguists.

There are a number of very strong structural factors which have kept linguists concentrating their scholarly efforts on the study of written language. One complex of factors has to do with cultural values traditionally associated with literacy and written language. Here, the activities of linguists (and other scholars) have also reinforced the positive evaluation of writing at the cost of speech, so there is obviously a reflexive relationship between commonly held value judgements and the scientific interests of scholars. But in addition to this, the limitations on available technology has strongly favoured the study of written language. In fact, writing is not simply a form of using a language (seen as an abstract symbol system), it is also the most important technology used in the study of language. Up until quite recently, when audio and video recorders became publicly available, writing was the only means of recording speech, and even today, spoken language can hardly be subjected to linguistic analysis without the use of written transcripts. Thus, even those who are determined to study spoken language on its own terms cannot entirely escape the effects that follow from the use of writing as a medium and written language as a metalanguage.

There can be no doubt that our way of conceptualizing language will be influenced by the form in which we encounter it, as spatially organized marks on a flat surface or as transient actions or acoustic events. Writing has encouraged a conception of language as a set of hierarchically organized abstract objects (e.g. a set of sentences). As Vološinov (1973, p. 78) puts it: "formalism and systematicity of the types so well illustrated in the practice of grammarians, lexicographers, logicians etc are the typical distinguishing marks of any kind of thinking focused on a ready-made and, so to speak, arrested object".

Language as a Property of the Individual Mind

The dominant traditions in linguistics treat language as a supraindividual system of abstract objects. As we have just seen, this is connected with the long-established focus on written language. In modern linguistics, especially generative transformational linguistics, this has met with a seemingly quite different intellectual tradition, i.e. cognitive psychology (cf. Chomsky, 1968). The two traditions produced a common offspring, psycholinguistics, a discipline which, according to many contemporary commentators, has suffered from a kind of hereditary schizophrenia. There is much to be said in favour of this sort of diagnosis, but in this context it may be more relevant to point out that the psychological traditions involved are also associated with a dependency on literacy and written language.

It is quite conspicuous and rather remarkable that the field of language psychology in general, not to speak of psycholinguistics, is so closely associated with individual cognitive psychology. Given that the natural habitat of everyday language is spoken interaction in face-to-face encounters, one would expect "the psychology of language" to cover a great deal of social psychology. Though the social psychology of language does exist as a field, it is still a very small one and regarded as more or less of marginal interest in linguistics as well as in psychology and sociology. There are obviously many causes of this state of affairs which I cannot go into here. What is essential in this context is simply that mainstream (American) psychology of language has such a consistent way of looking upon language almost exclusively as a medium for intraindividual information processing (as in monologic activities including writing and reading) rather than as a means for interpersonal communication. Language is regarded as a property of individual minds rather than as something that comes into existence in and through the dynamic interaction between people (or, if you will, between different people's minds). Activities like the production and understanding of text and discourse are exclusively treated as taking place within solitary individuals' mental systems for information processing. At a very concrete level, the impact of literate society on research in psycholinguistics is quite strong; most experiments on, for example, language comprehension or memory for linguistic material use written words, sentences, or texts as data, or if one works at all with spoken material, then it usually consists of decontextualized sentences or monologic texts (narratives) taken out of a natural communicative context. More generally, the ubiquitous emphasis on the solitary individual is, of course, quite compatible with widespread tendencies in a highly literate society, where only limited interest is devoted to everyday language use in oral contexts.

Language as an Intellectual Tool

Those who are familiar with the linguistic and philosophical literature on language will not fail to notice that very little attention is devoted to the topic of "language and emotion". Language is usually regarded almost exclusively as an intellectual tool, as a medium for the communication and representation of cognitive information. Again, this seems to be in perfect agreement with what one would expect if the proper and most important uses of language are the literate ones. It has often been claimed that Western literacy, centred around the technology of printing, fosters an intellectualized kind of human being (McLuhan). Such a view might turn out to be a rather gross exaggeration, but there is hardly any doubt that the various technologies associated with writing have greatly enhanced our capacity for storing information and performing cognitive operations. On the other hand, it is hardly self-evident that language has no important functions when it comes to the expression, evocation and representation of emotions, especially if we consider the fact that in speech, verbal language concurs with paralanguage, i.e. vocal and non-vocal signals of various kinds. What is evident, however, is that linguistics, with its traditional bias towards written language, is ill-equipped to cope with the relations between language and emotions. Let me draw attention to a few points in this context.

First, emotions are expressed, evoked and communicated by means of paralanguage rather than by language in a narrow sense, and more directly through speech than writing, while linguistics has dissociated itself from paralanguage, which is poorly or not at all represented in normal writing. Secondly, whereas emotions are tied to the language users acting under situated conditions, linguistics has been obsessed almost only with the structures of linguistic systems abstracted from the contexts of use. Thirdly, emotions are *shown rather than said* (according to a distinction going back to Wittgenstein), but linguistics has been concerned only with that which is verbally coded in a narrow sense, i.e. the meaning potentials of words and grammatical constructions. Linguistics has concentrated on the *what* of communication, where "what" means "what is verbally coded", but a more comprehensive theory of human communication must also consider the *why* of communication, where "why" has to cover such emotively loaded questions as "for what reason" and "to what effect" (cf. Linell, 1985).

Linguistic Units: The Role of the Sentence

Within linguistics, two kinds of units have competed for the status of "primary unit of language", i.e. "words" and "sentences". Of course, various modern linguistic theories have, at least at certain points, developed more sophisticated notions, but – by and large – both these unit types are based on needs experienced by those who have developed or analysed conventional writing systems; in short, words are units separated by blank spaces in printing and sentences are units demarcated by major punctuation signs. In impromptu speech, which is, after all, the most frequent type of spoken language in actual use, things are not that simple. There are grammatical criteria for analysing what is said in terms of word strings, but many word boundaries are not so easy to draw, certainly not by recourse only to phonetic facts (something which can be seen in young children's first written products). There are many problems connected with the definition of words here, and I have not even introduced the fundamental distinction between lexical items and (surface) word forms appearing in actual discourse, but I shall put these aside here and turn to the notion of sentence.

The role of the sentence is particularly interesting to us, since this very concept is so clearly an artefact of the literate culture. Moreover, in modern theoretical linguistics the sentence has taken over the role as the basic unit of analysis. I cannot go into a technical discussion of how to define "sentence"; the general idea of the kind of syntactic configuration demarcated by major punctuation marks in expository prose will suffice for my purposes here. Such units obviously have identifiable starting points and end points, they have certain structural properties such as (more or less) clear differences between main and subordinate clauses, and their constituent clauses have certain grammatical properties (they are analysable, at least in most cases and in most languages, in terms of subject and predicate, or verb plus arguments). Now the point is that there are no such clear-cut sentences in most cases of impromptu speech. Instead, talk consists of phrases and clauses which are more loosely related to each other, building up structures which are less clear and less hierarchical than in grammar books (and also actual writing). However, as members of a highly literate culture, where people have been – directly or indirectly, through schooling and education – accustomed to perceiving language in terms of units designed for written language, we are only marginally aware of this fact; laymen usually believe that they speak in full sentences, and only when they have listened to tape recordings, perhaps also supported by veridical transcripts, do they discover what the facts are.

The theoretical status of the sentence in modern linguistics may be epitomized by Chomsky's (1957) well-known definition of a language as a definite (infinite but enumerable) set of grammatical sentences. This view involves the written language bias in many ways. It pictures language as a set of objects (products rather than processes) (cf. above), it assigns a central importance to the notion of grammaticality, not an unproblematic concept when it comes to actual spoken language but traditionally quite important in grammar books dealing with (proper) written language, and it focuses on the unit of sentence. Apart from what has just been said about sentences, I will just mention one additional aspect: sentences are treated in grammatical theory as if they were simply strings of words without any prosodic structure (stress, intonation, rhythm, etc.). Of course, this is true of written language, but in speech, prosody is an integrating aspect of all utterances. Moreover, prosody is highly significant. For example, most of the emotive and social meaning invariably present in all face-to-face encounters is conveyed by prosody and paralanguage. Yet, this is treated in linguistics as outside, or at least peripheral to, a proper linguistic analysis. As a further case in point, one might note the discussion of "ambiguous sentences" like *Visiting aunts can be a nuisance* or *What disturbed John was being disregarded by everyone* (such sentences are discussed in most introductions to linguistic analysis). An orthodox analysis would maintain that these sentences have several readings (note the term reading!), and that these readings with their distinct meanings are *disambiguated* in speech. If speech had been considered primary, one would have to talk about ambiguation in writing rather than disambiguation in speech.

The Sound Structure of Spoken Language

Finally, let us consider the nature of the phonetic signals, i.e. the sounds produced and perceived in speech. These are obviously something which distinguishes spoken language from its written counterpart, and it would therefore be particularly revealing if the impact of literacy were manifest in phonetics too, i.e. in the field which deals specifically with sound structure. Indeed it is; we find some of the most beautiful examples of the written language bias in this area.

Phonetic behaviour and the resulting acoustic signals are continuous dynamic phenomena. The various phonetic gestures involved in speech production overlap and have no abrupt onsets and offsets. Yet it is generally assumed that there are abstract phonological structures, strings of discrete, static sound segments ("phonemes") underlying speech. In other words, phonological structures would be structurally similar to strings of alphabetic letters. Moreover, linguists use such letters not only in abstract phonological representations, they also use them – modified by various diacritical marks – in so-called narrow phonetic transcription, i.e. when the aim is to capture phonetic details. This means that our view of phonetic structure is influenced by the outer form of this written metalanguage.

There is hardly any reason to doubt that the idea of underlying segments has *some* kind of natural basis in speech production and perception (also for non-literate speakers and listeners). For example, there is substantial evidence for units like syllables, vowels, and consonants as units of production; common slips of the tongue like *spictly streaking* (for *strictly speaking*) and *struncture and fucture* (for *structure and function*) are but one type of evidence. Nevertheless, there is reason to believe that literacy has enhanced our experience of speech as being composed of segments (and nothing but segments). In lay conceptions of language, sounds and letters are seldom kept distinct (and it took linguists a very long time to become aware of the differences involved). It is also well known that once a person has acquired sufficient knowledge of conventional orthography, he will have considerable difficulties in hearing the actual phonetic details of his mother tongue (e.g. Ehri, 1985). At the same time we know, for example from spontaneous spellings by young children, that some of these details can be heard by the unprejudiced mind (Read, 1971). The impact of literacy thus seems to work also at the level of automatic speech perception.

The development of alphabetic writing constitutes a rather clear example of the reflexive relationship between theory and technology. When, in the beginning, the continuous and varying stream of speech behaviour was to be notated in writing, there arose a need for a parsimonious set of discrete signs, e.g., picture types or, at a more abstract level, letters. Ultimately, a workable notational system presupposed an analysis of speech in terms of segments of some sort. While there was a natural basis for this, the new emerging software, i.e. the alphabet, assigned to speech a more extreme, as it were more simplified, segmental structure than the phonetic facts seem to warrant. Some features of the stream of speech behaviour (or, if you prefer, in the flow of acoustic events) were amplified, while others, e.g. many prosodic aspects, were tuned down or even eliminated. Once this structure had been imposed on speech, it became virtually impossible to go back and imagine how it might be perceived without it.

This segment-based view governs thinking in linguistics as well as in lay conceptions of speech. Linguists, for their part, have stated the phonemic principle and developed intricate theories to reconcile the assumption of an underlying segmental structure with facts about the continuous phonetic signals. The general public, on the other hand, tends to take for granted that speaking consists of the pronunciation of strings of units, letters forming words and words forming clauses and sentences. Thus, there is a clear relation between what scientific theories and textbooks say and what the "innocent layman" believes (cf. Rommetveit, 1988, on Fregean semantics and the myths of literal meaning "lived by enlightened and literate citizens").

The Ubiquity of the Written Language Bias

I have now completed a very brief account of some elements of the written language bias in the language sciences. A more comprehensive treatment could have listed many more examples (see Linell, 1982). Some of these examples come from linguistics in the narrow sense, but many actually pertain to other disciplines, e.g. philosophy, psychology, sociology, pedagogy, literary studies and general communication theory. It is not only language as such which is approached within frameworks dependent on a preference for written language. A wide range of language-related phenomena are also understood in ways that are reflections of the same attitudes. For example, conventional ways of looking upon such concepts as "knowledge" and "learning", in educational sciences and elsewhere, seem to bear witness to this. Knowledge is often, in our culture, identified with fairly superficial pieces of information (factual knowledge) and with verbally coded (or codable) information; aspects involving complex interactions between the individual and the world, so-called tacit or personal knowledge, skills, etc, are often neglected or considered less important. In theories of learning and thinking, content is often treated as context-independent information units, as if this content could be assumed to exist prior to and independently of the contexts where learning and communication take place. Actually, processes of learning and communication are, of course, dependent on various contextual conditions, such as institutionalized premises of communicative activities, cognitive attitudes of the actors to the tasks involved etc. (see Säljö, 1988, and other contributions to this volume). But the theories of decontextualized content alluded to here are fully in line with prominent characteristics of the written language bias in our literate culture (e.g. the separation of form from content involved in the conduit metaphor of communication).

The written language bias is part of our overall culture of today and past times. It is not confined to linguistics and other language sciences. As I pointed out in my introduction, this is not hard to explain. Linguists and other scholars carry out their scientific activities on conditions defined by the surrounding cultures. Tasks and interests are related to political goals and practical needs existing in society at large, and the cultural values prevalent in society will, of course, also determine crucial features of the scholars' outlook on the world. Conversely, linguists and others have had a major role in developing these cultural values and theoretical conceptualizations. The schooling and educational systems in the Western world have always involved a great deal of linguistic cultivation, and certain kinds of uses of the written language have been systematically encouraged at school.

The impact of the linguists' scholarly activities can therefore be indirectly observed in the "linguistic folklore" that is passed down from generation to generation. Norms for linguistic correctness are strongly influenced by what grammar books say about (certain forms of) written language, and spoken vernaculars are almost invariably looked upon as less correct and less proper language (witness, for example, letters to the editors of so many newspapers and journals). Everyday language is replete with words and metaphors associated with the conduit view of communication (Reddy, 1979; Lakoff & Johnson, 1980). The lay terms for elements of language may be regarded as popular and simplistic versions of written language-biased concepts stemming from linguistics; terms like "word", "sound" (often confused with "letter"), "sentence" are but a few examples. Some words used about talking focus primarily on fairly "literate" forms of talk. As a single case in point, note that the everyday noun "speech" (countable: one speech, several speeches) refers to monologic speech events, not the more mundane and more frequent activities which in English are designated by Latin or Greek terms ("conversation", "dialogue").

Concluding Discussion

The written language bias in the language sciences is a very complex matter with many facets. One may discuss it in at least three different contexts;

written language as data, written language as metalanguage, and written language and literacy as part of the general cultural climate.If we consider the *data* which have been used and analysed by linguists, one may argue that they have traditionally been neither written language proper (i.e., real specimens of written language actually used) nor spoken language. Instead, in textbooks and in papers reporting on research from most subfields of linguistics we are faced with some sort of abstract, artificial language neutral with respect to medium. We find decontextualized linguistic specimens – isolated words and sentences – rather than coherent texts or discourses drawn from actual, or potential, communicative activities. (Such items are contextualized only at a secondary metalevel, that of the language lesson or the linguistic analysis itself.) The basic decontextualization, a process by which linguists, as it were, construct their own data (cf. linguists as "language makers", according to Harris, 1980), is regarded as a natural step, necessary if we want to study "language itself" (the system, *la langue*) rather than language use (*la parole*). This use of decontextualized specimens is characteristic of most subfields, not only theoretical grammar but also, for example, phonetics and experimental psycholinguistics. In phonetics, for example, one has traditionally used isolated words and sentences as data, and it is quite symptomatic that when phoneticians study longer stretches of speech, they choose monologic parts, often text paragraphs read aloud. Very few, if any, phoneticians have so far studied the phonetic mechanisms used in dialogue for regulating interaction.

Thus, there is a preference for "abstract, neutral" language data in linguistics. However, these data are shaped in ways which are strongly dependent on facts and ideals (and myths!) connected with specific sorts of actual written language, particularly expository prose. While it is true that some writing-specific traits, such as layout, punctuation, certain genre-specific features, have usually been eschewed in linguistics, it is a much *more* conspicuous fact that linguists have refrained from treating speech-specific features at their face values. This is especially true when it comes to spoken language used in interaction, in spite of the fact that conversation is the most natural habitat of language in everyday life.

Secondly, we have seen that written language has served as the *technology* and *metalanguage* of linguistic analysis, also when the data have indeed been drawn from situated speech communication. Phonetic structures are given in (modified) alphabetic notation, and dialogue analyses are carried out using written transcripts. Apart from the fact that transcription necessarily involves the elimination of a wealth of prosodic, paralinguistic and contextual features, it amounts to the transformation of a stream of transient, dynamic and interactive behaviour to a static, spatially organized, and, as it were, arrested object existing simultaneously in its totality. We can only speculate on what exactly is the impact of this transformation from speech to writing on the results of analyses (cf. Linell, 1986).

Thirdly, and perhaps even more importantly, linguistics (like other scientific activities) is embedded in an *academic literate culture*, a cluster of explicit theories and implicit assumptions about, among other things, language and the world, which have been developed and established over the centuries. As a whole, this acts like a huge filter which will bias the outcome of specific analyses. The whole complex involves a number of misleading or mistaken assumptions about the use of language in communication and thought. The conduit metaphor of communication, the notion of literal meaning, the alleged possibility of autonomous (decontextualized) use of language (meanings given and inherent in the texts as such), and language (or linguistic competence) as a well-defined set of items and rules are but a few examples. Even if the inadequacy of the specific theoretical claims involved in these and other cases pertains to both written and spoken language, it must be said that the inadequacy is more salient as regards spoken language.

In general, the written language bias in linguistics cannot be derived from properties of writing and written language per se. Differences between oral and literate cultures cannot be derived from inherent properties of the media in isolation but have to do with the social institutions in which the uses of spoken and written varieties are embedded. In our case, we are apparently faced with a somewhat fuzzy set of cultural traditions and conceptualizations, a special type of literacy developed in Western culture and possibly dependent on some accidental historical circumstances, as discussed by Street (1984). On the other hand, Rommetveit (1988) argues convincingly that some of the features that we have identified as typical of the written language bias in Western literate culture, e.g., the striving for invariant and stable meanings of words (literal meanings), is part and parcel of a need – on the part of "innocent lay people" – to believe in a "monistic, real world"; in Rommetveit's words, "something deep down inside us ... wants the myth of literal meaning to come true", and it still remains to be seen how universal this desire is.

Note. I have treated the issues involved in "the written language bias in linguistics" more extensively in Linell (1982), which is a next-to-final version of a book in progress. The short paper published here was presented at the symposium on *The Written Code and Conceptions of Reality*, held in Sydkoster, Sweden, on August 26–29, 1985, and at the LSA Summer Institute, held at Georgetown University, Washington, D.C., in July, 1985. I wish to thank the discussants at both places, especially Wallace Chafe, Florian Coulmas and James D. McCawley.

References

Chomsky, N. (1957). *Syntactic structures*. The Hague: Mouton.
Chomsky, N. (1968). *Language and mind*. New York: Harcourt, Brace & World.
Cooper, W. E. (1980). Syntactic-to-phonetic coding. In B. Butterworth (Ed.), *Language production, Vol.1: Speech and talk* (pp. 297–333). London: Academic Press.

Denes, P., & Pinson, E. (1963). *The speech chain*. Baltimore: Bell Telephone Laboratories.

Ducrot, O. (1972). *Dire et ne pas dire. Principes de semantique linguistique*. Paris: Hermann.

Ehri, L. (1985). Effects of printed language acquisition on speech. In D. Olson, N. Torrance, & A. Hildyard (Eds.), *Literacy, language, and learning. The nature and consequences of reading and writing* (pp. 333–367). Cambridge: Cambridge University Press.

Harris, R. (1980). *The languagemakers*. London: Duckworth.

Harris, R. (1981). *The language myth*. London: Duckworth.

Lakoff, G., & Johnson, M. (1980). *Metaphors we live by*. Chicago: The University of Chicago Press.

Linell, P. (1982). The written language bias in linguistics. *SIC 2*. Linköping: Department of Communication Studies.

Linell, P. (1985). Language and the communication of emotion. In S. Bäckman & G. Kjellmer (Eds.), *Papers on language and literature. Presented to Alvar Ellegård and Erik Frykman* (pp. 264–273). Göteborg: Acta Universitatis Gothoburgensis.

Linell, P. (1986). Problems and perspectives in the study of spoken interaction. In L. S. Evensen (Ed.), *Nordic research in text linguistics and discourse analysis* (pp. 103–136). Trondheim: TAPIR.

Olson, D. (1987). *The world on paper*. Unpublished manuscript.

Ong, W. (1982). *Orality and literacy. The technologizing of the word*. London: Methuen.

Parkinson, G. H. R. (1977). The translation theory of understanding. In G. Vesey (Ed.), *Communication and understanding* (pp. 1–19). London: Hassocks.

Polanyi, M. (1978). *Personal knowledge*. London: Routledge & Kegan Paul.

Read, C. (1971). Preschool children's knowledge of English phonology. *Harvard Educational Review*, *41*, 1–34.

Reddy, M. (1979). The conduit metaphor – a case of frame conflict in our language about language. In A. Ortony (Ed.), *Metaphor and thought* (pp. 284–324). Cambridge: Cambridge University Press.

Rommetveit, R. (1988). On literacy and the myth of literal meaning. In this volume.

Rommetveit, R., & Blakar, R. (Eds.). (1978). *Studies of language, thought and verbal communication*. London: Academic Press.

Säljö, R. (1988). A text and its meanings: Observations on how people construe what is meant from what is written. In this volume.

Saussure, F. de. (1916/1964). *Cours de linguistique générale*. Paris: Payot.

Searle, J. (1969). *Speech acts*. Cambridge: Cambridge University Press.

Street, B. (1984). *Literacy in theory and practice*. Cambridge: Cambridge University Press.

Street, B. (1988). Literacy practices and literacy myths. In this volume.

Vološinov, V. N. (1973). *Marxism and the philosophy of language*. (L. Matejka and I. R. Titunik, Trans.). New York: Seminar. (Original work published 1930)

CHAPTER 3

Literacy Practices and Literacy Myths

Brian V. Street

During the early 1980s there appeared in the United States, a number of collections of academic papers that claimed to represent the relationship between literacy and orality as a "continuum" rather than, as in much of the previous literature, as a "divide" (cf. Coulmas & Ehlich, 1983; Frawley, 1982; Olson, Hildyard & Torrance, 1985; Nystrand, 1982; Tannen, 1982b; Wagner, 1983; Whiteman, 1981). It appeared that the differences between literate and oral channels of communication had been overstated in the past and that scholars were now more concerned with overlap, mix and diverse functions in context. I shall examine some of these new representations, and argue that the supposed shift from divide to continuum is more rhetorical than real: that, in fact, many of the writers in this field continue to represent literacy as sufficiently different from orality in its social and cognitive consequences, that their findings scarcely differ from the classic concept of the "great divide" (cf. Goody, 1977). I shall argue that the implicit persistence of claims that the practitioners themselves would often explicitly reject can be explained with reference to the methodological and theoretical assumptions that underlie their work: in particular a narrow definition of social context, related to the split in linguistics between pragmatics and semantics; the reification of literacy in itself at the expense of recognition of its location in structures of power and ideology, also related to general linguistic assumptions about the "neutrality" of their object of study; and the restriction of "meaning" within traditional linguistics to the level of syntax.

I would like to suggest an alternative approach, which would avoid some of the problems generated by these assumptions and which genuinely moves us beyond the great divide. I have outlined elsewhere a distinction between "autonomous" and "ideological" models of literacy (Street, 1984, 1985, 1986, 1987) and I would now like to offer some further clarification (in view of some confusions that have arisen) and to locate the models in the broader context of linguistic and anthropological theory and methodology. In an earlier work (Street, 1984) I distinguished between an autonomous model of literacy, whose exponents studied literacy in its technical aspects, independent of social context, and an ideological model, employed by recent researchers whose concern has been to see literacy practices as inextricably linked to cultural and power structures in a given society. Some critics have taken the distinction to involve an unnecessary polarisation and would prefer a synthesis. I take the ideological model to provide such a synthesis, since it avoids the polarisation introduced by any attempt to separate out the "technical" features of literacy, as though the "cultural bits" could be added on later. It is those who have employed an autonomous model, and who have generally dominated the field of literacy studies until recently, who were responsible for setting up a false polarity between the technical and cultural aspects of literacy. The ideological model, on the other hand, does not attempt to deny technical skill or the cognitive aspects of reading and writing, but rather understands them as they are encapsulated within cultural wholes and within structures of power. In that sense the ideological model subsumes rather than excludes the work under-taken within the autonomous model.

I use the term "ideological" to describe this approach, rather than less contentious or loaded terms such as "cultural", "sociological", etc., because it signals quite explicitly that literacy practices are aspects not only of "culture" but also of power structures. The very emphasis on the "neutrality" and "autonomy" of literacy by many writers is ideological in the sense of disguising this power dimension. Any ethnographic account of literacy will, in fact, bring out its significance for power, authority and social differentiation in terms of the author's own interpretation of these concepts. Since all approaches to literacy in practice will involve some such bias, it is better scholarship to admit to and expose the particular ideological framework being employed from the very beginning – it can then be opened to scrutiny, challenged and refined in ways which are more difficult when the ideology remains hidden. This is to use the term "ideological" not in its old-fashioned Marxist (and current anti-Marxist) sense of "false consciousness" and simple-minded dogma, but rather in the sense employed by "radical" groups within contemporary anthropology sociolinguistics and cultural studies, where ideology is the site of tension between authority and power on the one hand and individual resistance and creativity on the other (Asad, 1980; Bourdieu, 1976; Hall, Hobson, Lowe & Willis, 1980; Mace, 1979; Strathern, 1985). This tension operates through the medium of a variety of cultural practices, including particularly language and, of course, literacy. It is in this sense that it is important to approach the study of literacy in terms of an explicit ideological model. I would now like to locate that model within the broader context of recent developments in linguistic and anthropological theory and methodology.

Within linguistics there has recently been a shift towards "discourse" ana-lysis, which takes as the object of study larger units of language than the word or sentence (cf. Benson & Greaves, in press; Coulthard, 1977; Stubbs, 1983). I will suggest that this trend towards "discourse" analysis in linguistics could fruitfully link with recent developments of the "ethnographic" approach with-in anthropology that take fuller account of theories of power and ideology. I shall briefly cite work from both discourse analysis, such as Blank and Tannen, and from the ethnographic method, such as Heath, and argue that they pro-vide a useful basis from which to construct a synthesis that develops beyond either approach in isolation. With respect to research in orality and literacy this merging of disciplines and methodologies, within an ideological as opposed to an autonomous model of literacy, provides, I would argue, a means to replace the concept of the great divide with richer, and less ethnocentric concepts. In particular I would like to employ and develop further the concepts of "literacy events" (Heath, 1982), "literacy practices" (Street, 1984) and "communicative practices" (Grillo, 1986).

Heath defines a "literacy event" as "any occasion in which a piece of writing is integral to the nature of participants' interactions and their interpretive processes" (Heath, 1982). I employ "literacy practices" as a broader concept, pitched at a higher level of abstraction and referring to both behaviour and conceptualisations related to the use of reading and/or writing. Literacy practices incorporate not only "literacy events", as empirical occasions to which literacy is integral, but also "folk models" of those events and the ideological preconceptions that underpin them. Grillo has extended this notion still further to the notion of communicative practices in general, which obviously owes much to Hymes' work on the "ethnography of communication" (Hymes, 1974). Grillo construes the concept of communicative practices as including "the social activities through which language or communication is produced", "the way in which these activities are embedded in institutions, settings or domains which in turn are implicated in other, wider, social, economic, political and cultural processes" and "the ideologies, which may be linguistic or other, which guide processes of communicative production" (Grillo, 1986, p. 8). For Grillo, then, "literacy is seen as one type of communicative practice", within this larger social context, moving the emphasis away from attempts to attribute grand consequences to a particular medium or channel.

Central to development of this conceptual apparatus for the study of literacy is a re-evaluation of the importance of "context" in linguistic analysis. Linguists, with some justification, have been reluctant to allow the floodwaters of "social context" to breach defences provided by the rigour and logic of their enterprise. They sense that "context" is so unbounded and loose that it would swamp their own very precise and bounded studies. One explanation for this fear might be that, whereas linguists recognise the need for rigorous theory and method in studying grammar and syntax, they see the "social" as something that anyone can comment upon without the need for academic discipline: as Chomsky argued at a recent conference, it is simply "commonsense" (Boston Conference on Language Development, 1986). For these and other reasons, many linguists have attempted to exclude context altogether from their domain. Pratt points out in a recent article on anthropology and linguistics:

> Although it is often stressed that language is, amongst other things, a social fact, the importance of this dimension is diminished by the way the levels of "semantics" have been constructed, in particular the claim (made by Lyons, amongst others, 1981, p. 28) that word and sentence meaning are "to a high degree context independent" (Grillo, Pratt & Street, 1987, p. 11).

Even when they have paid attention to social context, it has been in terms of a narrow definition:

> In linguistics the term social tends to be reserved for personal interaction, whereas most anthropologists would want to emphasise that even the native speaker intuiting is a social being...
>
> (Furthermore) when in the analysis of utterance meaning, attention is turned to the social context, the main focus of enquiry has been pragmatics, doing things with words. This is undoubtedly an important area of enquiry, and at least one anthropologist (Bloch) has recently made extensive use of the concept of illocutionary force. However, this should not diminish the attention paid to social context in the analysis of the use of language to make propositions about the world, since this is also fundamentally a social process (ibid. p. 11).

When they do turn to sociology for assistance in the analysis of "context", linguists have tended to borrow mainly from "network" theory, or from Goffman-inspired "interactionalism", which refers only to those aspects of context that are directly observable and to such immediate links between individuals as their "roles", obligations, "face-to-face encounters", etc. This is true for post-Firthian linguistics which, for all its emphasis on language in context, is still bound by its inheritance from Malinowski of his narrow conception of "context of situation", along with the problems of his functionalism that have been largely superseded by subsequent theoretical developments within social anthropology (cf. Bailey, 1985). In his recent book on pragmatics, for instance, Levinson explictly and self-consciously excludes wider interpretations of "context" and admits:

> A relatively narrow range of contextual factors and their linguistic correlates are considered here: context in this book includes only some of the basic parameters of the context of utterance, including participants' identity, role and location, assumptions about what participants know or take for granted, the place of an utterance within a sequence of turns at taking and so on (1983, p. x).

He does acknowledge the existence of wider interpretations of "context":

> We know, in fact that there are a number of additional contextual parameters that are systematically related to linguistic organisation, particularly principles of social interaction of various sorts of both a culture-specific kind (see e. g., Keenan, 1976) and universal kind (see e. g., Brown & Levinson, 1978) (ibid.).

But he excludes them because his aim is to faithfully represent the philosophico-linguistic tradition in the United States and Britain, rather than, for instance, that on the continent where the tradition he notes is "altogether broader" (p. ix) (cf. also Dillon, Coleman, Fahnestock & Agar, 1985, and Bailey, 1985, for explorations of recent developments in post-Firthian linguistics, particularly with regard to discourse analysis and pragmatics).

I would like to argue that the analysis of the relationship between orality and literacy requires attention to the "wider parameters" of context largely under-emphasised in Anglo-American linguistics. Within social anthropology, for instance, these would be taken to include the study of kinship organisation, conceptual systems, political structures, habitat and economy etc., which are seen as "systems", and analysed in terms of function and structure rather than simply of "network" or "interaction". There is little point, according to this perspective, in attempting to make sense of a given utterance or discourse in terms only of its immediate "context of utterance", unless one knows the broader social and conceptual framework that gives it meaning. This involves not just commonsense, but the development of theories and methods as rigorous as those employed in other domains. It is these theories and methods that provide some guarantee that attention to social context need not swamp or drown the precise aspects of language use selected for study with linguistics.

In recent years the methods and theories employed to study social life in cross-cultural perspective have been subject to rigorous criticism. In contrast with the static, functionalist approach implied in, for instance, Malinowski's "context of situation", recent approaches within anthropology have emphasised the dynamic nature of social processes and the broader structure of power relations. This has frequently taken the form of exploration of the concept of ideology and of discourse (see Agar, 1986; Agar & Hobbs, 1983; Asad, 1980; Bloch, 1986; Grillo et al., 1987; Parkin, 1984; Strathern, 1985). In this sense "discourse" refers to the complex of conceptions, classifications and language use that characterise a specific sub-set of an ideological formation. It borrows something from Foucault's usage, although that refers to whole periods of European history, whereas the anthropological usage is often more specific with reference to a given sub-culture of the scale normally investigated through ethnographic method. It remains, however, rather broader than normal usage of "discourse" within linguistics, where it frequently indicates simply chunks of language larger than the sentence. The boundaries between the senses of the term in the different disciplines remain unclear and can frequently overlap. Far from being a source of confusion, however, this ambiguity may be turned to constructive use, providing a means to pursue issues that are perhaps harder to grasp within the language and definitions of either discipline separately.

Recent developments in discourse analysis within linguistics, for instance, such as Brown and Yule's concern to "link thickly described discourse to larger patterns of action and interaction" (quoted in Dillon et al., 1985, p. 456) provide a method which can be more sensitive to language in use than traditional ethnography has been. The method, however, needs to be allied with a linguistic theory that conceives of language as essentially a social process, and which takes full account of more sophisticated theories of language than simple interactionalism, network analysis or commonsense. Similarly, the methods employed by anthropologists do not on their own guarantee theoretical sophistication: it is possible, for instance, for ethnographic accounts of literacy to be conducted within the autonomous model, with all the problems and flaws that entails. However, when ethnographic method is allied to contemporary anthropological theory, emphasising ideological and power processes and dynamic rather than static models, then it can be more sensitive to social context than either linguistics in general or discourse analysis in particular have tended to be. It is at the interface between these linguistic and anthropological theories on the one hand, and between discourse and ethnographic method on the other, that I envisage future research in the field of literacy studies being conducted. This should enable us to replace previous accounts of literacy, based on inadequate methods and theories, with accounts that provide a firm basis for sound cross-cultural comparison and generalisation. Until then, we would be well advised to refrain from generalisations, particularly those of the grandiose sort indulged by writers like Ong and Goody, but also even the more modest claims being made within some of the "collections" on literacy published in the 1980s.

I would now like to examine some of these "modest" claims more closely and to suggest that, through their reliance on traditional methods and theories regarding the study of literacy, they are still implicitly embedded in the great divide framework that many of their exponents would wish explicitly to reject. I have space to examine only one or two examples of these recent "literacy myths": the notion that written discourse encodes meaning through lexicalisation and grammar, while oral discourse does so through paralinguistic features, leading to consequential differences between the potential of the two mediums and to an implicit reinstatement of the great divide; the notion that written discourse is more "connected" and "cohesive", while oral discourse is fragmentary and disconnected; and finally the myth that written language delivers its meaning directly via the "words on the page", whereas oral language is more "embedded" in the immediate social pressures of face-to-face communication.

These myths are both rejected and revived in a collection of essays edited by Deborah Tannen entitled *Spoken and Written Language: Exploring Orality and Literacy* (1982b). In the preface Tannen signals the contemporary trend away from traditional linguistic approaches to literacy:

> Many of the papers in the present collection owe much to the insight of anthropological and literary work on orality and literacy. However, they go beyond this dichotomy to investigate the characteristics and effects of changing traditions, and to suggest that distinctions between orality and literacy on the one hand, and spoken vs. written language on the other, do not suffice to characterize real discourse. For one thing, there are various oral and literate traditions, and there are different ways of realizing these in both spoken and written language ... A number of the chapters consider the relationship of literary to conversational language and find them closer, and distinctions between them foggier, than had previously been thought (p. xi–xii).

Similarly in *The Myth of Orality and Literacy*, which was published in another collection of essays on literacy at this time, Tannen challenges two "myths" of literacy that have been prominent in linguistics: the myth "1) that writing is decontextualised and 2) that text-focused discourse is found only in writing" (1982a, p. 41).

The theory of a great divide between literacy and orality was generally under attack at this time and one might have looked to the many collections of essays being published in the field to develop alternative positions. And yet Tannen herself is typical of many contributors in her tendency to reintroduce the notion, albeit in "softer" guise. She relates, for instance, how she found "the notion of oral vs. literate tradition – or more precisely, an oral/literate continuum reflecting relative focus on involvement vs. content – useful to my own research on discourse". Despite her reference to "discourse" here, Tannen's account does not represent the shift away from the traditional view of literacy that I am suggesting could be facilitated by a combination of recent discourse analysis with those versions of the ethnographic method that are rooted in theories of power and ideology. Her use of the term remains closer to traditional, and narrower aspects of linguistic theory and method and does little to detach her from the autonomous model of literacy. Her association of orality with "involvement" and literacy with content in practice replicates classic features of great divide thinking and her use of it cannot help but revive the dichotomy even amidst protestations to the contrary. I would like to pursue here just one strand of her argument, in which she relates the distinction between "involvement" and "content" to a further supposed difference between orality and literacy, which she terms "the cohesion hypothesis".

"Spoken discourse", according to Tannen, "establishes cohesion through paralinguistic features whereas written discourse does so through lexicalisation" (1982a, p. 41). In speaking, Tannen argues, paralinguistic features, such as tone, facial expression etc., reveal the speaker's attitude towards the message and serve to establish cohesion, that is, to show the relationship between ideas, highlight relative importance, etc. "One cannot speak without showing one's attitude to the message and the speech activity" (1982a, p. 41). In writing, by contrast, "features of nonverbal and paralinguistic channels are not available" (ibid). The writer may wrinkle his or her face but it does not show up on the written page. So the relationship between ideas and the writer's attitude to them must be lexicalised. This is done through choice of words, by explicit statements and by conjunctions and subordinate clauses, which do the work that in speaking is done by paralinguistic means. The implications of these differences are that speaking exhibits greater attention to the involvement of participants, while in writing there is a greater emphasis on the content of what is said. However, this does not mean that individuals or groups can be simply labelled either "oral" or "literate": "Rather, people have at their disposal and are inclined to use, based on individual habits as well as social conventions, strategies associated with either or both in speech and writing" (Tannen, 1982a, p. 47).

Some research she conducted on middle-class dinner parties in the United States, shows how some participants may employ "literate-like" strategies in their conversation, while others are employing "oral-like" stategies, leading to miscommunication and mutual dissatisfaction. For instance, one group which she labels "literate-like", want the emphasis in stories to be placed upon content and the point to be made explicit, while the other "oral-like" group dwell upon personal details and emotions and want the point to be inferred from the dramatic structure rather than stated explicitly. The two groups also have trouble over turn-taking and sequence: the oral-like ones frequently talk at the same time while the literate-like group prefer one person at a time to talk and will themselves halt the flow of conversation by refusing their turn and remaining silent if they are "interrupted".

The justification for applying the labels "oral-like" and "literate-like", which slide into simply "oral" and "literate" at times, is that the groups exhibit features that are associated with orality and literacy according to the cohesion hypothesis. Waiting one's turn, for instance, is literate-like or literate in the sense that it involves putting emphasis on the content of what is said, while overlapping is oral in the sense of emphasising personal involvement, at the expense of "the clear relay of information". Those who prefer "explicitness" are literate in the sense that the cohesion hypothesis shows writing to require more explicitness, through lexicalisation and syntax, whereas those who prefer the message to be inferred, or conveyed by other than direct verbal expression, are oral-like in the sense, again according to the cohesion hypothesis, that oral communication places more emphasis on paralinguistic means of conveying the feelings of the speakers.

These claims seem to me to be fairly dubious and are of a kind with the myths of literacy that Tannen herself rightly rejects. The persistence of such myths derives, I would suggest, from the underlying methodological and theoretical framework. The argument that writing does not exhibit features of "nonverbal and paralinguistic channels", for instance, derives from viewing written production within a narrow definition of "social context". If we approach "context" in the broad sense suggested above, where discourse analysis and ethnography overlap, and where the methods are rooted in theories of power and ideology and of language as essentially social, then the characteristics of written channels of communication will appear somewhat different. We will find, for instance, a whole range of paralinguistic features by which meaning is expressed through writing, at least as complex and rich as those of oral discourse. To take an example close to home: when a piece of writing appears in an academic journal, its standing and the attitude the reader brings to it rests on more than "lexicalisation" alone: the status of the journal itself, even the quality and style of the paper and covers, all contribute to the "meaning" of the propositions contained within it and to the degree of attention it is deemed to deserve from an "academic" reader on the one hand or, on the other, whether it is worth a "lay" person bothering with it at all. A neatly bound and well-produced book with a Cambridge University Press imprint gets different attention than a scruffy pile of A4 computer paper, even though the lexicalisation in both cases may be exactly the same. To take an example from further afield, Bledsoe and Robey (1986) describe how the Mende of Sierra Leone impart meaning to written products in a variety of ways:

> Writing has secondary means for communicating meanings other than those literally transcribed on the paper. Elegant paper, typewritten script, and a clean, multicoloured airmail envelope are signs of respect for the person addressed as well as for enhancing the prestige of the message. Conversely, if the writer wishes to show disrespect, he might write the message in red ink (an insult) (p. 225).

The "secondary means" described here are precisely those paralinguistic and nonverbal features that Tannen and others find only in oral discourse. Bledsoe and Robey, in fact, show how the message may be the same orally or in writing but the very act of sending it in written form itself indicates something about the message:

> Writing often substitutes for speech, even when the latter might just as well communicate a direct message. The Mende frequently approach someone of high status for a favour by handing him a written letter. This circumvents face-to-face "shame" on the part of the supplicant, even if he delivers his own message in person, as he often does. Although in some instances writing may enhance communication by avoiding stuttering and embarrassing pauses, the Mende emphasise that writing is intended to enhance the importance of a message and to show that the sender feels respect for the receiver (p. 224).

Shame, respect and status, then, may all be conveyed by paralinguistic features of writing: the furrow on the brow of the writer or the bow towards the receiver can be enscribed despite Tannen's claim that they "will not show up on the written page" (Tannen, 1982b, p. 41): they show up in the fact and nature of the sending and may, in her terms, be encoded in other than lexical features of the message. Bledsoe's and Robey's work also suggests more subtle and less obvious features of writing as a means of establishing secrecy and maintaining control of, or as she puts it "managing", knowledge. Writing is absorbed by Mende secret societies into a tradition of secrecy and exclusion, where hierarchies of access to knowledge maintain degrees of power and control over others. We cannot really claim to make sense of items of script produced within this framework if we attend only to the meaning of the "words on the page" and to the lexical devices for encoding meaning: these represent only one aspect, Bledsoe and Robey suggest, of the "potential" of writing and to ignore others is to miss much of what gives it meaning in "real-life" situations. Observation of these, moreover, is to be understood not simply in terms of the immediate context of utterance but of such broader features of social and cultural life as the secret societies of the Mende and their institutional control and definition of hierarchies of power. It is, then, this broader meaning of the term "context" to which Bledsoe and Robey are referring when they argue for understanding literacy in its cultural context:

> Writing is assuredly a medium of great potential in social interaction, but we underscore that different social use of writing are culturally limited or enhanced in

different societies. In itself writing does not mechanically produce social results. The cultural context greatly influences the social role of writing, both as a mode of communication and as a type of knowledge. By treating literacy as a resource in this way, moreover, we de-emphasize the dichotomy of speech versus writing... We view the two modes as more similar than different in their sociological impact ... (and so much of the discussion) could apply to oral competence as well (p. 203).

This stress on the similarity, rather than the difference, between written and oral discourse is also brought out by another recent study that makes explicit the extent to which it was the methodological framework of traditional linguistics that helped reinforce the myth of the great divide. Marion Blank (1982), in an article on pre-school language use, examines a number of characteristics classically attributed to literacy and which have frequently been used to emphasise a great divide between written and spoken language, notably that literacy is "disembedded", "sustained and sequential", and has "implicit connectedness". These assumptions, she suggests, derived from the traditional linguistic method of decoding separate components of an utterance – in Lyons' terms, word meaning and sentence meaning are taken to be "to a high degree context independent" (1981, p. 28). This led to the study of oral language as consisting of separate chunks or fragments, often "imperfectly grammatical", as though it lacked cohesion and connectedness. Written language, on the other hand, was studied in larger chunks in which a thread could be discerned running through the parts. From this it appeared to follow that literacy was intrinsically characterised by connectedness and cohesion and orality by fragmentation. However, Blank notes that recent research in linguistics has shifted away from the methodology that helped sustain such distinctions, and towards analysis of organised, connected text or discourse, whether oral or written, and this has considerable implications for traditional assumptions about orality and literacy. By applying discourse analysis to oral production it is beginning to become apparent that there are implicit rules of cohesion that were missed by the previous, atomistic methodology. Conversation analysis, for instance, focuses on "the structure and cohesion rules that make a chunk of talk 'a conversation'" (Blank, 1982; cf. also Craig & Tracy, 1983). Blank gives examples where children's talk was tape recorded and later analysis showed how early references in a discussion were sustained in later comments:

> For example, in a lunchtime conversation between a mother and her 5-year-old child, the mother said, "Now eat your carrots". Then she paused and, changing tone, said "Oh, I forgot to plant the tomatoes". The conversation continued for a while and suddenly the child altered the flow by saying "I know why you said tomatoes. When you said carrots, it made you think of tomatoes, and that's why you did it" (1982, p. 85).

Blank interprets this as demonstrating that "the child was saying she expects a conversation to be connected, that the grouping of tomatoes and carrots in that context was peculiar but that there must be some logic available by which that combination could be explained – and indeed, she found the logic" (loc. cit.). Oral discourse, then, may be more "cohesive" than previously assumed, if only we were to study it in an appropriate way. "Cohesion" may not be such an important criterion for distinguishing oral from written language as many earlier researchers had assumed.

On the one hand, as Blank says, oral discourse studied in this way may turn out to be more cohesive than previously assumed. On the other hand, we may also need to examine more closely the assumed intrinsic cohesiveness of written production. The examples that linguists tend to use, and that Blank herself employs, are most often drawn from "literary" writing, or from the "essay-text" tradition. These, of course, have a "built-in" cohesion since the conventions by which they are written require a thread of connectedness throughout a whole piece and since they are usually written by a single author whose own presence sustains and implicitly links the parts. There are, however, many other uses of literacy in everyday life, and those to which the majority of people are exposed most of the time do not belong to this particular tradition: they consist, rather, of apparent fragments – signs, labels, lists, advertisements, etc. There is a cohesion to these too, but it is not to be found at the overt level of the authored script but at deeper levels of culture and ideology, levels missed by traditional linguistic methodology, with its tendency to dwell on a particular, culture-specific form of literary writing.

Since the discourse methodology that will provide insights into these submerged levels of cohesion in writing and in oral discourse alike is only relatively recent, there is consequently little comparative data available on which to make general claims for difference between orality and literacy based on this feature. It is therefore unsound on empirical as well on theoretical grounds to use "cohesion" as a criterion for contrasts between orality and literacy as such. The cohesion hypothesis is another literacy myth.

If both oral and literate practices are frequently part of a sustained narrative whose connections lie deep in the culture, so that it is difficult for them to be observed at the overt level or in the immediate context, then what methodological framework can be employed to investigate them? Blank's article suggests that the shift towards discourse analysis within linguistics offers a useful beginning. The analysis of deeper levels of discourse cohesion and communicative exchange in both oral and literate modes also requires, I would suggest, an extension of discourse analysis into an ethnographic approach, such as represented in the work of Shirley Brice Heath. I will conclude with a brief discussion of how the concepts and methods she employs can be extended to provide a basis for the kind of literacy studies that I am proposing.

Heath's work challenges, in particular, a further myth of literacy generated by traditional linguistic methodology, that is, the assumed autonomy of written language, where the meaning is taken to reside in "the autonomous text" (Olson, 1977, p. 268). Oral language, in contrast, was seen as quintessentially a social exchange, in which any "true" or unambiguous meaning was usually swamped by the social pressures exerted by the participants' relative status, power, etc. I have examined these propositions elsewhere, as they appear in strong form in the work of researchers such as Olson, Ong and Goody. I am concerned now to note that recent work at the interface of linguistics and anthropology has also challenged this myth and suggested a methodology for studying similarities between orality and literacy in relation to features traditionally taken as indicative of a great divide.

Heath, for instance, has employed an ethnographic approach to demonstrate how written language as well as oral can work as a form of exchange in situations of face-to-face communication. The Piedmont people she studied may open a letter on their verandahs and discuss its meaning with friends and neighbours, constructing a reply in collaboration (see also Shuman, 1983, on "collaborative literacy"). The links and underlying cohesion of the reading and of the writing in this situation derive from the interaction of the participants' rather than being the product of a single "author", composing in isolation. Written language, then, cannot be divided from oral language on the grounds that it lacks the quality of immediate exchange characteristic of face-to-face communication. Moreover the situation that she describes where Piedmont people are negotiating the meaning of a letter is part of larger "context" than the immediate one of the participants' interaction on the verandah: to understand it requires further knowledge of the culture and ideology of the participants and of a range of other literacy events and practices in which they engage than simply those under immediate scrutiny. A crucial feature of this broader context is relations of power between the various participants. "Official" letters often represent an exercise of power over the recipient, in this case a school board determining where a child will be sent, while delivery of a response may represent a form of local autonomy and resistance to central dictates. The words on the page do not carry independent meaning but depend upon their location in this power struggle for their active meaning: the literacy events that can be observed as letters arrive, are read and replied to, are part of a larger literacy practice that includes local/state relations, and broad ideological assumptions about the "power" of the written word, that are less easily observed or described empirically. The participants themselves take these into account in interpreting and constructing the "meaning" of written items but it has proved difficult for autonomous linguistics to do so due to its insistence that language and literacy can be studied independently of this level of social context.

Recent work at the interface of anthropology and linguistics, discourse and ethnography, however, has provided a way out of this difficulty by challenging the myths of orality and literacy that have dominated research in this area for too long. Literacy, it is now apparent, cannot be divided from orality on the grounds either of cohesion, or of connectedness or that it employs paralinguistic as opposed to lexical features of language. Nor is it true to suggest that oral language is more embedded in social situations and "exchange", while written language remains independent and autonomous. The attention to these supposed differences between literacy and orality that helped sustain belief in the great divide, even when its grosser features were being rejected, can now itself be seen as a product of traditional linguistic methodology and of the cultural conventions of the linguists themselves. It is to be hoped that the collections of essays and papers to be published in the second half of the decade can make a cleaner break with the myths of the past and begin to represent the full cultural and ideological significance of literacy discourses.

References

Agar, M. (1986). *Independents declared*. Washington: Smithsonian.

Agar, M., & Hobbs, J. (1983). Natural plans: Using AI planning in the analysis of ethnograhic interviews. *Ethos, 11*, 33–48.

Apple, M. (Ed.). (1982). *Cultural and economic reproduction in education*. London: Routledge & Kegan Paul.

Asad, T. (1980). Anthropology and the analysis of ideology. *Man, 14*, 604–627.

Bailey, R. W. (1985). Negotiation and meaning: Revisiting the 'context of situation'. In J. D. Benson & W. S. Greaves (Eds.). (in press). *Systemic functional approaches to discourse*. Norwood: Ablex.

Benson, J. D., & Greaves, W. S. (Eds.). (in press). *Systemic functional approaches to discourse*. Norwood: Ablex.

Blank, M. (1982). Language and school failure: Some speculations about the relationship between oral and written language. In L. Feagans & D. Farran (Eds.), *The language of children reared in poverty* (pp. 75–93). New York: Academic Press.

Bledsoe, C., & Robey, K. (1986). Arabic literacy and secrecy among the Mende of Sierra Leone. *Man, 21*, 202–226.

Bloch, M. (Ed.). (1975). *Political language and oratory*. London: Academic Press.

Bloch, M. (1986, June). *Literacy and enlightenment*. Paper presented at Anthropology/Linguistics workshop, University of Sussex.

Bourdieu, P. (1976). Systems of education and systems of thought. In R. Dale, G. Esland & M. MacDonald (Eds.), *Schooling and capitalism* (pp. 192–200). London: Open University/Routledge & Kegan Paul.

Brown, P., & Levinson, S. (1978). Universals in language usage: Politeness phenomena. In E. Goody (Ed.), *Questions and politeness: Strategies in social interaction* (pp. 56–289). Cambridge: Cambridge University Press.

Coulmas, F., & Ehlich, K. (Eds.). (1983). *Writing in focus*. New York: Mouton.

Coulthard, M. (1977). *An introduction to discourse analysis*. London: Longman.

Craig, R., & Tracy, K. (1983). *Conversational coherence: Form, structure and strategy*. London: Sage.

Dillon, G., Coleman, L., Fahnestock, J., & Agar, M. (1985). Review article of discourse analysis and pragmatics. *Language, 61*, 446–460.

Frawley, W. (Ed.). (1982). *Linguistics and literacy*. Proceedings of the Delaware Symposium on Language Studies. New York: Plenum.

Goody, J. (1977). *Domestication of the savage mind*. Cambridge: Cambridge University Press.

Grillo, R. (1986, April). *Aspects of language and class*. Paper presented at Lancaster Conference on Linguistics and Politics.

Grillo, R., Pratt, G., & Street, B. (1987). Linguistics and anthropology. Mimeo. To appear in J. Lyons (Ed.), *New horizons in linguistics*, (Vol. 2). London: Penguin.

Hall, S., Hobson, D., Lowe, A., & Willis, P. (Eds.). (1980). *Culture, media, language*. London: Hutchinson.

Heath, S. B. (1982). What no bedtime story means: Narrative skills at home and at school. *Language in Society*, *11*, 49–76.

Heath, S. B. (1983). *Ways with words*. Cambridge: Cambridge University Press.

Hymes, D. (Ed.). (1964). *Language in culture and society*. New York: Harper & Row.

Hymes, D. (1974). *Foundations in sociolinguistics: An ethnographic approach*. Philadelphia: University of Pennsylvania Press.

Keenan, E. L. (1976). The universality of conversational implicature. *Language in Society*, *5*, 67–80.

Levinson, S. (1983). *Pragmatics*. Cambridge: Cambridge University Press.

Lyons, J. (1981). *Language, meaning and context*. London: Fontana.

Mace, J. (1979). *Working with words*. London: Chameleon.

Nystrand, M. (Ed.). (1982). *What writers know: The language, process and structure of written discourse*. New York: Academic Press.

Olson, D. (1977). From utterance to text: The bias of language in speech and writing. *Harvard Educational Review*, *47*, 254–279.

Olson, D., Hildyard, A., & Torrance, N. (Eds.). (1985). *Literacy, language and learning*. Cambridge: Cambridge University Press.

Parkin, D. (1984). Political language. *Annual Review of Anthropology*, *13*, 345–365.

Shuman, A. (1983). Collaborative literacy in an urban, multi-ethnic neighbourhood. In D. Wagner (Ed.), Literacy and ethnicity. *International Journal of the Sociology of Language*, *42*, 69–81.

Strathern, M. (1985). Feminism and anthropology. Unpublished manuscript.

Street, B. (1984). *Literacy in theory and practice*. Cambridge: Cambridge University Press.

Street, B. (1985, October). *Literacy and orality as ideological constructions: Some problems in cross-cultural studies*. Paper presented at the Copenhagen Conference From Orality to Literacy and Back.

Street, B. (1986). Walter Ong on literacy. *Aspects*, *1*, 2–16.

Street, B. (1987). Literacy and social change: The significance of social context in the development of literacy programmes. In D. Wagner (Ed.), *The future of literacy in a changing world (pp. 48-63)*. Oxford: Pergamon Press.

Stubbs, M. (1983). *Discourse analysis*. Chicago: University of Chicago Press.

Tannen, D. (1982a). The myth of orality and literacy. In W. Frawley (Ed.), *Linguistics and literacy* (pp.37–50). Proceedings of the Delaware Symposium on Language Studies. New York: Plenum.

Tannen, D. (Ed.). (1982b). *Spoken and written language: Exploring orality and literacy*. New Jersey: Ablex.

Wagner, D. (Ed.). (1983). Literacy and ethnicity. *International Journal of the Sociology of Language*, *42*.

Whiteman, M. (Ed.). (1981). *Writing: The nature, development and teaching of written communication. Vol. 1. Variation in writing: Functional and linguistic and cultural differences*. New Jersey: Erlbaum.

CHAPTER 4
Language Practices and the Visibility of Language. Reflections on the Great Divide in the Light of Ethiopian Oral Traditions

Karin Aronsson

It once so happened that an Ethiopian donkey driver met a learned and famous man who quite unexpectedly bowed quite low to him, politely bidding him good morning, *endet adderatchu* (literally: "how was the night (for you)?" Later, the humble donkey driver told his friends about this flattering incident, only to learn that he had been ridiculed. Since the greeting was phrased in the second person plural (*adderatchu* rather than the second person singular, *addereh*) the poor man had been placed in the same category as his donkey. Levine (1972) recounts this anecdote in his book about traditional Amhara culture and about characteristic Amharic ways of playing with language, a type of verbality which is particularly well developed in the poetic tradition of *semenna werq* – "wax and gold". This refers to a figurative use of language, originally rooted in the religous poetry *qene*. *Qene* couplets can be recognized by their play on overt versus covert sentence meaning. The "wax", or surface mould, hides the latent "gold" of the underlying meaning, whether it be an erotic allusion, ironic critique, a threat or a political message. The wax-and-gold tradition originates in the learned culture of orthodox Coptic schooling. Yet, historically, it has been developed to excellence in the oral contexts of daily bickering. In the everyday language of irony, speakers thus play with language complexity, making use of sentence ambiguities.

Levine offers examples of erotic allusions as well as political or belligerant ones; e.g.

> *yemin tiqem talla yemin tiqem tajji*
> *tallat sishanu buna adargaw enji*
>
> of what use is beer, of what use is mead?
> when seeing an enemy off, serve him coffee

The ambiguity resides in *buna adargaw*, which may be read either as "serve him coffee" or "reduce him to ashes" (through elision, *bun-adargaw*). The Amharic language is highly agglutinative. For instance, verbs carry information not only about tense and subject (gender, number, deference) but also about object, negation, voice and intensity (e.g. *al/seberr/en/ew/im* = not/broke/we/it/not = we didn't break it). Moreover, several common morphemes (such as *ye*) are ambiguous in that they may be used for quite different functions, which means that ambiguous sentences can be constructed relatively easily.

With respect to forms of address, the Amharic language marks both addressee's sex and familiarity/status. Divergences from the established rules are at times used intentionally, e.g. the feminine form of address may be used to tease or belittle a male friend. Minor deviations from expected usage are particularly useful as ironic devices. In the donkey driver episode, the use of the polite form of address, *adderu* would have constituted too obvious a deviation from the expected form. In the way that the greeting was formulated, the provocation was, however, less obvious – a hidden "golden" one – only to be revealed to more observant minds than that of the donkey driver.

Qene couplets, like puns, make use of double meanings based on alternative grammatical segmentations of one specific sentence, which means that language play occurs on a syntactic level. In order to appreciate the joke or the *qene* couplet, the listener must be aware of the alternative interpretations and of the very fact that there are two "readings" (two different interpretations) of the same text. This type of language play is cognitively fairly advanced, and in Western cultures, children's appreciation of puns develops relatively late. Non-literate children (preschoolers) generally do not understand puns or more complex riddles (Hirsh-Pasek, Gleitman & Gleitman, 1978). These results can be interpreted in terms of literacy. The possibility to reinspect and fixate a specific line would then explain the older school children's greater success in disclosing the double meanings. However, success is not reached upon learning to read but some years later (after a few years' reading) which means that literacy per se does not constitute the crucial explanation.

Also, puns and riddles exist in many non-literate cultures which means that literacy cannot be a necessary prerequisite for attendance to language form. On the contrary, the understanding of puns and riddles could be seen as a preparation for literacy. As shown by Lundberg, Olofsson and Wall (1980), preschoolers who are able to solve segmentation tasks also tend to learn to read with greater success than those who do not show such metalinguistic abilities.

As human beings, we live within language. We express ourselves through the spoken mode and others affect us in various ways by speaking to us, thereby expanding the here-and-now (talking about other times and other worlds). The listener is expected to attend to meaning, not to form. Thus, content overrides form in importance. In the everyday discourse of many people, form seldom carries any functional significance in social interaction. However, form becomes visible when errors are made or when implicit rules are broken (e.g. inappropriate choices with respect to formal/informal style). Thus, only when form is distorted does language become visible. Jokes and insults which play with language thus reveal the role of form. Theoretically, linguistic awareness would thus develop to a greater extent, or at an earlier stage, in cultures where language play is highly valued.

When reading or when solving a syllogism, we have to attend to language form. Unless we attend to formal properties of language, it is not possible to read or write or to draw a syllogistic conclusion. Western type societies at times make quite heavy demands on the reader's/listener's ability to separate form from content. How is this separation fostered, and what are the factors conducive to a normal or rapid development? How does language awareness develop? Or, phrased differently, how is language made visible?

In the following, I will comment on the relation between language visibility and language practices from the vantage point of Ethiopia, a multilingual society in which literacy is a new phenomenon for the population at large. Before the revolution in 1974, it is estimated that only 7% of the population was literate compared to the official figures of about 60% in present-day Ethiopia. However, even in far-away rural communities, not yet literate, there are rhetorical and multilingual traditions with a bearing on language awareness. My comments will focus on the oral traditions and their implications for the so-called great divide (between literate and non-literate cultures).

Language Awareness and the "Great Divide"

Several theories on literacy emphasize the crucial importance of literacy for general cognitive development, including language awareness (and the separation of meaning from form). Language visibility would thus increase notably with the advance of literacy. Metalinguistic development is seen as one of several changes contingent on breaking the written code. Underlying this reasoning is a view of literacy as a short cut to logic, "civilization" and to the modern world. A most articulate critique of this idealistic interpretation has been formulated by Street (1984). Street has undertaken a thorough analysis of literature on literacy and cognition. In this analysis, he challenges some of the underlying normative elements in earlier writings. Also, he claims that several effects, ascribed to literacy per se ("autonomous" effects) should rather be analysed in terms of cultural changes – material conditions, ideologies, knowledge.

In his refutal of the great divide, Street also takes a stand in the old controversy concerning language deficits versus language differences. Like Labov (1972) in his frequently cited critique of Bernstein (as read by Labov), Street seems to end up in a position of "beyond"; i.e. a no-difference perspective. Not only is a specific culture not deficit, it is, moreover, not really "different". The basis for the comparisons, the criteria of the highly literate culture, is not regarded as legitimate which in turn implies that comparisons are not possible. If any comparisons are to be made, they should rather be made on the premises of the minority – rather than on the premises of the dominant culture (or at worst, the premises of what Street refers to as the "academic language culture").

In an earlier review of the field, Goody (1977) challenged the old dichotomy between oral and literate cultures, underpinning his discussion with descriptions of complex oral habits with restricted literacies. Street goes even further than Goody in emphasizing the overlaps between oral and literate cultures; how specific oral practices are highly demanding in terms of discourse planning and discourse organization (requiring a high degree of language awareness), whilst certain types of literacies are indeed but restricted literacies, far removed from what he refers to as the more complex "essay-type" literacy.

One important part of Goody's reformulation of the great divide is that the dichotomy should be formulated as a polarized field (with continua) rather than as a gulf. If we adopt the view of oral/literate continua, it would also follow that different language activities would be associated with different complexity gradations. When we return to Street, it can be seen that he contrasts complex oral practices with restricted literate ones, implicitly equating "literacy" and "restricted literacy", comparing the overlapping areas of the oral/literate continua (Fig. 1). Thus, in his criticism, Street tends to relativize literacy, as if literate and oral practices would, for all purposes, be the same (normatively, this may indeed be a useful standpoint, but from a specific perspective such as that of, say, language awareness, it is untenable).

Street offers detailed and illuminating descriptions of different types of restricted literacies in Islamic communities in Iran, in relation to economy and commerce. Also, he refers to work by others on different types of restricted literacies which have but negligible effects on cognition. In particular, he draws on the work of Scribner and Cole (1981). In their work on Vai literacy, they show how it is fruitful to make fine-grained analyses, teasing out the relative effects of schooling and literacy. Scribner and Cole compare "self-taught" and schooled Vai literates, and they demonstrate how literacy has purely marginal effects on cognition. Schooling, or rather, more extensive schooling, seems to be the decisive factor in explaining different cognitive skills. At first glance, these results support the position of Street in that they illuminate the role of education (and tradition of culture) rather than technology per se. On the other hand, the same results could be interpreted in terms of *extensive* literacy. It could well be argued that essay-type reading and

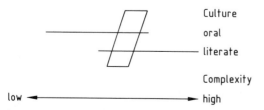

Fig. 1. Cultural continua and language practices (circumscribed area: overlap)

writing only assume importance after some years' schooling, which would then explain the sleeper effect of literacy. Thus, the cognitive achievements which do appear after some years' schooling are, in fact, due to more experience with expository reading and writing. Olson (1970) demonstrates how performance and perception are inextricably interwined. If we apply such an Olsonian type analysis to the Vai data, it seems quite reasonable that the fairly superficial rote learning of early schooling should not have the same effects as, for instance, the practice of writing or working with more complex texts.

The whole investigation of Scribner and Cole is above all concentrated on the role of literacy, which is also indicated in the title (*The Psychology of Literacy*). Consequently, it should not surprise the reader that other factors, such as the role of bilingualism, are not treated. In their results' section, they present some advantages of Vai-Arabic biliteracy. However, bilingualism is not explicitly discussed as a phenomenon with potential bearing on language awareness or literacy. Literacy is focused to the exclusion of other language practices of relevance for the visibility of language.

Earlier, in the present text, we indicated that language play is one factor symptomatic of and conducive to metalinguistic development. Thus, literacy is seen here, not as the one and only road to language visibility, but as one specific practice with relevance for linguistic awareness, along with language play. One more global practice of relevance is bilingual functioning. In translating between languages, the listener/speaker becomes aware of word nuances and of word order import.

Bilinguals as Grammarians

Leopold (1978) claimed that his daughter was more aware of linguistic matters than children of the same age in general, ascribing this increased sensitivity to her bilingualism (German-English). Similar interpretations have been made by Slobin (1978). However, these claims are somewhat difficult to interpret in that these bilinguals have grown up in elite groups in terms of education. We do not know to what extent language awareness is an effect of specific language activities in the home or to what extent there is indeed a bilingual advantage.

If we temporarily leave this matter unresolved, there are substantial theoretical reasons for expecting a bilingual advantage. According to our previous reasoning, language only becomes visible if or when there are problems in connection with communication. Such problems arise for the bilingual when he, for instance, makes interference errors. In those cases when he himself notices such errors, language structure becomes open to scrutiny, being for a moment the object of analysis, rather than merely a medium for analysis. Also, language becomes visible when words fail in one language, and when the bilingual speaker becomes painfully aware of his relative weaknesses in the two languages. Thirdly, language structure becomes visible in everyday translations. In most bilingual communities, translations are required more or less often in everyday encounters – in the market place, at school or in court. When translating, language structure may become quite visible, perhaps most so in poor matches at a sentence level; i.e. when literal translations result in ungrammatical or awkward sentence structures.

Work on the grammatical awareness of bilinguals would clarify the role of bilingual practices. One such study has been undertaken, and in this case the subjects were all non-literates. Aronsson (1981) studied the grammatical awareness of bilingual preschoolers (immigrant children of working class origin). Bilingual preschoolers were significantly more advanced than matched monolingual children in matching judgements of sentence grammaticality (detecting errors in "silly sentences").

Furthermore, bilinguals have been shown to be less inclined to reify words than monolinguals. In a series of word- referent tasks – bilingual children were more proficient than monolinguals of the same age at keeping form and meaning apart (Ben-Zeev, 1977; Ianco-Worrall, 1972; Cummins, 1978). There is no real evidence that monolingual (or bilingual) children regard words as concrete properties of objects, as suggested in the early writings of Piaget (for a critique, cf. Aronsson, 1981). Yet, there is a distinct bilingual advantage when it comes to flexibility in word-switching games of the Piaget-Vygotsky type (e.g. Ben-Zeev, 1977). Feldman and Shen (1971) demonstrated how there is only such a bilingual advantage if the child has to switch between meaningful terms (e.g. *cow* for *dog* and vice versa). If the child is required to use a nonsense term (e.g. *wug*) instead of a meaningful term (*dog/cow*), monolinguals perform as well as bilinguals. These results indicate that the young children in question do not hold animistic views of language, rather they are unaccustomed to focusing on form. To sum up, the bilingual advantage has to do with attention to form.

A Multilingual Case Study: Reflections on Language Visibility and Language Practices in Ethiopia

One important avenue to knowledge about language awareness and language practices is to study language communities which differ widely with respect to their concrete language situations and language practices. The Ethiopian language scene is of specific interest in that multilingualism is indeed quite common.

Amharic is only one of the nation's many languages. There are four different language groups – the Semitic (e.g. Amharic, Tigrinya), the Cushitic, the Nilotic and the Omotic. Since about two thirds of the population have mother tongues other than Amharic, bilingualism is quite common. There are about 60–80 different languages (depending on the type of division made), and primary schooling is offered in several of the languages. In view of the many languages, it is not possible to offer schooling in all the languages. Thus, many children become bilingual during the primary grades (learning Amharic as a second language or increasing earlier bilingual mastery).

English is used as the language of secondary schooling, which means that monolingual Amharic speakers are confronted with a second language, and other children with a third language. This type of trilingualism is not uncommon in African countries and in other parts of the world where there are both several indigenous languages and an international language used for secondary schooling and for communication with the international community.

Ethiopian multilingualism involves multiliteracy (Ethiopian, Roman and/or Arabic script). Scribner and Cole's study on Vai literacy shows how syllabic literacy is also acquired outside formal schooling. Syllabic scripts are, in some ways, probably easier to acquire than alphabets in that the script units are more closely tied to linguistic structure (morphemes). If we consider the case of Amharic and the Amharic syllabic script, the great success of the Ethiopian literacy campaign seems to bear this out. Or, at least, the impressive increase in literacy does not contradict such a theory. Were it the case that syllabic scripts are more difficult than alphabets, the increases in literacy rates would be hard to explain.

Analysed from a different perspective, other things being equal, Amharic literacy should perhaps also entail increased grammatical awareness and, most likely, more so than for many types of Roman alphabet literacies. Amharic, the major language of early schooling (and the mother tongue of about one third of all Ethiopians) is, as pointed out, highly agglutinative. The learning of the 251 fidels (typically, consonant + vowel, CV) also entails the identification of many highly productive prefixes and suffixes (such as -ye/ye-, -me/me-, ti-, te- etc). When learning the CV fidels, morphemic structure is often made visible.

Structurally speaking, the Amharic language allows for multiformity (cf. Bender, Bowen, Cooper & Ferguson, 1976). Word order is of a relatively free subject + object + verb (SOV) type, and several of the morphemes may operate both as parts of verbs and as parts of nouns (e.g. ye), which means that sentences must be closely attended to in order to be correctly deciphered. Not only verbs, but also nouns are dense with information – about number, gender, case, possession, definitiveness. For instance, the conjunction "and" can be used either as a separate conjunction or in a suffix form (e.g. ye/ bet/occ/achin/inna = of/house/s/our/and). Thus, when heard out of context, Amharic sentences may at times be ambiguous. Moreover, Amharic allows for a relative freedom of expression with respect to plurals, pronouns, gender, etc. Gender is, for instance, generally determined by the speaker, depending on his/her conceptualization of the gender of a specific object. Furthermore, the Ethiopic script offers personal choice in that the same words can be written in several different ways. For instance *hassab*, an "idea", can be written in 22 different ways. This is due to the presence of a great number of redundant fidels and it is also dependent on the basic ambiguity of the so-called sixth vowel order. In the syllabic matrix of 31 consonants x seven vowels, the fidels of the sixth order are either pronounced as vowels or as CV fidels depending on the word context. Word context also determines when gemination is necessary, since the script does not tell if a specific consonant involves a short or long sound. However, the meanings may be completely different, which again allows for play with word meaning (e.g. *ale* = he said; *alle* = there is). Thus, structurally, the Amharic language allows for puns and other types of word play relatively easily.

When writing about *semenna werq* and Amharic word play, Levine (1972) points out that Amharic has at times been referred to as the "language of ambiguity". Multilayered or figurative language use is greatly enjoyed in traditional Amhara culture, and there is a saying that "weighty verse (multilayered), like heavy clothing warms the inside" (cf. Levine, 1972). In present-day Ethiopia, such verse may be heard in bars (jocular insults sung to fellow guests by special singers). Also, figurative language has always been important in making political jokes. Cultural esteem has been attached to a rich and multilayered use of language, and less competent speakers have been referred to as *daraq* "dry". Conversely, people from non-Amhara parts of Ethiopia sometimes speak of Amharic speakers as hard to understand – not because of language differences per se but because of their veiled talk "they always bury the real meaning" as a Tigray friend said to me.

Amharic speakers are themselves aware of the multiplicity of meaning in everyday talk. One British expatriate, who is a fluent speaker of both Amharic and English (brought up bilingually from an early age) told me that he prefers English for business purposes in Ethiopia. Whenever business is conducted in Amharic, he never quite knows what decisions have indeed been reached. For the sake of clarity, he therefore prefers English to Amharic even though his Ethiopian counterparts may at times be somewhat handicapped in terms of tempo or nuances. Still, discussions conducted in English are preferable to him because of their greater distinctness. Once he switches to Amharic, he has observed that both his counterparts and he himself tend to switch to the "code of ambiguity". Thus, the language switch as such also entails an opening towards word games and double meanings.

Shemageles and Everyday Litigation

Skilful use of language thus involves indirectness. Such indirectness is also exhibited by the elders, *shemageles*, in their negotiations and conflict resolutions. Traditionally, many conflicts (boundary disputes, quarrels, breaches of contract, marital problems, etc.) are referred to the *shemgelena* institution.

There are regional variations, but in the prototypical case, two litigants will each appoint one *shemagele*, who in turn appoint a third one, who will be the final arbitrator. The *shemageles* will carefully investigate the conflict in question before trying to reconcile the two parties in the *shemgelena* procedure. The *shemageles* tend to be old and trusted members of the community (upkeepers of local history) and their conclusions tend to be phrased in allegorical or metaphorical form (e.g. couched as proverbs, sayings and everyday precedents).

In present-day Ethiopia, this institution has been adapted by the municipal local government – the *kebele* – where trusted persons are appointed as *shemageles* for different zones within the *kebele* (two for each zone). A third person is appointed as secretary, which means that the two *shemageles* need not be literate. The *shemgelena* procedure is an old one, and it certainly predates large-scale literacy. Rich and skilful use of allegory has always been highly valued in these contexts, and the *shemagele* who finds the most poignant and appropriate proverb or simile is also the one who will clinch the case.

Oral excellence is highly valued in the *shemgelena* procedure. Such sophistication may, of course, be related to other complex verbal practices, such as the *semena werq*-type puns. However, neither type of practice can conclusively be seen as a prerequisite for the other type, even though several such practices involve indirectness and veiled talk. If anything, the different types of practices would rather reinforce each other in recursive ways.

For complex verbal practices, embedded in cultural matrices, unidirectional causal reasoning is misleading whether it be couched in the language of the great divide or in the so-called ideological model (Street, 1984), where the effects of essay-type literacy are teased out from the effects of restricted literacies. Street acknowledges the role of, for example, oral, political rhetorics, but the majority of his analyses are confined to literacy as such (varying within a restricted/extensive continuum) related to cognitive changes in a causality type model.

Language Visibility – Spiral Development

Writers on literacy are inclined to discuss literacy effects on cognition, rather than the inverse effects (i.e. cognitive effects on literacy). However, Lundberg (1978), and Lundberg et al. (1980) and others have shown how previous cognitive development is reflected in literacy rates. Several of the cognitive advances which are ascribed to literacy seem to predate literacy rather than the other way round. Children know how to segment words into syllables, and syllables into phonemes, before learning how to read and write. Phonemic awareness is thus one aspect of metacognitive development which precedes literacy. Also, in our discussion on bilingualism, we showed how bilingualism enhances grammatical awareness. Theoretically, we would thus expect favourable effects of bilingualism on language awareness, and awareness effects on bilingualism.

Werner and Kaplan (1964) describe language development as a spiral development where new forms generate new functions which, in turn, generate new forms. From their theoretical standpoint, literacy would form a moving point in such a spiral development. Only in a very restricted sense would it be reasonable to see literacy as the one and only avenue to linguistic awareness. Rather, language awareness should be analysed as contingent on a set of language practices, such as litigation, wordplay, literacy and bilingual practices. In terms of the great divide, literacy is then defocused, being seen as but one of several practices with a bearing on language awareness. Simultaneously, language awareness is still linked to essay-type literacy and extended literate practices (including active performance, such as expository writing). The main shift in focus is that literacy is analysed as one of several practices of importance.

Unidirectional hypotheses do not seem to hold in such a complex field as that of language awareness. Rather, language development is inextricably embedded in a matrix of mutually influential forces. For instance, language play influences language awareness and vice versa, and bilingualism affects literacy and the other way round.

Thus, literate practices as well as poetic or bilingual practices all have specific impacts on language visibility (Fig. 2). If language practices are analysed from the perspective of such a spiral development, it also becomes more clear how restricted literacy may have purely marginal effects on cognitive development. Literacy is seen neither as a causal agent, in any mechanistic fashion, nor as the sole agent of awareness raising.

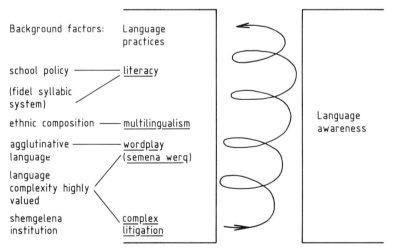

Fig. 2. Language visibility and language practices. – Spiral development

In Ethiopia, we can see how language structure facilitates indirect and complex oral practices. However, we may also argue that language structure as such is shaped by culturally determined needs and preferences.

References

Aronsson, K. (1981). The bilingual preschooler as grammarian. *Psychological Research Bulletin, 21*, 10–11.

Bender, M. L., Bowen, J. D., Cooper, R. L., & Ferguson, C. A. (1976). *Language in Ethiopia*. London: Oxford University Press.

Ben-Zeev, S. (1977). The influence of bilingualism on cognitive strategy and cognitive development. *Child Development, 48*, 1009–1018.

Cummins, J. (1978). Metalinguistic development of children in bilingual education programs. In M. Paradis (Ed.), *Aspects of bilingualism*. Colombia, South Carolina: Hornbeam Press.

Feldman, C., & Shen, M. (1971). Some language-related cognitive advantages of bilingual five-year olds. *The Journal of Genetic Psychology, 118*, 235–244.

Goody, J. (1977). *The domestication of the savage mind*. Cambridge: Cambridge University Press.

Hirsh-Pasek, K., Gleitman, L. R., & Gleitman, H. (1978). What did the brain say to the mind? A study of the detection and report of ambiguity by young children. In A. Sinclair, R. J. Jarvella, & W. J. M. Levelt (Eds.), *The child's conception of language*. Berlin, Heidelberg, New York: Springer Verlag.

Ianco-Worrall, A. D. (1972). Bilingualism and cognitive development. *Child Development, 43*, 1390–1400.

Labov, W. (1972). The logic of non-standard English. In A. Cashdan & E. Grugeon, *Language in education*. London: Routledge & Kegan Paul.

Leopold, W. F. (1978). A child's learning of two languages. In E. M. Hatch, (Ed.), *Second-language acquisition*. Rowley, Mass: Newbury House.

Levine, D. N. (1972). *Wax and gold*. Chicago: The University of Chicago Press.

Lundberg, I. (1978). Aspects of linguistic awareness related to reading. In A. Sinclair, R. J. Jarvella, & W. J. M. Levelt, (Eds.), *The child's conception of language*. Berlin, Heidelberg, New York: Springer Verlag.

Lundberg, I., Olofsson, Å., & Wall, S. (1980). Reading and spelling skills in the first school years predicted from phonemic awareness skills in kindergarten. *Scandinavian Journal of Psychology, 21*, 159–173.

Olson, D. (1970). *Cognitive development*. New York: Academic Press.

Scribner, S., & Cole, M. (1981). *The psychology of literacy*. Cambridge, Ma.: Harvard University Press.

Slobin, D. (1978). A case study of early language awareness. In A. Sinclair, R. J. Jarvella & W. J. M. Levelt (Eds.), *The child's conception of language*. Berlin, Heidelberg, New York: Springer Verlag.

Street, B. V. (1984). *Literacy in theory and practice*. Cambridge: Cambridge University Press.

Werner, H., & Kaplan, B. (1964). *Symbol formation*. New York: Wiley.

CHAPTER 5
Computer Literacy and Procedural Knowledge

Steen Folke Larsen

Introduction

With the rapid introduction of information technologies into all sectors of industrialised societies, many people have argued that the ability to understand and use such devices has become a necessary part of general education. The term "computer literacy" has been coined to refer to this ability. This chapter deals with cognitive characteristics and implications of computer literacy.

"Computer literacy" is still a very vaguely defined and hotly debated concept. There is sharp disagreement concerning what should count as computer literacy. Is ability to use an application program (like a word processor or a book-keeping program) sufficient, or should some level of skill in writing one's own programs be required? More fundamentally, it is by no means clear whether the suggested analogy with traditional literacy – mastery of written language - is valid at all. Some have claimed that computer literacy is antithetical to traditional literacy and threatens to eradicate it. Others view computer literacy as an extension of traditional literacy which will increase the importance of reading and writing skills and cause them to develop further.

The present argument (see also Larsen, 1986) is based on a view of computer systems as a new medium of expression and communication, both for the programmer and the user. Therefore, the problem of computer literacy is approached by considering more generally the relation between cognition and media of expression, in particular natural language. I shall argue that proficiency with computers is cognitively similar to spoken and written language abilities; it makes certain kinds of knowledge explicit and consciously accessible and it develops certain patterns of thinking. But computer skills are also cognitively very different from natural language skills. First, computers require a level of explicitness of expression which is an order of magnitude above that of written language (Olson, 1985a, 1985b). Secondly, I shall suggest that computers are media of expression which focus on a kind of knowledge that natural language is badly suited to deal with, namely *procedural knowledge*, and that the use of computers for expression will promote an ability to think in terms of procedures. The cognitive skills of using computers may therefore with some justification be called "procedural literacy", as proposed by Sheil (1980), rather than "computer literacy".

Expression and Explication of Knowledge

It is an old idea that the language we use influences our knowledge of the world. In radical theories of linguistic relativity like the classical proposals of von Humboldt, Sapir and Whorf, the individual's native language is seen as a mould into which knowledge of an amorphous reality is cast to acquire its form. This view almost inevitably leads to agnosticism and solipsism. Besides, it is empirically wrong. Studies of natural language concepts over the past couple of decades (Rosch, 1974, and numerous other investigators) have shown that the structure of concepts is jointly determined by the inherent structure of the real world, the structure of the human biological system, and the nature of the activities by which the individual relates to his or her environment. The latter point is particularly important. Human beings interact with their environment (including other humans) in order to make it serve their purpose, and they select and organise information in accordance with the requirements of these purposive activities. For instance, when knowledge about plants is organised into concepts like "vegetables" and "weeds", it is clear that this structuring owes more to the custom of human activities like eating and gardening (in a particular culture) than it owes to properties of the plants themselves or to the language which supplies words to label the concepts. As Olson and Bruner (1974) put it, "we have a picture of reality that is biased by or coded in terms of our actions upon it; knowledge is always mediated or specified through some form of human activity" (p. 128).

Does this mean that language and other symbolic systems are completely neutral with respect to the knowledge they are used to express? This conclusion would be too hasty because the use of a symbolic system is itself a "form of human activity". But Olson and Bruner's view implies that we should consider what happens when a symbol system is actually used, rather than looking at its structure in vitro. Thus, in their discussion of instructional media, Olson and Bruner (1974) point out that verbal instruction may contribute to students' knowledge in two ways: first, by stating information in a form which has greater generalisability than their previous knowledge, and secondly, by developing the student's skill in using the particular form of language which is employed for instruction. The second point is straightforward. Using a language, whether for receiving or expressing information, improves the skills required (though reception and expression may not involve the same skills, of course). Subsequently, the student will be able to apply these skills more easily and to a wider range of information than before. Therefore, if the given language has any influence on the student's knowledge, this influence should affect an ever increasing part of his or her knowledge base. The effects of using a medium of expression will spread like ripples in a pond as the expressive skills are developed and applied to an ever wider range of knowledge.

The first point made by Olson and Bruner concerns the nature of the influence of language on knowledge. They may be said to claim that knowledge already possessed by students is *transformed* by verbal (or written) expression – its *form* is changed into one of more general applicability. To put it strongly, the format of existing knowledge may be altered by linguistic expression, but "no new information can be conveyed through language" (Olson & Bruner, 1974, p. 141). This statement appears untenable in the context of students who *receive* verbal instruction; even though language is always interpreted in terms of the receiver's previous knowledge, it does seem possible to acquire new information through language. However, in the present context I am concerned primarily with the *expressive* use of language, and here Olson and Bruner's point seems well taken. The information that is expressed in linguistic form does not come from the language itself, it must already be possessed by the person who expresses it. This previous knowledge may still undergo change and transformation in the act of expression, however. Let us consider this more closely.

In Olson's (1975, 1977) later analyses of the cognitive implications of oral and written language, he develops the hypothesis that the primary demand of writing is that meanings and intentions be made *explicit* in the text. In oral communication, speaker and listener share the present situation, they usually know each other and have a common cultural background. Therefore, much can be taken for granted without saying, and most potential ambiguities, such as implicit references and imprecise lexical choices, never surface or are resolved immediately. Writing is used to communicate across differences in time, place, personal acquaintance and even culture, however. Much less information on the part of the reader can therefore be presupposed, so the writer's intended meaning should be explicitly stated in the text if he wants to be sure that it gets across. Moreover, since writing makes the words of language into enduring objects that can be scrutinised again and again, the distinction between an explicit meaning preserved in the text and a, possibly different, implicit meaning intended by the author is almost forced upon both writer and reader. In sum, literacy should promote thinking in terms of explicit meanings, and thus help to make one's own knowledge explicit – to explicate knowledge that was previously available only implicitly.

Two recent papers by Olson (1985a, 1985b) apply this explication theory to computers and computer literacy. Olson notes that "even 'user friendly' computers require a greater degree of explicitness in language than that involved in ordinary conversational language" (1985a, p. 7), because computers cannot interpret ambiguous expressions at all. Everything one wants the computer to do must be stated explicitly in the command or program. Working with computer systems is therefore expected to make children (and adults) realise any differences between the meaning they intended and the one they expressed, and in general to increase their skill in making meanings fully explicit. "Computers set a new standard of explicitness" (Olson, 1985a, p. 6) which is an order of magnitude above that of writing, but in principle of the same kind. In this way, computer literacy may be seen as a skill of "radical explication of expression" that builds upon, extends and actually perfects traditional literate competencies.

Olson's theory is attractively simple and yet it puts the cognitive consequences of computerisation in a rather surprising perspective: are they that well known, even trivial? Do computers really make literate people even more literate? Are there no lurking dangers at all? Even though I believe the theory to be on the right track, the issues are probably more complicated. To take Olson's account one step further, let us note that in no symbolic medium can just any information or intention whatsoever be expressed with equal ease and completeness. Media are always selective in what they allow to be expressed from immediate experience. This is a weaker version of the linguistic relativity thesis: things or ideas vary in codability within language. Each medium or language is developed to code and thus explicate certain kinds of knowledge, to maintain it for conscious consideration, and thus to support a certain range of practical and mental activities (division of labour, long-term planning, preservation of knowledge, exploration of hypothetical situations, etc). What are the classes of knowledge that the major kinds of symbolic media are specialised for explicating?

A Classification of Knowledge

Since antiquity, a large number of classifications of the knowledge that may be acquired by human beings has been put forward by philosophers and psychologists. I have recently made a proposal (Larsen, 1984) that builds upon a classification of types of memory described by the Canadian psychologist Tulving (1983, 1985). For convenience, I shall take Tulving's scheme as a point of departure because it makes it easy to identify a number of important issues which motivated the classification I am proposing.

Tulving's Three Memory Systems

Tulving's hypothesis is that there are three different memory systems, each of which is specialised to perform a particular set of memory tasks. The systems are interrelated in what he terms a "mono-hierarchical arrangement of three levels", where each higher-level system depends on the lower system but also possesses unique capabilities. Each system is characterised by specific ways of representing information, specific methods of acquiring it, specific possibilities for expressing it and specific kinds of consciousness. Tulving assumes that the neuro-psychological basis of memory systems is a set of elementary operating components, some of which are shared by the systems whereas others are unique to a specific system. Finally he speculates that the systems have emerged at different stages in the evolution of the human species and that they emerge at different stages in the ontogenetic development of the individual.

At the lowest, most primitive level is *procedural memory* which "enables organisms to retain learned connections between stimuli and responses, including those involving complex stimulus patterns and response chains, and to respond adaptively to the environment" (Tulving, 1985, p. 387). Information in the procedural system is represented in a prescriptive form, it is action orientated, it is acquired by "tuning" of the organism's capabilities, it can only be expressed directly by overt response, and it is characterised by what is called "anoetic" (non-knowing) consciousness. At the next level, *semantic memory* gives "the additional capability of internally representing states of the world that are not perceptually present ... to construct mental models ... that can be manipulated and operated on covertly, independently of any overt behaviour" (p. 387). Information in the semantic system is descriptive, detached from any particular action and isomorphic with what it represents. The characteristic way of acquiring this information is by restructuring, it can be expressed flexibly, under conditions far removed from those of original learning, and it is associated with "noetic" (knowing) consciousness which allows introspective awareness of the internal and external world. At the highest level is *episodic memory* which "affords the additional capability of acquisition and retention of knowledge about personally experienced events and their temporal relations in subjective time" (p. 387). Information in the episodic system is also descriptive and it includes the relations of represented events to the rememberer's personal identity. It is acquired by accretion, it is typically expressed in recollective experience, and it is accompanied by "auto-noetic" (self-knowing) consciousness which consists of the individual being aware of his or her own identity and existence in subjective time, extending from the past through the present to the future.

Generally speaking, I am quite sympathetic to the classification proposed by Tulving. In particular, I find it important to consider the evolution of different kinds of memory, and I agree with the view that in both phylogenetic and ontogenetic development, procedural memory precedes semantic memory which precedes episodic memory (see Larsen, 1983). However, it seems to me that too many and too loosely defined properties are lumped together in the three proposed memory systems, and that some of the suggested relationships are highly questionable. Therefore, it appears somewhat premature to commit oneself to a particular set of memory systems. This was also the conclusion of the majority of reviewers of Tulving's summary of his 1983 book in the journal *Behavioral and Brain Sciences* (Tulving, 1984). Let us take an alternative view on Tulving's theory.

Contents of Knowledge and Forms of Consciousness

According to the ecological approach to memory advocated by Neisser (1985), the basic questions to ask do not concern memory systems or memory mechanisms but rather the nature of the information which is remembered. In other words, what are the different kinds of knowledge that are remembered? Only if it is the case that such kinds of knowledge are handled differently by the organism may it be necessary, or even meaningful, to postulate separate memory systems. When Tulving's scheme is stripped for assumptions about separate memory systems, methods of acquiring and processing information, and suggested kinds of consciousness, there appears to be at the heart of it a ternary classification of the contents of knowledge possessed by human being.

Procedural knowledge is concerned with general properties of the individual's own activity. It is the kind of knowledge that underlies physical and mental skills, but also the tactics and strategies of planning and executing purposive, goal-directed behaviour and thinking. It includes knowledge of the external world, but only in the sense that the individual's activities are adapted to real-world properties and therefore reflect them – as the skill of typing reflects the properties of the keyboard. *Semantic knowledge* is concerned with general properties of the world, represented independently of any particular actions, purposes, needs, and wants of the individual. It is knowledge that is at least to some extent valid across different activities. But it also reflects the nature of these activities by representing the world in terms of its relevance to them, similar to the affordances described by J. J. Gibson. *Episodic knowledge* represents specific, unique events, usually including their temporal relationships and information about the context of and the role of the individual in the events.

In Tulving's account, procedural memory seems to be very different from semantic and episodic memory (which he, in some cases, refers to collectively with the term "propositional memory"), in particular because it is associated with a peculiar "non-knowing consciousness" which is meant to "refer to an organism's capability to sense and to react to external and internal stimulation" (1985, p. 388). This capacity seems to have nothing at all to do with consciousness, as it is obvious in the case of the tropisms of plants which Tulving uses as an illustration. Only in human beings (and perhaps some higher animals) may sensing and reacting to stimulation be accompanied by full consciousness of what is sensed and reacted to.

What is alluded to by the concept of non-knowing consciousness may be that the processes used to control the pick-up of sensory information and reactions to it are not known by the subject – this procedural knowledge is not conscious, it is used automatically without conscious control. This restriction of conscious access is not limited to procedural knowledge, however, it characterises some semantic and episodic knowledge, too. For instance, it is well known that people have great difficulty in telling which features they use to determine membership of a conceptual category whereas they can usually decide with ease whether a specific instance is a member of the category or not. Again, in producing and comprehending language, conceptual knowledge is obviously involved and can be expressed without effort. To call such non-conscious knowledge "propositional" begs the question of why it cannot be stated in actual propositions. Tulving (1984) seemed to realise this difficulty when he admitted that the most perspicuous example of semantic knowledge, so called lexical memory, should perhaps be counted as part of procedural memory because it is not really propositional! Episodic knowledge may like-wise be difficult or impossible to make conscious, although not to the same extent as semantic knowledge. For instance, in the déjà vu phenomenon it is probably information about a specific previous situation that we cannot con-sciously remember which gives rise to the feeling that "I have experienced this situation before". The feeling that a face or a place is familiar may similarly be based on non-conscious episodic information. Contextual features from the situation where something is learned may greatly influence whether it can be recalled later on, even though the subject is not consciously aware of such features (see Baddeley, 1982). Most recently, studies of priming in simple tasks like word recognition and word completion have shown that information about single episodes may be active but not accessible to consciousness (Graf & Schacter, 1985).

The opposite case, where procedural knowledge is consciously accessible, also occurs. For instance, if problems are encountered in carrying out a pro-cedure, people will usually not just give up or try the same procedure again. They will rather begin to think about what they were doing, consciously reflecting on their procedures. This may be difficult and often only partially successful, but it is not entirely impossible. Experts are people who are not just highly skilled, be it in a physical or cognitive domain, but also very good at consciously accessing the procedures they use. The 'mental practice' employed by some athletes is an example of procedural knowledge being developed and refined by conscious thinking. Also, many common everyday skills are developed from consciously controlled actions, or even from verbal or written instructions, by automatisation. Even though consciously thinking about an automatised skill may interfere with its execution, it would be strange to assume that the initial explicit knowledge of the procedure must disappear completely when it is automatised.

Implicit and Explicit Knowledge

Instead of Tulving's proposal that each type of knowledge is associated with a specific kind of consciousness (because they belong to different memory sys-tems), I suggest that procedural, semantic and episodic knowledge may exist in two forms or formats which differ in accessibility to conscious reflection. The resulting scheme is shown in Table 1 which also indicates the place of Tulving's three memory systems in this framework.

Table 1. Two-way classification of knowledge

Contents of knowledge	Form of knowledge	
	Implicit (operational, usable)	Explicit (declarative, knowable)
Procedural (generalities of own activity; skills)	"Procedural memory"	Instructions Directions Methods
Semantic (generalities of world; concepts)	Lexical decisions Categorisations Affordances	"Semantic memory"
Episodic (specific events; experiences)	Familiarity *Déjà vu* Priming	"Episodic memory"

Let us call the formats "implicit" and "explicit" knowledge. Knowledge in implicit form is assumed to be tacit in the sense that it can only be expressed by demonstration, by being used. It is context dependent, the present context of use must be similar to the context of acquiring the knowledge. And it is automatic in the sense that its execution does not require conscious control or effort. On the other hand, explicit knowledge can be expressed by description in a variety of ways and independently of the present context. Therefore, it can be manipulated and modified voluntarily, and its expression and use require conscious decision, control and effort. Implicit knowledge appears to be primary both in evolution and in individual development. This means that knowledge is initially acquired in implicit form and that the later emergence of explicit knowledge presupposes the existence of a certain basis of implicit knowledge.

Obviously, the distinction between implicit and explicit knowledge is similar to several earlier ones, in particular Polanyi's (1966) concepts of tacit and explicit knowledge. It is also related to Winograd's (1975) dichotomy of procedural and declarative representations, most notably by assuming that we are dealing with two different *formats* of knowledge that may well concern (i.e. be knowledge of) the same phenomena in the real world. However, I prefer to avoid Winograd's terms which invite confusion with the memory system concepts of procedural and propositional memory used by Tulving and others. Finally, the present distinction is similar to Graf and Schacter's (1985) concepts of implicit and explicit memory with which they propose to explain differences between amnesic and normal subjects' episodic memory. Though amnesics were unable to recall being presented with some words (explicit episodic memory), the words affected their later performance on tasks like word completion (implicit episodic memory) just as much as in normal subjects who did recall the presentation episode. Thus, implicit and explicit memory of episodes seem to be functionally distinct, and Graf and Schacter suggest that they are based on different sets of "memory traces", that is, different formats of knowledge.

Explicit Procedural Knowledge and Computing

With the classification developed above, we are ready to consider a second proposal about the cognitive requirements of computing. A few years ago, Sheil (1981) put forward the view that thinking in terms of explicit procedural knowledge has achieved unprecedented importance because of developments in information technology. Sheil called this kind of thinking "procedural reasoning" which he defined as "the process by which one determines the effects of a set of instructions or, alternatively, the set of instructions that will achieve a particular effect" (p. 8). He claimed that procedural reasoning is a fundamentally new way of thinking and that it is a skill underlying appreciation of programmed artifacts as well as programming itself.

Sheil argued that since information processing devices are controlled by explicit procedures put down in their programs, efficient utilisation of such devices – not to speak of programming them – requires at least some procedural reasoning. Even moderately complex devices can only be understood if we have a cognitive model of how they work. If it is a programmed device, the only kind of model that will make sense of its behaviour is a procedural model. The user who does not have an elementary grasp of procedural reasoning will probably rely on a cognitive model he is familiar with. One alternative is a mechanical model which basically corresponds to a list of facts saying that "this button gives this function". Such a model is far too simple and the result is that the user will be restricted to a small part of the facilities provided by the device. Another alternative model for comprehending programmed devices is the anthropomorphic model which errs in the direction of being far too complex. Here, the user views his role as analogous to giving instructions to another person whom he naturally expects to understand the meaning of the instructions and to carry them out according to their intentions just as he, the user, would be able to do himself. The design and marketing of information technology, particularly personal computers, encourage this inappropriate model, for instance by naming the computer "friend" or "partner", by having it respond "Good morning" or "Hi, Ann" when Ann turns it on, and so forth. No wonder people complain about the stupidity of computers. In the case of the antropomorphic model, this is the only conclusion when the user fails to make the machine "obey" simple orders.

In view of the ever-increasing use of complex programmed machinery, Sheil asserted that procedural reasoning is becoming "a modern survival skill" (Sheil, 1980). But how can procedural reasoning be developed? Sheil believed this to be a matter of acquiring some, otherwise not defined, basic programming skills which he terms "procedural literacy", in analogy with written language skills. However, he also believed that procedural literacy is difficult to acquire because of its novelty. Even though he admitted that people have "some kind of procedural framework which is widely used to formulate, follow and reason about procedures...a *naive procedural semantics...*" (p. 24, author's emphases), procedural literacy was seen as lacking an appropriate base of pre-existing skills to build on. I would not consider that to be entirely true, however. The whole import of my argument up to now is that adult human beings possess a large amount of implicit procedural knowledge which is actually much richer than the rather limited repertoire of algorithms that are used in programming. The real problem is that by far the major part of this knowledge is not accessible to conscious thinking and therefore cannot be used to understand or design programmed artifacts. The format of most procedural knowledge is solely implicit, not explicit.

At this point, Olson's explication hypothesis of written language and computing may be used to put the problem in a new perspective. I suggest that Olson's hypothesis be generalized to say that explicit knowledge is the result of expressing implicit knowledge in a language. Instead of just talking about levels of explicitness from oral through written to computer language we are thus led to consider if the languages, or symbolic media, are differentially suitable for explicating and communicating the three classes of knowledge outlined above. More specifically, what language is appropriate for explicating the procedural knowledge necessary to computing?

The Specialization of Languages for Knowledge Explication

In all probability, spoken language originally served to support the regulation of practical activities during cooperative work. Therefore, it must be able to express simple orders and to direct attention to relevant features of the situation. In so doing, some procedural and semantic knowledge is explicated. But since speaker and listeners share the present situation, there is no need for complete descriptions or unambiguous references. Furthermore, most of the skills which are used to do the cooperative work will be part of a common cultural background and therefore need not be talked about. We may say that spoken language is specialised for highly context- and person-dependent information. When the descriptive powers of a spoken language are increased, it is therefore understandable that it focuses on specific, personally experienced events, i.e. episodic knowledge, which in explicit form comes to make up the person's autobiography. The mental skill of selecting information for and composing such event descriptions has been called "narrative thinking" (Robinson & Hawpe, 1986) and it has been formalised into various cultural forms, like stories, myths and rituals.

Written language was invented to support communication across time, space and differences in cultural backgrounds. To achieve this context independence, the precision of references to objects must be increased, presuppositions must be explicated, a standardised vocabulary must be developed, and more general concepts must be formed to accommodate irrelevant local variations among referents. The individual's semantic knowledge is thus explicated and developed towards greater generality by using written language; words move beyond being self-explanatory vehicles for communication, they become objects of discussion and thinking by themselves. This is often called "logical thinking", though it need not involve the use of formal logic at all (Johnson-Laird, 1983). However, classical formal logic may be viewed as a refinement of written language in which context independence is carried to its limit to enable expression of conceptual relations without even considering their contents. The purpose of a formal language like classical logic is not to communicate information but to enable calculation, i.e. to control and prove the validity of conscious explicit thinking and to draw correct conclusions from completely hypothetical assumptions.

So far, I have argued that spoken language is particularly suited to making episodic knowledge explicit, communicable and consciously accessible, and that writing allows the same to be done with semantic knowledge. But what about procedural knowledge? Procedures are seldom expressed in oral language because they are self-evident, they are already intimately known by participants with a shared cultural background. What is new and important to talk about is conditions in the environment which the person's activity must take into account – obstacles to overcome, dangers to avoid, opportunities to take advantage of. Thus, the implication was that there is no need to talk about procedural knowledge, only properties of the situation to which the procedure must be adapted have to be explicitly communicated. However, skills have to be transmitted to young people through instruction, and it is often useful to be able to describe procedures in writing, e.g. in recipes and directions for using various devices. It is plain to see in these cases that describing procedures is not a trivial task. Skills instruction is very often more easily and efficiently done by demonstrating how to carry out the procedure or by guiding the learner as he attempts to do it.

Procedural Literacy

In contrast to both oral and written language, programming languages seem to be specialised for describing procedures. It is true, as Olson emphasises, that programming requires a higher level of explicitness and precision than speaking and writing because the major part of the meanings that are coded in a program concerns neither specific episodes nor conceptual relationships, but rather procedures that one wants the computer to perform. (Though it might appear so, I do not think that so-called logic programming is an exception to this assertion. If the programmer does not take into account the procedures used by the machine to process his "declarative" statements, the program will soon run into trouble.) To succeed with programming or operating a computer system, one must, therefore, first be able to figure out, on the basis of previous experience and present information, how a task should be done or a problem solved. Secondly, one must also be able to describe one's knowledge of the procedure explicitly in the system's language. In other words, the activity of using computer systems, especially experience with programming languages, requires that procedural knowledge is explicated, and the system offers a symbolic medium designed for expressing such procedures. Just as proficiency with written language serves to make semantic knowledge conscious and explicit, programming experience may thus bring implicit procedural knowledge within the reach of consciousness and controlled use. In this sense, the term "literacy" is well chosen to label the kind of competence with computers and programming that many current educational efforts strive for. However, Sheil's term "procedural literacy" is more fitting than "computer literacy"; after all, we do not talk about "book", "pencil", or "typewriter literacy" in the case of reading and writing – the physical realisation of the technology is less important than its psychological contents.

If the present hypothesis – let us call it the "procedure explication hypothesis" – is correct, then interesting consequences may be foreseen. First, procedural literacy should not be viewed as something that is presupposed in order to learn to program, as Sheil implies; quite the opposite, procedural literacy is a result of learning to use a programming language. This does not mean that there are no obstacles to acquiring programming skills and procedural literacy, as I shall discuss in the next section. Secondly, the influence of procedural literacy on knowledge organisation should spread so that an increasing proportion of the person's knowledge of procedures becomes explicit and conscious. Thirdly, as procedure explication skills develop, the person should become increasingly sensitive and therefore able to detect information that specifies procedures underlying concrete actions – his own as well as those of other people. Fourthly, to the extent that not only physical activities but also social interactions (like communication and cooperation) can be expressed in suitable procedural languages, the underlying routines of such behaviours may become more open to inspection, too. Fifthly, when procedures are made accessible to conscious reflection, the person should become more able to imagine alternatives to present procedures and thus be prepared to change them. Finally, one should perhaps not overlook the risk that thinking in terms of explicit procedures may give rise to a certain blindness or even aversion towards behaviours and processes that do not lend themselves to being expressed in the procedural media that happen to be around.

Each of these conjectures deserves much more discussion and empirical investigation. However, I shall finish the present chapter by considering some of the possible barriers to developing procedural literacy.

Obstacles to Procedural Literacy

When acquiring the basic programming skills necessary to procedural literacy proves difficult, we should ask two questions: (a) whether the learning process takes sufficient advantage of pre-existing procedural knowledge; and (b) whether the programming language is suited to explicate the implicit knowledge of procedures that the learner already possesses. In both respects, most current educational efforts are probably off the mark. The solution to the first problem should be relatively straightforward since it is a matter of choosing contents and examples which relate to previous experience and established skills of the learners. The second problem goes deeper since it questions the appropriateness of ordinary programming languages for explicating relevant implicit knowledge. Instead of formalised algorithmic languages, maybe we should look for analogical procedural systems of expression which cannot be guaranteed to lead to the desired result but lend themselves more easily to the representation of commonly known situations. This suggestion is based on a suspicion that the strict *formalisation* of programming languages is a major obstacle to their mastery, and to harvesting the benefits of explicating one's procedural knowledge at the same time.

Among other factors that may render our everyday procedural thinking difficult to express in a programming language, one seems to be concerned with the *level of details*, as is apparent in the instructions we give other people. Usually, we talk at the level of actions and the goals they are expected to achieve whereas we take for granted the more elementary operations which are employed to reach the goal under the circumstances that happen to prevail. For the distinction between "actions" and "operations", see Leont'ev, 1959/1981; Reiser, Black, & Abelson, 1985, used a similar distinction of activities versus general actions and showed that episodes are usually not only talked about but also remembered in terms of purposive actions (activities) rather than operations (general actions).

In the context of a traditional example, the hammer-and-nail situation, one would typically instruct another person to "nail the loose board on the roof" or just "fix the roof", not "bring the ladder, take the hammer and a nail, . . . ". The former would seem to be the standard level of instructions, similar to the basic level of naming categories (Rosch, 1974), perhaps because mastery of the necessary operations may normally be presupposed as I suggested earlier. However, if the person who is going to carry out the instructions is lacking in these skills, we may be more specific: " . . . hold the nail steady with your left hand at the point where you want it to go in, then take the hammer in your right hand . . . hold it by the end of the shaft in order to make full use of its weight when you hit . . . " It would be hard to move to a still finer level of specification, like "if the hammer is down, lift it by raising your right arm . . . ", and it would be totally pointless unless you were trying to program an artificial arm. The task only becomes impossible if one would want to move still further down to the level of individual muscle movements, a situation resembling programming in machine code. Fortunately, it is not necessary to specify operations that closely with the high level languages of current information technology. But even high level languages require much more detailed specification of procedures than the basic level of everyday verbal instructions. Therefore, the level of detail required by present computer systems may be a serious obstacle to procedural thinking.

A related problem is that instructions at the level of actions can leave the means to achieve the goal of an action unspecified and to be performed according to the parameters of the concrete situation of the actor. But the program for an automatic device must contain almost every conceivable operation together with their criteria of application because the precise circumstances at the time of executing the program cannot be foreseen. The demand of coming close to *exhaustive* specification of alternatives may be a very difficult one to satisfy when we attempt to explicate procedural knowledge.

Sheil (1981) proposed another factor that tends to make procedural reasoning difficult, namely the *separation of intent from action*. This means that the user has to specify all the actions to be performed before any of them are carried out. In practical action, we have the advantage that we can see the outcome of our previous activity before we decide on what operations to apply next. The requirement of advance specification does not seem to be radically different from what we have to do in planning practical activities. The problem boils down to having a sufficient repertoire of alternative operations at one's disposal at each decision point, i.e. the problem we have just discussed.

The difficulties of acquiring procedural literacy may seem formidable, at least to people beyond school age. However, many youngsters apparently learn to use and program computers without much effort, if only they try. Motivation will come when the things one can do with computers are clearly useful or fun. All the same, present-day programming languages could do much more to ease the way towards making computers serve people's purposes (as distinct from serving the purposes that manufacturers believe people have). The design of programming languages is too *machine dependent* which means that arbitrary constraints are placed on what procedures may be expressed straightforwardly. A change of direction is desirable towards designing languages and computer systems that take their point of departure in the way humans think about procedures (cf. Winograd & Flores, 1985).

References

Baddeley, A. D. (1982). Domains of recollection. *Psychological Review*, *89*, 708–729

Graf, P., & Schacter, D.L. (1985). Implicit and explicit memory for new associations in normal and amnesic subjects. *Journal of Experimental Psychology: Learning, Memory, and Cognition*, *11*, 501–528.

Johnson-Laird, P. N. (1983). *Mental models*. Cambridge: Cambridge University Press.

Larsen, S. F. (1983). Erindringens natur og historie (The nature and history of recol-lection). *Psyke & Logos, 4*, 277–307.

Larsen, S. F. (1984). Kognitionens logikker: Handling, sprog og datamater (The logics of cognition: Thinking, logic and computers). *Psyke & Logos, 5*, 221–242.

Larsen, S. F. (1986). Procedural thinking, programming, and computer use. In E. Hollnagel, G. Mancini & D. Woods (Eds.), *Intelligent decision support in process environments* (pp. 145–150). Berlin, Heidelberg, New York, Tokyo: Springer-Verlag.

Leont'ev, A. N. (1981). *Problems of the development of the mind.* Moscow: Progress. (Original work published 1959).

Neisser, U. (1985). The role of theory in the ecological study of memory. *Journal of Experimental Psychology: General, 114*, 272–276.

Olson, D. R. (1975). The languages of experience: On natural language and formal education. *Bulletin of the British Psychological Society, 28*, 363–373.

Olson, D. R. (1977). From utterance to text: The bias of language in speech and writing. *Harvard Educational Review, 47*, 257–281.

Olson, D. R. (1985a, May). Computers as tools of the intellect. *Educational Research-er, 14*, 5–8.

Olson, D. R. (1985b). *Intelligence and literacy: On the relations between intelligence and the technologies of representation and communication.* Unpublished manuscript.

Olson, D. R., & Bruner, J. S. (1974). Learning through experience and learning through media. In D. R. Olson (Ed.), *Media and Symbols: The forms of expres-sion, communication, and education* (73rd yearbook of the NSSE) (pp. 125–150). Chicago: National Society for the Study of Education.

Polanyi, M. (1966). *The tacit dimension.* New York: Doubleday.

Reiser, B. J., Black, J. B., & Abelson, R. P. (1985). Knowledge structures in the organization and retrieval of autobiographical memories. *Cognitive Psychology, 17*, 89–137.

Robinson, J. A., & Hawpe, L. (1986). Narrative thinking as a heuristic process. In T. R. Sarbin (Ed.), *Narrative psychology* (pp. 111–125). New York: Praeger.

Rosch, E. H. (1974). Linguistic relativity. In A. Silverstein (Ed.), *Human communi-cation: Theoretical perspectives* (pp. 95–121). Hillsdale, N.J.: Erlbaum.

Sheil, B. A. (1980). Teaching procedural literacy. *Proceedings of the 1980 ACM National Conference.* Nashville.

Sheil, B. A. (1981). Coping with complexity. *Xerox Research Center, Report No. CIS-15.* Palo Alto: Xerox Corporation. Also in R. A. Kasschau, R. Lachman, & K. R. Laughery (Eds.), *Information technology and psychology* (pp. 77–105). New York: Praeger, 1982.

Tulving, E. (1983). *Elements of episodic memory.* Oxford: Clarendon Press/Oxford University Press.

Tulving, E. (1984). Précis of "Elements of episodic memory". *The Behavioral and Brain Sciences, 7*, 223–268.

Tulving, E. (1985). How many memory systems are there? *American Psychologist, 40*, 385–398.

Winograd, T. (1975). Frame representations and the declarative-procedural contro-versy. In D. G. Bobrow & A. Collins (Eds.), *Representation and understanding* (pp. 185–210). New York: Academic Press.

Winograd, T., & Flores, F. (1985). *Understanding computers and cognition: A new approach to design.* Norwood, N.J.: Ablex.

CHAPTER 6

Writing, Time and Memory in the Perspective of Socio-cultural Evolution

Arild Lian

The main conceptions of memory which have been presented in philosophical and psychological literature seem to have been formed, more or less, as metaphors of writing. Plato, in *Theatus* compared memory with a wax tablet, and Aristotle (*On Memory and Reminiscence* in Dennis, 1948) likened the memory image to the "imprint of a seal ring" on this tablet. The term "engram", which means "inscription", is based on this metaphor. Later writers have dealt with the "engram" as a potentially locatable object, i.e. as a residual neural trace of a stimulus.

In this way, the metaphors of writing also lead to a general idea of memory storage. For example, Augustine (*Confessions X*, 13) spoke about "the great cave of memory" and Locke (*Essay Concerning Human Understanding*) about "the storehouse of our ideas". In our century, neuropsychologists, who have tried to identify the physiological substrata of learning and remembering, may be said to have availed themselves of the same conceptions of memory storage. Yet, important objections to mechanical storage models were raised as early as in 1950 when Lashley summarized his lifelong endeavours in his symposium paper *In Search of the Engram*. (For later contributions in this field, see Orbach, 1982.)

Writing metaphors of memory, though seemingly oversimplified to the modern researcher, have never been fully abandoned in cognitive psychology and cognitive science. With the computer, these metaphors have been extended and refined. The wax tablet and writing paper are substituted by magnetic discs. "The imprint of a seal ring" is turned into an electric signal in the track of a disc, or to the position of an electronic switch in a network wiring. The RAM of a computer has served as a concrete model for human memory storage, just as computer terminology itself has been formed, to some extent, by conceptions of memory which are commonly advanced in the Western culture.

Just as writing leaves a trace on a particular surface, sensory input also leaves an "image", a "representation" or an "impression" in the mind of the individual. Moreover, such an image can be reactivated or apprehended in the act of remembering. But, according to *The Representative Theory of Memory* (Shoemaker, 1967), the image is not the input or the past event remembered. Rather, it constitutes an 'inner representation' of such an event or episode.

The question is whether we could ever have conceived of such a representation without a written code.

Truly, writing and writing technology have greatly affected the way we think about memory. We may also ask, whether writing, considered as a cultural and technological innovation, has in the long run affected the bio-logical capacity of memory. This question pertains to the more general one concerning cultural influences on behaviour. Therefore, the relationship be-tween writing and memory should be considered in the context of socio-cultural evolution. Contrary to dominant trends in research literature, me-mory itself should be studied from a developmental point of view, particularly with respect to phylogenetic and historical aspects. With an upsurge of ex-perimental research on animal memory (Honig & James, 1971; Wagner & Pfantz, 1978; Smith & Spear, 1979) many investigators have stressed the points of contact rather than the differences between man and animal. Pa-radoxically, therefore, an extension of memory research to subhuman subjects has served to obliterate rather than focus on differences between the species and developmental trends in the evolution of memory.

Some researchers, however, have stressed the differences. Winograd (1971) argued that theories of animal and human memory will be different. Leont'ev (1981) has pointed out that "the transition from primitive, biological forms of memory to its highest, specifically human ones is the result of a long, complex process of cultural and historical development" (p. 327).

In the present paper, I shall deal with the ways development of a written code and the growth of literacy may have influenced the evolution of human memory functions as well as common knowledge and conceptions of memory in predominantly literate societies. This influence probably does not apply equally well to all forms of memory. Consequently, to limit the scope of my inquiry, I shall call attention to some recently advanced distinctions between types of memory. In other words, I shall try to define the memory concept which will be used in this work.

Memory as Awareness of Time

James (1890) distinguished between "primary" and "secondary" memory. Bergson (1910) distinguished between "habit memory" and "pure memory". Since then, we have had a long tradition of dividing memory into at least two types. In particular, Hunter's work (1913, 1920) with delayed response and delayed alternation in animals led to a widely held distinction between "sym-bolic memory" versus "non-symbolic memory". Later, Ryle (1949) suggested a distinction between "knowing how" and "knowing that". Thereafter, the following distinctions are the most celebrated ones: "memory without record" versus "memory with record" (Bruner, 1969); "episodic" versus "semantic memory" (Tulving, 1972); "reference memory" versus "working memory" (Honig, 1978).

From the literature on artificial intelligence (see in particular Anderson, 1981, 1982), a distinction is drawn between memory for "procedural" knowledge and memory for "declarative" knowledge. The former refers to information which is represented implicitly in cognitive processes, operations or procedures; whereas the latter refers to information formed explicitly as a set of facts or data structures. Thomas (1984) argued for a somewhat similar distinction between "dispositional memory" (involved in conditioning and discrimination learning) and "representational memory" which involves images, representations, etc. of previous events.

These distinctions have several aspects in common. They do not represent alternative theories or models of memory. Rather, they may be considered as supplements to each other. Regardless of the differences in terminology, the researchers seem to have been concerned with the same fundamental difference in learning: on the one hand, habituation and learning of skills provide for specific capacities and thereby change the ways individuals are "wired" to their present environment. On the other hand, previous experiences are "represented" and coded temporally as past events in the remembering mind. The fact that both types of memory affect the individual's interaction with the present environment does not contradict the distinction mentioned.

In the present work, I shall be concerned with the type of memory which involves representation of past events, and which has been termed "episodic", "declarative" or "representational". It is my contention that development of a written code has greatly influenced this type of memory.

To show more specifically how this influence has come about, it is important to focus on certain aspects of "declarative/representational memory" which are almost neglected in current research literature. The explication of these aspects, which have to do with the awareness of time, will, I think, increase the precision of common definitions of "declarative/representational memory".

Actually, it is quite surprising that the time perception aspect has been so little focused on in the current literature on memory. In classical literature, the time perception was considered an integral part of remembering. Thus, Aristotle claimed that "all memory . . . implies a time elapsed; consequently only those animals which perceive time remember, and the organ whereby they perceive time is also that whereby they remember" (quoted from Dennis, 1948, pp. 1–2).

Bergson said that 'pure memory', which man alone possesses, serves to record the events of daily life *as they occur in time*. Janet (1928) presented a joint treatment of time and memory, and while he portrayed a common view among philosophers, he asserted that memory always involves "knowledge of the past" (p. 183).

We might say that memories are 'time coded'. This means that they are dated as either recent or remote events, i.e. the person remembering knows approximately what time the original event took place. The question is, what is the nature of a "time code" and, how is it "cracked" by the nervous system?

Amnesics, particularly those who are suffering from anterograde amnesia after damage to the central nervous system, can generally learn new skills and even remember news items, but they find it very difficult to place them in time (Hirst & Volpe, 1982).

A speculative approach to the "chromomnemonics" of the mind was made by Deutsch (1984). He pointed out that 'time-tagging' of memories cannot be based on the strength of an association (or the synaptic connection underlying the association). This would leave the individual with a most ambiguous indicator of time. He argued that an analoguous problem has been solved by the eye. Just as the eye can locate the wavelength of light almost independently of intensity, so the brain might be able to assign a memory to a particular time, independent of the strength of that memory.

In vision, three inverted U-curves represent three basic processes underlying hue perception. Each hue or wavelength is assigned a value for each of the three curves, and these values are fed into two different mechanisms: one sums up the values to provide information about overall intensity, and one computes the ratio of the three values to provide information about position in the spectrum. Deutsch argued that this system can be applied to memory. Rather than assuming a single process for each memory trace, he suggested that each one is

> . . . represented by a number of processes, simultaneously initiated, but increasing and decreasing in strength at different rates. This would produce the signals that would be fed into the two kinds of mechanisms that are used by the eye. One of these mechanisms would sum the intensities produced by the two processes that increase and decrease with time at different rates. The output of this mechanism would signal the strength of the memory or habit, while losing all information about when the memory was laid down. The second mechanism would extract the ratio between the strength of the signals that had been simultaneously initiated. This second mechanism would thus measure the age of the memory, while losing information about its strength (1984, pp. 159–160).

This approach to chromomnemonics leaves us with two questions. One has to do with the way empirical support can be documented. How can we demonstrate the existence of several processes, initiated by one stimulus event, which increase and decrease at different rates? Deutsch dealt with this question in a report on the memory blocking effect of anticholinesterases. He administered these drugs to rats at different time intervals after their initial learning of a habit. Using the two peaked curves of vulnerability to anticholinesterases, he argued that the memory trace of initial learning may be represented by more than one process. On the basis of the data reported, this possibility cannot be ruled out. At the same time, it should be stressed that Deutsch seems to have been concerned with a "dispositional" type of memory in which time tagging may not occur. The chromomnemonic mechanism, though, may be common to all types of memory. However, the information provided by a "comparator of process strengths" may only be used in certain cases, depending on the situation or task demands.

The second question is a theoretical one. Given that we can account for a multiprocess substrate of memory, why should a comparator of process strengths give rise to a time tagging of memories? If it does, would it work independently of the neural processing underlying memories having other time tags?

In the case of such independence of function it might be said to provide for an absolute timing of events in memory, and hence it would contradict phenomenological evidence and explain too much. Events which are retrieved from memory are ordered temporally rather than assigned absolute time values. The "age" of a memory is, to a great extent, derived from the context.

Deutsch, however, argued against a contextual interpretation of time tagging. A retrieved event may be placed in time relatively independent of other mnemonic processing, he said. Moreover, the mechanism invoked by the model, presupposes that time is "sensed" like hue and brightness. In this way, chromomnemonics was considered as a biological, relatively culture-free function of the mind.

It seems to me that Deutsch has invented a capacity which hardly exists in the human mind. Certainly, memories are time coded, but with a lack of contextual cues this code is a very imprecise one. Also, memories may carry a sense of pastness, while the rememberer is incapable of telling the time of the retrieved event. This shows great variation in the chromomnemonic power of one person, and when it comes to comparisons between persons, these variations may be even greater. Therefore, I think it is rather unlikely that memory, considered as an awareness of the past, should be possible to explain with reference to a biological mechanism of the type described by Deutsch.

Memory involves more than the dating of individual events, memory provides *the time perspective* which serves as a basis (or measure) of all episodes remembered by the individual. Without the personal time perspective, there could be no time coding of memories. This perspective brings together events, facts, situations, knowledge, etc., into a coherent time axis of life. Memory, so to speak, ascertains the continuity of life from a distant past to the present, and from the present to expectations of the future. Moreover, a coherent temporal scheme of life warrants a *personal identity*.

Ontogeny involves a constant expansion and differentation of an individual's time perspective. Only neurological and cerebrovascular impairments underlying senility and amnesia by Alzheimer and Korsakoff patients cause a slowdown or halt to this process. In some cases, the personal time perspective may actually shrink to cover only parts of the life span of the individual. Furthermore, neurological damage or traumas may erase parts of the personal time perspective and, for a while, the identity of the individual.

The cultural setting, however, may exert an even greater influence on the time perspective of an individual. *Rites de passage* are supposed to structure the life of the individual temporally. These transitions mark off intervals in the life span, with each individual being mainly responsible for events which have taken place since the latest *rites de passage*. This interval marks a period in which the individual is supposed to remember events well. For the most part, this period becomes the time perspective of the individual. Therefore, social transitions often have an impact on the perception of time.

We are now in a position to qualify current definitions of "declarative/representational memory". These definitions are generally made with reference to a formal structure of knowledge. If no further specifications are added, they may turn out to be inadequate ones. Thus retrieved events, which are not recognized as events experienced by the person in the past, may easily be considered as examples of declarative/representational memory.

Reference to a formal structure of knowledge is essential but insufficient. We should add the specification that *retrieved events are extracts from a personal history*. Without this specification we cannot know whether instances of déjà vu, hallucination or fantasy should be included in the declarative/representational category of memory.

Knowing Time

Becoming aware of time, especially linear time, and developing mnemonic capacities of the type I have mentioned may be considered different aspects of the same cognitive endeavour, i.e. the human consciousness.

This development, which is no doubt based on biological assets of *Homo sapiens*, is inextricably linked with socio-cultural evolution. It is, I think, an integral part of that evolution. Particularly conceptions and measurements of time may be said to mirror socio-cultural evolution and the emergence of civilizations.

Leach (1971) raised the question of how prehistorical man, without clocks, calendars or any system for recording temporal events, could experience time. He assumed that, eventually, the category of time rests on two types of experiences:

(a) that certain phenomena of nature repeat themselves (and)
(b) that life change is irreversible (p. 125)

Certainly, these experiences must have been critical ones for the establishment of a time concept by man. Yet, the two types may have had different impacts on the way man conceived of time. I shall, therefore, consider each of them in turn, starting with the experience of irreversible change.

The observation that all living things are born, grow old and die may have been a potent factor in the early formation of an idea of time. We must, however, add the qualification that natural changes should neither be too slow, nor too fast; they should be comparable with human events. Under these conditions, we can say that irreversible changes in nature provide for a "time flow" in human consciousness. On the other hand, they do not necessarily provide for a time perspective. This, I think, may be more dependent on the former type of experiences, namely the experiences of events repeating themselves.

Again, we should add a qualification, an event which repeats itself must have a recognizable temporal structure. For example, the growing of crops in which sowing comes before harvest. In such an event, the changes run unidirectionally towards an *end state*. Therefore, when the event repeats itself, it will give rise to an expectation of a goal, and this expectation may be essential to the development of a certain time perspective.

The event which includes an end state may be called a "goal-directed episode" or "goal-directed action". If a goal-directed action is blocked, and if the individual is strongly motivated to attain the goal, this blocking will provide a very strong feeling of time. Some will say that this blocking will cause a feeling of duration, but this term carries the implicit connotation of measured time. Therefore, "duration" is not a good term. What I allude to is a feeling of "time flow", not a feeling of minutes or hours passed.

Consequently, natural events give rise to an idea of time and they also encourage an expectancy of future events. Thus, development of a time perspective is initiated by repeatable events in nature, but this perspective is probably quite a restricted one.

The problem for prehistorical man may have been to take account of a considerable span of the past. However, man may not have conceived of the past as a matter of great interest until certain productive systems evolved. Thus, when man settled on more or less permanent sites and started to "experiment" with simple forms of gardening and agriculture, *a need for communication about duration* was created. Because man had to take the past into account, a form of primitive time reckoning came into existence. Social settings and economy on the one hand, and communication and conceptions of time on the other may have mutually influenced each other. In any case, communicative requirements invoked the development of *units of time*. Without such units, communication about duration would be difficult.

When human society reached a certain degree of complexity, the control and regulation of activities covering a certain time span became of prime importance. This control could only be obtained by some form of time measurement, an achievement that required the apprehension of an adequate time unit and the invention of a counting system. Such a system may be said to form part of a communicative technology in prehistoric societies. This technology may have drastically changed the very conception of reality.

Prior to the invention of a recording system, man, I assume, had a predominantly "cyclic" conception of time. Certainly, the observation of irreversible changes gave rise to the perception of a certain time flow. But these observations did not necessarily encourage a 'linear' way of thinking about time. The 'linear conception' may have come about as a solution to practical problems which were connected to the new production systems in permanent sites. These systems required a more rigorous planning of actions, i.e. planning based on *estimates of time passed rather than expectations of the reoccurrence of a natural event.*

Socio-cultural evolution encouraged a distinction between repetitive and non-repetitive events. Comprehension of the former is facilitated by a number of phenomena in nature. The latter, however, is not easily comprehensible from the observation of nature alone. Since so much repeats itself, everything, even the life cycles of individuals, might be supposed to repeat itself. Leach, for example, pointed out that people in traditional societies may have repudiated the final truth about irreversible changes in nature; and that religion in particular has denied the reality of death. Thus, birth and death were said to be the same thing – "that birth follows death, just as death follows birth" (Leach, 1971, p. 125).

A general expectation of the reoccurrence of events in nature may have prevented an understanding that many episodes happen just once and are gone. Communication about duration, however, requires a clear distinction between the *beginning* and *end* of something, a distinction which may be hard to maintain if time moves in a "cyclic" fashion. To overcome this difficulty, temporal events must be represented by permanent and discriminative objects.

As pointed out, however, the need to communicate about duration can be found primarily among people established on permanent sites. Also, I think, the distinction between repetitive and non-repetitive events was clearly made, for the first time, among people who lived and worked for a living on one site throughout most of their life.

On the other hand, nomadic people or others who are non-sedentary may come up with a different conception of time. For example, people who constantly abandon sites upon depletion of the vegetation seem to be concerned with a more concrete space-time reality (Sørum, 1984). Particularly when these people move in a fixed "migration circle", past events may be recounted by referring to sites or places. Thus, Barth (1975) reports that to the Baktaman of New Guinea "places also serve to recall events in the past – stories and anecdotes that I was unable to elicit in conversation in the men's house would suddenly surface in the forest with the opening 'this is the place where'. . . ." (p. 18).

Establishment in permanent sites may seem to have encouraged a certain dissociation of space and time. However, this dissociation is not due to a sedentary form of life per se, but rather to the communicative technologies developed in these social settings. Time has never been fully abstracted from space. Modern computer and telecommunication systems may further encourage the dissociation process, particularly since man has almost instant access to information over vast distances in space. The *recording procedures*, not geographic mobility, determine the extent to which space and time are interlinked in human cognition.

Written records have thus encouraged a change from a predominantly cyclic to a linear or unidirectional conception of time. But the latter conception of time never fully replaced the former. Evolution has provided a temporal framework for remembered events, i.e. a framework which ascertains a coherent structure of the personal past, and this structure serves as a basis for all remembering by humans. Without this structure, the individual still 'records' and retrieves events, but he does so in a more or less detached way. The retrieved event cannot be clearly located in a temporal framework, or the person is not aware of having experienced the event himself. This is an ordinary post-hypnotic phenomenon and it occurs in some forms of psychopathological states.

Metamemory

Communication about past events, especially events which do not repeat themselves, requires, of course, memory of these events. Moreover, such communication requires some recognition of the memory capacities of oneself and those of others. Hence, communication about a recent and common past involves *metamemory*. Thus, the growing awareness of time, the evolution of memory functions, and the recognition of such functions by man are closely linked in behavioural development.

Metamemory means knowledge and awareness of mnemonic activities. The acquisition of this knowledge can be studied ontogenetically, as an aspect of child development and historically as an aspect of behaviour evolution. Until recently, most research on this subject was done with children.

Flavell and Wellman (1977) have shown that metamemory changes with age and that it depends very much on other cognitive functions of the child. Research into mnemonic strategies have shown that young children do not know the appropriate strategies for remembering and therefore do not apply them well. Soviet psychologists (cf. Meacham, 1972; Smirnov, 1973) have argued that children do not perform well when memory is set as a goal. Their performance is much better when mnemonic activities are required as a means to attain another end or purpose.

This shows, I think, that awareness of the memory function and the intentional retrieval of a past event is a matter of great abstraction, and that it can be achieved only in a relatively late stage of cognitive development. The evolution of metamemory by early man may have taken a different course. As part of man's self-consciousness, this capacity must have been a relatively late achievement. Thus, in this respect, ontogenetic and historical development are similar. Also, metamemory in early man was part of a more general cognitive development. In the following, I shall argue logically about the other cognitive capacities that have been linked to metamemory.

Naturally, metamemory is part of a general knowledge system and, in my opinion, the main ingredients of this system apply to the time perspective and the awareness of non-repetitive events in the past. This awareness makes possible a basic distinction between an *original version* (of a story, event, etc.) and a later *reproduction* or retelling of the event. Communication about the past does not change the events which have taken place, it only changes our *understanding* of them.

Olson (1988) has recently called attention to a similar distinction, namely the one between *observation* and *interpretation*. It differentiates between the information "given" and the "inferences assigned". In texts, for example, it is represented by literal statements ("what the text says, asserts, claims . . ."), versus an interpretation of such statements. These are conceptual distinctions which are linked to metamemory. This means, I suggest, that man could not communicate or raise a problem of memory unless he could make these distinctions. The problem is how these distinctions have been acquired. Most probably, these, as well as other cognitive capacities, have been acquired in the attempt to solve social and practical problems. They may also be closely linked to the emergence of primitive systems of production in early societies. In short, conditions of metamemory may be found in the *praxis* of early man.

More specifically, I assume that these conditions were provided when man developed a primitive form of a recording system. Discriminative objects or marks could "represent" past and distant objects and events. A "conservation" of the past was made possible, and this conservation was sanctioned by the group by the invention of a specific code. Naturally, a recording system does not in itself warrant a metamemory among its users, but it greatly encourages a development in this direction. Also, we can say that the very invention of a recording system involved the recognition of memory requirements in gardening, agriculture, trade and other activities in ancient societies.

Until now, metamemory has been described as a cognitive *capacity*. This description is not quite accurate. Metamemory is most probably also the product of an attitude and a way of life. As such, it is wholly dependent on social institutions and interpersonal relationships. In societies where such relationships are regulated by myths rather than written records, the type of conceptual distinctions mentioned above are not encouraged. Hence, there is no way of evaluating recounts of history independently of present social practices.

An interesting case in point was reported by Goody and Watt (1968) who studied the oral poetic traditions of the Gonja of Ghana. These people were said to have no category for "the very words" or for the 'verbatim' repetition of a story. Hence, they had great difficulties in distinguishing between an *original* version of a story and various *reproductions* of the story. People in this society regulated their lives according to "the myth of the state" (the Bagre of Gonja). The story was recorded twice, 60 years apart, and in this interval some major changes occurred. The myth goes somewhat as follows:

Ndewura Jakpa conquered the indigenous inhabitants, enthroned himself as head of the state and proclaimed his sons as rulers of its territorial divisions. Goody and Watt, who recounted the story, called attention to certain details that appeared in the first recording at the time the British extended their control over the area. This version said that Jakpa had seven sons "corresponding to the number of divisions whose heads were eligible for the supreme office by virtue of their descent from the founder of the particular chiefdom". When the British arrived, two of the seven divisions disappeared. And "sixty years later, when the myths of the state were again recorded, Jakpa was credited with only five sons and no mention was made of the founders of the two divisions which had since disappeared from the political map" (p. 33).

I think it would be missing the point if changes in the myths were attributed to losses of memory by the people who maintained the oral poetic tradition. Such losses attribute meaning only in so far as deliberate attempts are made to record history. However, genealogies of traditional societies tend not to serve this function, rather they seem to "act as charters of present social institutions" (Goody & Watt, 1968, p. 33).

Yet, I would warn against overstating the point. At any time, the genealogy of the group is well defined. Therefore, those who retell the myth are not free to construct it according to their own wishes. From the point of view of the group, it is quite possible to be wrong about the past.

However, the past is not a recorded past, i.e. it does not constitute original events independent of later societal changes. The conceptual distinction between an *original* and its *reproduction* may be virtually non-existent, or is not a prominent one in some traditional societies. Hence, the basic conditions for *raising* a problem about memory, or communicating about memory, are absent.

Control of Memory

Metamemory, which involves awareness of remembering, is accompanied by a type of control which we may call "active elaborative processing". This type of control takes place in both encoding and retrieval, and it characterizes the memory activities of healthy normal adults. Most probably, metamemory is a direct prerequisite to an active, elaborative processing of the materials to be remembered. In the present section, I shall argue that this type of control is evolutionarily related, on the one hand, to changes in early man's attitudes towards memorizing and, on the other, to cognitive operations involved in the recording and use of a written code. Hence, writing changed human memory functions in the sense that it invoked a new type of control. First, however, I shall address myself to the general question of whether mnemonic activities by man submit to different types of control operations. An issue relating to my question concerns the alleged difference between recognition and recall memory.

In general, it has been shown that subjects perform better in recognition tasks than recall tasks. Kintsch (1970) proposed that the latter would require generation of the item before it could be recognized, whereas in recognition tasks, the generation is done by the experimenter. The subject needs only to recognize the item provided. However, the difference in performance depends on a comparison between recognition and *free recall*. Performance in *cued recall* tasks may sometimes be better than performance in recognition tasks (Flexer & Tulving, 1978, Jones, 1978; Wallace, 1978). This means that an interpretation which does not require a superiority of recognition may, therefore, gain some attention. Griffith (1975) assumed essentially the same memory system, but postulated different control processes for the two forms. Subjects may code the material differently depending on whether they expect a recall or a recognition test.

According to the position taken by Leont'ev (1981), the relationship between recognition and recall cannot be explicated by way of experiments alone. Rather, experimental data should be supplemented by other types of data showing the historical development of human memory capacities. If there are genuine differences between recognition memory and recall memory, these differences should be considered in the context of socio-cultural evolution.

Leont'ev assumed that there exists some form of memory which is biologically based, and which operates relatively independently of man's cultural and social setting. This form he called "direct memory" or "the natural capacity for impression and reproduction". To get an idea of how direct memory differs from "higher forms of memory", Leont'ev turned to descriptions of the memory disorders of patients with the so-called Korsakoff syndrome. Until recently, it was generally assumed that these patients retain information in their working memory, but are unable to transfer it to permanent memory. It has now been shown that Korsakoff patients preserve learning of perceptual-motor and cognitive skills as well as certain repetition-priming effects, while they show memory impairments as regards specific items or facts (Cohen, 1984). In other words, they appear to have lost some of their declarative/representational form of memory, while they still perform normally on tasks which involve dispositional memory.

On the other hand, it has been shown that both Korsakoff patients and other amnesics may show retention of specific items, to the same extent as normal persons, as long as the testing procedure does not require awareness of having experienced that item in the past. Thus, Cermak, Talbot, Chander and Wolbarst (1985) reported that prior presentation of a word enhances subsequent identification of the word, an effect which is independent of recognition memory.

Hence, it does not seem to be memory for specific materials or events that is impaired, but rather memory activities that require awareness of remembering. Higher forms of memory, which, according to Leont'ev, required mediated recall, always involve an awareness of remembering. The distinction between the higher forms which are lost, and the direct memory which is preserved in amnesia is most characteristically described by Leont'ev in one of his remarks about the patients:

> Active recall is impossible for them; when we present words to a patient that have been read to him prior, he recognizes them; by "pushing" him onto them, we can evoke remembrance of having learned them in him, but he is unable to remember them independently (1981, p. 338).

This does not mean that Korsakoff patients have recognition memory, but are deprived of active recall. The preserved ability of the patients was called "evoked remembrance" by Leont'ev. This is not directly comparable to recognition memory as used in modern literature. Rather, evoked remembrance may be likened to 'state-dependent memory'. This is the type of memory which is evoked by similarity of states, moods and the supportive aspects of the current environment. Memories which are retrieved by contextual cues may also have been learned incidentally. However, this is not a critical condition. Primarily, "evoked remembrance" means that retrieval cannot take place in the same way as direct recall.

Here, we have come to the main point concerning the development of memory. It deals with the locus and form of control of remembering. Having developed a "technology" for comprehending time as a flow of non-repetitive events, man also acquired a certain capacity to control memory. That is to say, the individual took over part of the control which had previously been the sole domain of physiological and situational determinants.

Physiological factors underlying moods, emotions, smells, etc., have always been recognized as having a great impact on memory. Thus, a good deal of processed material seems to be "dissociated" from normal memory in that it has been stored or acquired in a contextual or drug altered state (Weingartner, 1984). Situational determinants also include rituals and ceremonies performed by the group. Such rituals may have been very strong triggers of memories and, therefore, the cult of the people has served as a 'technical device' for controlling memory. In fact, it may have been hard to distinguish between the memory of the individual and the memory of the group or the culture.

This situation changed radically (although the transition may have taken centuries) with the development of a recording system and a written code. The trigger mechanisms of rituals and ceremonies did not satisfy the memory demands of new production systems. Consequently, to solve social and economical problems, procedures were invented which could be used by individuals. Naturally, these were simple forms of memory aids which are more or less a part of everyday life. They have, nevertheless, served as a kind of *mnemonic technology* connecting memory to material objects. Thus, Janet writes:

> The man who wants to recall a memory takes something into his hand; he ties a knot in his handkerchief, puts a little pebble into his pocket, takes a piece of paper or a leaf from a tree. These are what we still today call souvenirs (1928, p. 262).

The use of such remedies testifies to man's conscious attempts to master his memory – the memory aids, we can say, indicate *intent* to remember. Therefore, it will be important to trace the use of such aids in prehistoric times. Their first occurrence may have marked a major step in the development of human cognition. Moreover, memory aids in the form of concrete objects varying in size and shape, may have been precursors to writing. Schmandt-Besserat (1982) has provided some main arguments in this direction. The Uruk texts, representing the first form of writing known to date, consisted, not of concrete pictographs, but highly abstract ideographs inscribed on clay tablets. Epigraphers have, therefore, assumed that art at that time had already reached an advanced level. Schmandt-Besserat argued that cues to the precursors of Uruk writing could be found in characteristics of the clay material used. Objects unearthed from Nuzi, a city existing in Iraq in the second millenium B.C., revealed similar characteristics. And according to later analysis, these were said to constitute tokens used in an elaborate counting system:

> For example, one token of a particular kind might represent each of the animals in the palace herds. When new animals were born in the spring, the appropriate number of new tokens would be added; when animals were slaughtered, the appropriate number of tokens were withdrawn (p. 82).

Tokens with a variety of forms such as spheres, disks, cylinders, etc., were also found at Susa, the great Elamite site. This is said to have levels which are more than 1500 years older than those of Nuzi. Pierre Amiet (cf. Schmandt-Besserat) could also confirm that these tokens had served as an elaborate counting system.

With this background, Schmandt-Besserat collected and systematically analysed a large number of clay artifacts from sites in the Near East. She found a great number from the Neolithic period in the area which had most likely been used for counting and book-keeping purposes. The earliest tokens known to date can be dated back to around 8500 B.C., when people still tended flocks but eventually started to experiment with crops.

In passing, it should be noted that the transition to writing is indicated by the double book-keeping system used in Nuzi and Susa. On the former site, egg-shaped, hollow tablets had been used to store or "deposit" tokens. The so-called "bullae" from Susa had a similar function. Inscriptions on their surfaces matched the number of tokens inside. On the bullae, surface impressions also matched the shape of tokens inside.

There is also anthropological evidence from our own century that concrete memory aids are used as a kind of substitute for writing. A case in point was provided by Weule (1915) who analysed the use of so-called letter sticks (*Botenstäbe*) among the Australian aborigines. These were notched, round sticks or rectangular wooden tablets used for communication between tribes living far apart. The notches, which were cut by the sender, represented a particular message. Yet the notches were not conventional symbols which could be read by several people. Rather, they signified to the bearer, particular persons, places, animals, objects and numbers which occurred in the message to be transmitted. In other words, they served as important cues to that message.

It could be said that the notches served as a means of controlling memory. In this way, an indirect or mediated form of memory evolved. According to Leont'ev, "mediation of the act of recall . . . alters nothing in the biological law of this function; only the structure of the operation as a whole is altered" (1981, p. 330).

However, I do not want to put too much emphasis on the distinction between "direct" and 'mediated' memory. In a sense, all memory is mediated or cue dependent. Thus, retrieval may be dependent on contextual cues and physiological, or motivational states. These contingencies form the structure of the operation. The main point to be noted is that man has deliberately changed this structure by *selecting the cues while he is in the process of acquisition*. He has decided, beforehand, under what circumstances the message is to be retrieved. Leont'ev says that subsequent development takes place along two lines: (a) as a refinement and differentiation of external aids – this line of development leads to writing; (b) conversion of external aids to internal ones – this leads to free recall.

Apparently, we could say that a higher form of memory has been added to the biologically more primitive one. The distinction between the two is reflected in the way we talk about remembering. A person uses the expression "that reminds me" when cued by more or less accidental circumstances. When deliberately intending to retrieve a memory, the expression used is 'I recall that'.

It seems as if memory functions have been extended in evolution. Yet, it is hard to say whether a "new" type of memory has been added to the cognitive repertoire of man. I think we can only ascertain an adaptability in the way man has responded to the memory demands of his society. Specific control procedures have been developed and deliberately used in interactions between people. These procedures do not necessarily indicate any change in the biological capacity of memory, but they do show man's awareness of his own memory capacity. Hence, control of memory and metamemory are two aspects of the same thing. Together, they form the *psychological basis* for the development of writing. And writing, once in progress, further encourages a development of memory along the lines described here.

The Transformation of Memory

Olson (1988) argued that nothing would be "more systematically misleading" than to say that writing extends memory. Instead, he proposed that writing *transforms* memory. The point is an important one, however, and I think it needs some explication. Most probably, we cannot speak about "transformation of memory", if "transformation" is to be used in the cybernetic sense of the word. This terminology requires two states of memory: the definition of the "set of operands" (memory A); and the "transforms" (memory B). Memory A is "transformed" into memory B under the influence of an "operator", i.e. the written text (Ashby, 1957). At present, I do not think we have reached the level of specification required in the cybernetic description of "operands" and "transforms". Yet, I think we can deal with transformation of memory in a non-specific, intuitive fashion. Furthermore, we have empirical evidence showing that some form of transformation may take place, for example, when text is converted into memory; and later, when memorized material is retrieved in the form of verbal reports.

Most researchers today agree that memory for text is seldom verbatim. Of course such remembering may take place in rote learning of poems, lists of meaningless syllables, etc., but learning in these cases requires much effort and the use of rhythmical and pause-bound groupings of the material. It is generally easier to memorize a text if it can be structured by the reader in a meaningful way.

Bartlett's (1932) analysis of the recall of narrative stories shows the way memorized material can be restructured and distorted by the individual. Also, in the recall of such stories fragments could be added so the material would adhere to the stereotyped situations people were familiar with. This analysis has convinced many researchers that memorization of text and discourse is first and foremost a product of comprehension.

In general, memorization seems to be successful to the extent that the reader is able to capture the "gist" of the story. In part, this is built up by inferences from propositions in the text. Hence, new sentences complying with these inferences, which are presented to the subject in a recognition test, are frequently said to have occurred in the text (Thorndyke, 1977).

The gist captured depends, of course, on the prior knowledge possessed by the subject. Thus, what is retained of a sentence is, in part, a "knowledge-based model" of the situation rather than some propositional analogue of the text itself. Consider, for example, a study of cued recall by Garnham (1979) in which subjects were presented with the following sentence: *The housewife cooked the chips*. In general, people know that chips (French fries) are fried not cooked. Therefore, when subjects were cued by the word "cooked", they were less likely to remember the sentence than when they were cued by the word "fried".

However, "gist", and possibly even "knowledge-based model", are elusive things to define. Consequently, it is difficult to specify the type of transformation taking place when text is converted to memory. Some researchers have proposed ways of dealing with the "gist" of a story; these attempts have been reviewed and discussed by Sanford and Garrod (1981). Most systems tend to focus on (a) main propositions; (b) main goals; and (c) main actions, in order to give an adequate representation of the gist. But the problem still remaining is to show how these elements are combined in the type of "model" used by the reader for comprehension and memory.

Perhaps all we can say at present is that the *temporaneity of text* is converted into the *contemporaneity of a model* in the mind of the reader. That transformation of memory is best modelled after some trade-off function between space and time. But we might also say that what is retained in memory is some contemporaneous pattern which is similar to the "invariant" of a perceptual event. Consider, for example, a Johansson scene of lights (i.e. points of lights against a dark background) which move in programmed paths. Mathematically, the description of these paths is enormously complex. The lights, however, are attached to a person moving in an otherwise dark space. Suddenly the event is seen as a meaningful one, a person walking with regular steps in one direction. Most probably, the perceptual event and the memorized pattern have homologous structures.

The transition from a syntagmatic chain of text to a contemporaneous model in the mind of the reader, may be compared to the metaphoric transformation which, according to Levi-Strauss, takes place in successful inter pretation of myths. (For a brief summary of the main principles of myth interpretation, see Leach, 1976.) Actually, the transformation is one between *metonymy* and *metaphor*. In metonymy "a part stands for a whole", as when a crown is said to be a sign of royalty. This also means that a sign is related to a whole by contiguity. A metaphor, however, depends on an asserted similarity between objects or events from different cultural domains. In this way, metonymy and metaphor form opposites, like the syntagmatic and paradigmatic axes of speech (see Blache, 1978).

The temporally ordered segments of text are not metonymically linked unless an instantaneous pattern can be detected in each of the segments. In myth interpretation, Levi-Strauss proceeds by breaking up the story into a suitable number of episodes. By considering each one of these as a metaphoric transform of each of the others, he looks for a common pattern or structure. When this pattern is detected, the original episodes can be linked by metonymy. This warrants a final interpretation of the myth.

Leach asserted that episodes of a story are linked by metonymy insofar as the beginning implies the end and vice versa. As an example, he mentioned the Christian European custom in which brides are veiled and dressed in white and widows are veiled and dressed in black. The two episodes are "part of the same message. A bride is entering marriage, a widow is leaving it" (Leach, 1976, p. 27).

When segments of a text are linked by metonymy, the whole text can be treated as one chunk by the reader, and hence retention will be easy. The metaphoric transform, therefore, can be looked upon as a "cognitive gestalt" or "organized whole". Consequently, my standpoint is that the myth interpretation analogy serves a heuristic function in the study of memory. It provides an essential clue to the understanding of how text, text comprehension and memory are related. Moreover, it may also serve as a reference framework for integrating studies of memory with studies of perception.

At the same time, it should be admitted that the model has clear limitations. First of all, written language is generally not like the myths of oral poetic traditions. Metonymy and metaphoric transforms are characteristics belonging to the latter. As a result of these characteristics, personal recollections of myths, narratives, etc. have been possible in non-literate societies. Oral transmission of culture is heavily dependent on the type of structures revealed in myths.

As long as the elements of a story are linked by metonymy, the listener (or reader) can maintain the same orientation to the message, so there will be no elements of surprise. The parts, i.e. segments, paragraphs, etc., of written language are not necessarily linked by metonymy. Thus, reorientations, reinterpretations and surprises are possible, and sometimes expected, in the continuous reading of text. In this way, written language contrasts with myths and makes memorizing more difficult.

Yet text, when converted to memory, must be segmented and restructured by the reader in a way that makes metaphoric transforms possible. The extent to which memorizing is successful depends, of course, on the type of text being read. Thus, written text may also have characteristics in common with oral poetic traditions. If not, there will be a demand for new knowledge-based models to control memory. Otherwise, individuals will be more dependent on the written medium. Reinspection of the material will replace recall.

Concluding Remarks

Literacy has encouraged the conception of time as a flow of non-repetitive events. In this way, literacy has also made man more attentive to his own memory capacities, and he has availed himself of various means for control of memory. The structure of written text can be said to contrast with the contemporaneity of a memory pattern. Hence, writing transforms memory. But despite these various effects, it is not possible to show that literacy has changed the biological capacity of memory.

Most importantly, however, the written code has brought an implicit definition of memory into the culture, which has formed the basis of memory research from Ebbinghaus to the present. This implicit definition involves the distinction between an "original" and its "reproduction". Hence, evaluation of memory requires a system for recording original or non-repetitive events in time. By way of such a system, reports of retrieval will, therefore, have to be compared to original events at the time of acquisition.

Actually, writing has provided the main recording system used in memory research. As a consequence, we can only show that the content of recall memory is that which can be written. Most probably, this frame of reference prevents us from capturing the essence of memory structures. Changes in the written code, or any recording code, will have little effect on this state of affairs as long as the recording of events is syntagmatically ordered.

Finally, it should be emphasized that culture has treated memory as awareness of non-repetitive events in the past. Thus, memory itself has implicitly been considered a recording system, and past time as the domain of events for which this system is to be used. Based on this background, it has been impossible, for example, to deal with memory as a creative, cognitive system.

References

Anderson, J. R. (1981). *Cognitive skills and their acquisition.* Hillsdale, N.J.: Erlbaum.

Anderson, J. R. (1982). Acquisition of cognitive skill. *Psychological Review, 89,* 369–406.

Ashby, W. R. (1957). *An introduction to cybernetics.* (2nd ed.). New York: Wiley.

Barth, F. (1975). *Ritual and knowledge among the Baktaman of New Guinea.* Oslo: Universitetsforlaget.

Bartlett, F. C. (1932). *Remembering.* Cambridge: Cambridge University Press.

Bergson, H. L. (1910). *Matter and memory.* (N. M. Paul & W. S. Palmer, Trans.). London: Allen.

Blache, S. E. (1978). *The acquisition of distinctive features.* Baltimore: University Park Press.

Bruner, J. S. (1969). Modalities of memory. In G. A. Talland & N. C. Waugh (Eds.), *The pathology of memory* (pp. 253–259). New York: Academic Press.

Cermak, L. S., Talbot, N., Chandler, K., & Wolbarst, L. R. (1985). The perceptual priming phenomenon in amnesia. *Neuropsychologia, 23,* 615–622.

Cohen, N. J. (1984). Preserved learning capacity in amnesia: Evidence for multiple memory systems. In L. R. Squire & N. Butters (Eds.), *Neuropsychology of memory* (pp. 83–103). New York: The Guildford Press.

Dennis, W. (1948). *Readings in the history of psychology* (pp. 1–9). New York: Appleton-Century-Crofts.

Deutsch, J. A. (1984). Chromomnemonics and amnesia. In L. R. Squire & N. Butters (Eds.), *Neuropsychology of memory* (pp. 157–164). New York: The Guildford Press.

Flavell, J. H., & Wellman, H. M. (1977). Metamemory. In R. V. Kail & J. W. Hagen (Eds.), *Perspectives on the development of memory and cognition* (pp. 3–33). Hillsdale, N.J.: Erlbaum.

Flexer, A. J., & Tulving, E. (1978). Retrieval independence in recognition and recall. *Psychological Review, 85,* 135–171.

Garnham, A. (1979). Instantiation of verbs. *Quarterly Journal of Experimental Psychology, 31,* 207–214.

Goody, J., & Watt, I. (1968). The consequences of literacy. In J. Goody (Ed.), *Literacy in traditional societies* (2nd ed., pp. 27–68). Cambridge: Cambridge University Press.

Griffith, D. (1975). Comparison of control processes for recognition and recall. *Journal of Experimental Psychology: Human Learning and Memory, 10,* 223–228.

Hirst, W., & Volpe, B. T. (1982). Temporal order judgements with amnesia. *Brain and Cognition, 1,* 294–306.

Honig, W. K., (1978). Studies of working memory in the pigeon. In S. H. Hulse, H. Fowler, & W. K. Honig (Eds.), *Cognitive processes in animal behavior* (pp. 211–276). Hillsdale, N.J.: Erlbaum.

Honig, W. K., & James, P. H. R. (Eds.). (1971). *Animal memory*. New York: Academic Press.

Hunter, W. S. (1913). The delayed reaction in animals and children. *Behavior Monographs, 2*, 1–86.

Hunter, W. S. (1920). The temporal maze and kinesthetic sensory processes in the white rat. *Psychobiology, 2*, 1–17.

James, W. (1890). *The principles of psychology* (Vol. 1). New York: Holt.

Janet, P. (1928). *L'évolution de la mémoire et de la notion du temps*. Paris: A. Chahine.

Jones, G. W. (1978). Recognition failure and dual mechanisms in recall. *Psychological Review, 85*, 464–469.

Kintsch, W. (1970). *Learning, memory and conceptual processes*. New York: John Wiley & Sons.

Lashley, K. S. (1950). In search of the engram. In *Symposia of the Society for Experimental Biology*, No. 4 (pp. 454–482). Cambridge: Cambridge University Press.

Leach, E. R. (1971). *Rethinking anthropology*. London: The Athlone Press.

Leach, E. R. (1976). *Culture and communication. The logic by which symbols are connected*. Cambridge: Cambridge University Press.

Leont'ev, A. N. (1981). *Problems of the development of mind*. Moscow: Progress Publishers.

Meacham, J. A. (1972). The development of memory abilities in the individual and in society. *Human Development, 15*, 205–228.

Olson, D. R. (1988). *Interpretation and observation in the world on paper*. Unpublished manuscript.

Orbach, J. (Ed.). (1982). *Neuropsychology after Lashley. Fifty years since the publication of Brain Mechanisms and Intelligence*. Hillsdale, N.J.: Erlbaum.

Ryle, G. (1949). *The concept of mind*. London: Hutchinson.

Sanford, A. J., & Garrod, S. C. (1981). *Understanding written language. Exploration in comprehension beyond the sentence*. New York: John Wiley & Sons.

Schmandt-Besserat, D. (1982). The earliest precursor to writing. Readings from *Scientific American*. San Francisco: Freeman.

Shoemaker, S. (1967). Memory. In *The Encyclopedia of Philosophy, 5*, New York: Macmillan.

Smirnov, A. A. (1973). *Problems of the psychology of memory*. New York: Plenum.

Smith, G. J., & Spear, N. E. (1979). Reactivation of an appetitive discrimination memory following retroactive interference. *Animal Learning and Behavior, 7*, 289–293.

Sørum, A. (1984). Om tid og rom i Bedaminis verdensbilde (On time and space in the world-view of the Bedaminis). *Antropolognytt, 6* (3/4).

Thomas, G. J. (1984). Memory: Time binding in organisms. In L. R. Squire & N. Butters (Eds.), *Neuropsychology of memory* (pp. 374–384). New York: Guilford.

Thorndyke, P. W. (1977). Cognitive structures in comprehension and memory of narrative discourse. *Cognitive Psychology, 9*, 77–110.

Tulving, E., & Thompson, D. M. (1971). Retrieval processes in recognition memory: Effects of associative context. *Journal of Experimental Psychology, 87*, 116–124.

Wagner, A. R., & Pfantz, P. L. (1978). A bowed serial position function in habituation of sequential stimuli. *Animal Learning and Behavior*, *6*, 395–400.

Wallace, W. P. (1978). Recognition failure of recallable words and recognizable words. *Journal of Experimental Psychology: Human Learning and Memory*, *4*, 441–452.

Weingartner, H. (1984). Psychobiological determinants of memory failures. In L. R. Squire & N. Butters (Eds.), *Neuropsychology of memory* (pp. 203–212). New York: Guildford.

Weule, K. (1915). *Vom Kerbstock zum Alphabet*. Stuttgart: Kosmos.

Winograd, E. (1971). Some issues relating animal memory to human memory. In W. K. Honig & P. H. R. James (Eds.), *Animal memory* (pp. 259–278). New York: Academic.

Part 2
Literate Practices and Human Cognitive Repertoires

CHAPTER 7
Interpreting Texts and Interpreting Nature: The Effects of Literacy on Hermeneutics and Epistemology[1]

David R. Olson

Harold Innis writing in 1949 (Innis, 1951) and Marshall McLuhan writing only a few years later (McLuhan, 1962) brought about a decisive change in our orientation to the study of literacy. Prior to their writing on the "bias" of communication media, literacy was generally considered to be a simple, unadulterated good, a mark of progress and of civilization. True, there were some counter arguments such as those presented by Plato in the *Phaedrus* (cited in Goody & Watt, 1968) to the effect that writing would destroy memory and Rousseau's argument in *The Origin of Language* (1749/1966) that writing would dehumanize language by separating the author from his text, but by and large the prevailing assumption was that language is what makes us human, and literacy is what makes us civilized.

But with the writings of Innis and McLuhan, literacy came to be seen not as the solution to every other problem, but rather as a problem in its own right, indeed the central problem in coming to understand ourselves and the modern world. Complemented by such contemporary and seminal works as Eric Havelock's *Preface to Plato* (1963), Jack Goody and Ian Watt's *Consequences of Literacy* (1968), literacy came to be seen as a decisive factor in the evolution of modernity – in the development of Protestantism, modern science, law and government, and even consciousness. Decisive in this transformation was the invention of the alphabet and the invention of printing. And further, they argue that the effects of literacy were more or less invisible to us; what we took to be natural was, in many cases, the consequence of the particular biasing of alphabetic literacy.

These writers, while agreeing about the consequences of literacy, differed in their hypotheses as to how these effects were brought about. Havelock thought that the alphabet permitted explicitness of representation such that decoding could be distinguished from understanding, Goody and Watt sug-

1   The argument presented in this paper is developed more fully in a forthcoming book with the working title, "The World on Paper." This research was supported by grants from the SSHRC, the Spencer Foundation, and a Fellowship from the Center for Advanced Study in the Behavioral Sciences, Stanford, California, for the year 1983–84. An earlier version of this paper was published in *Visible Language*, 1986, *20*, 302–317.

gested that writing made language into an object of reflection, and McLuhan and Innis argued that writing altered the sense ratios. No one hypothesis has received general, let alone empirical, support.

The hypothesis I shall advance is closely related to that recently advanced by Brian Stock in his study of literacy in the Middle Ages, *The Implications of Literacy* (1983). In that work Stock documents the increasing use of writing and of written documents for such purposes as law, theology, philosophy and science. In those domains, uses of literacy regularly and systematically altered those institutions and the individuals participating in them. To cite a single example: in the early Middle Ages, a variety of forms of evidence could be presented at a trial to determine the innocence or guilt of a person charged with a crime. Some of these forms of "evidence" now strike us as decidedly odd. Eyewitness testimony was used but so were, he points out, dreams, prophecies, and visions. If someone had a dream that the accused had committed a crime, that was an important form of evidence for his guilt. That changed with literacy. Stock points out that some new conceptual distinctions came to be drawn (or old distinctions came to be honored more systematically) as judges and courts became more literate. Oral testimony and dreams came to be regarded as unreliable, while written records came to be regarded as evidence. Simultaneously, the distinctions made in the administration of law came to be made in other domains such as writing up the lives of the saints and their miracles. What were these distinctions? Here is the crucial point: a distinction was made between texts and their interpretations and between facts and their interpretations. The former were coming to be seen as objective while the interpretations were coming to be seen as subjective, personal, and invented or fabricated.

Here, I believe, we have our link between literacy and modernity – the systematic distinction between something which is taken as given, fixed, autonomous, and objective and something which is taken as interpretive, inferential and subjective. My hypothesis is that the contrast between texts and their interpretations provided the model, and more than that, the precise cognitive categories or concepts needed for the description and the interpretation of nature, that is, for the building of modern science. To state this somewhat grandly, hermeneutics, the interpretation of texts, provided the conceptual categories needed for scientific epistemology, what I referred to above as the "interpretation of nature." This schema is presented in Fig. 1. In the remainder of this paper, I will spell out the relation and provide some evidence for the hypothesis.

The Conceptual Change Hypothesis

The Reformation, the rise of modern science and mentalistic psychology are, of course, social movements but they all rested, I argue, on a new conceptual distinction. What is that distinction and how was it derived from writing and

Book of Scripture		**Book of Nature**	
Hermeneutics		Epistemology	
read	interpret	see	know
say	mean	observation	inference
	intention	fact	theory
		evidence	claim
given	interpretation	given	interpretation

Francis Bacon (1605)
> The book of God's *word* and The book of God's *work*.

Thomas Browne (1643)
> There are two books from whence I collect my divinity; that written of God, [and that] written of Nature.

Fig. 1. The conceptual relations between hermeneutics and epistemology

literacy? A written text preserves only part of language. What is preserved is the form, and the meaning has to be regenerated from that form by the reader. The preserved part we can talk loosely of as being "given," "fixed," "permanent"; the reconstructed part we can call, roughly, the "meaning," the "intention," the "interpretation."

That distinction is implicit in speech but the relation between a text and an interpretation becomes problematic *only in literacy*. In oral language, the form and meaning form an indissoluble pairing. When we do not understand a sentence/utterance we say, "what do *you* mean?" not "what does *it* mean?", focusing upon the person doing the communicating, not on the utterance. Furthermore, we use much beside the linguistic form to gather a person's intentions with the result that it is virtually impossible to distinguish what was said, the form, and what was meant by it, the meaning. In speech, then, form and meaning are indissolubly linked or at least perceived as such by speakers. Children and nonliterates both show little distinction between them as I will show presently. The relation between texts and their interpretation is the problem of hermeneutics. And the development of a sharp distinction between texts and their interpretation gave rise to Luther and the Reformation.

Hermeneutics

Literacy created hermeneutics. It did not create interpretation, of course. It created a theory or concepts of interpretations. The development of a distinction between statements and texts on one hand and their interpretation on the other was a consequence of literacy. Two examples of how the literate distinctions altered orientation to language will help to make this point.

Preliterate societies, both the preliterate Greeks and the preliterate Azande studied by Evans-Pritchard in the 1930s, used oracles for giving advice and making predictions. The oracles would utter a prediction and with remarkable frequency these oracles told the truth, or were at least taken as telling the truth. Recall Shakespeare's *Macbeth* in which the promise made by the oracular witches that Macbeth was secure until Birnam Wood came to Dunsinane was fulfilled by the attacking soldiers carrying boughs of Birnam wood as camouflage in their attack on Dunsinane. The interesting point about oracles is that they largely disappeared with literacy. Why?

The conceptual hypothesis offered above can take this in stride. In a preliterate society there is little or no distinction between a text and its interpretation. The preliterate attitude is that the interpretations arrived at by the listener were actually said by the speaker. There is no recognition of the ambiguity of the pronouncements and the role of the listener in arriving at an interpretation. Later events, taken as fulfillment of the oracle, were seen as having been intrinsic in the pronouncement. Again, there was no distinction between what the oracle said and its *interpretation* by the listener. Any interpretation arrived at by the listener was ascribed to the speaker. Oracles fell to literacy because literacy involved an awareness of that distinction. If the interpretation could not be ascribed to the oracles, the oracles lost their power. The horoscope is, of course, a modern-day version of the oracles which, I believe, we still read with a tingle of the possibility of prescience. But serious reading lets one see their enormous "openness" to interpretation; the texts are written to be ambiguous. Writing, by preserving the words but not their meanings, invites the distinction between a text and its interpretation.

A second example comes from the remarkable work on witchcraft and oracles among the Azande, a nonliterate or traditional society, in which Evans-Pritchard (1937) commented on a peculiarity of interpretation: he noted anything a suspected witch may say was "interpreted in a different sense from the one the speaker intended to give his words" (p. 133). Evans-Pritchard was surprised that these "interpretations" were attributed directly to the speaker and used to prove his guilt. The same is true of the language of ritual. Leach (1966) points out that "a great variety of alternative meanings are implicit in the same set of categories" (p. 408). Clearly, these were not interpretations in a literate sense – they were not thought of as having been made up by the hearer as we would think of them. Rather, any interpretation made by the listener was ascribed to the speaker. The Azande interpret language, of course, but they do not distinguish their interpretations from what the speaker actually said. Their interpretive stance is quite similar to that taken by children in our society when they encounter the ambiguity of language. They, too, assume that the intention or interpretation is exactly what the speaker said. When they arrive at an interpretation, they are convinced that the sentence could not be interpreted any other way (Beal & Flavell, 1984).

Again, the point to note is that the Azande make little distinction between what is said and its interpretation. This is not because they are "primitive" or child-like but because that distinction is a literate one – one shaped up for dealing with written texts. Literacy involved the preservation of a part of language – what was actually said, the "given," which could be contrasted with the interpretations assigned and the intentions that lie behind it. In an oral society there were, of course, "texts," fixed bodies of ritual and poetry, along with intentions and interpretations. All language necessarily involves all of those. But literacy provides the means for splitting those things apart, fixing part of its meaning as the text and permitting interpretations to be seen for the first time as *interpretations*. Goody (1985) has shown how religious reform movements rely upon just this distinction, calling for the abandonment of interpretations and a "return to the book."

The twist in the understanding of interpretation which has been studied most carefully is the change in interpretation associated with the Reformation and the Counter-Reformation. As Brian Stock has shown, the problem of heresy in the Middle Ages was almost exclusively associated with literacy. "Heretics had a highly developed, if somewhat personal, style of 'rationality' which depended on individual interpretation of theological texts" (pp. 110–120). Heretics considered the teachings of the Church to be mere interpretation, if not fabrication. Yet while heretics recognized the interpretations of the Church as interpretations – they were recognized as man-made – they did not recognize their own interpretations as mere interpretations. They, like the medieval church, took their interpretations to be the ones intended by God and, hence, they died, apparently happily, at the stake for them.

The Church's view of interpretation prior to the Reformation, as expressed for example in Aquinas' *Summa Theologia* (written 1267–1273), was that Scripture had several levels of meaning including literal meaning, spiritual meaning and moral meaning. All levels of meaning were given in the text. Reformation theology, as exemplified in Luther, denied that all these meanings were in the text: the literal, historical meaning was in the text, all the rest was "tradition" and "dogma." Reformation theology, in a word, involved a sharp distinction between what was given by the text and the interpretations that one could make of a text. The latter were suddenly seen as subjective, fanciful, and a product of the imagination. Thus, part of the meaning was moved from being seen as given by the text to being seen as invented by the reader. The interpretive principle of the Reformation, as expressed for example in Luther's attitude to Scripture, was that Scripture is "autonomous," it does not need interpretation, it needs reading; it means what it says. All the rest is made up – a product of fancy or tradition. It was this distinction between the given and the "interpreted" which launched the Reformation and which, a century later, opened "the book of nature" to modern scientists, to make it readable to anyone "with a faithful eye" as Robert Hooke, one of the first of the seventeenth century British empiricists, said.

Epistemology

Returning to Fig. 1, the hypothesis connecting hermeneutics with scientific epistemology is that hermeneutics provided the conceptual distinction between something taken as fixed or given and something else taken as contributed by the reader, that is, as interpretation. The scriptural text and its interpretation was seen as exactly parallel to the natural world and its interpretation.

It was commonplace in the Middle Ages to speak of nature as God's book. The metaphor came to have a new meaning in the seventeenth century. Francis Bacon spoke of "the book of God's word and the book of God's work." Thomas Browne, a seventeenth century British cleric, talked of God's two great books, Scripture and nature. At first we may be tempted to believe that this is a mere metaphor. To us it is a metaphor; to the seventeenth century scientists it was literally true; modern science was the product of applying the distinctions needed for understanding the book of Scripture, namely that between the given and the interpreted, to the book of nature. For modern science, the given was the world of observed facts; all the rest, hypotheses, final causes, interpretation and inferences were invented, made up by man. These distinctions are fundamental to scientific epistemology. Modern science rests on the distinction between observation and inference, observations being objective and reliable while the inferences are theoretical interpretations of those observations. In this century the distinction has come in for considerable revision. These categories, which were taken as absolute in the seventeenth Century, have been completely relativized in the twentieth, yet they remain important epistemological concepts (see Olson, 1986).

The modern scientists, Galileo, Francis Bacon, William Harvey, Robert Hooke, Robert Boyle, and Isaac Newton consistently and systematically distinguished facts from "hypotheses." Science, Bacon said, consisted of the "statement of observed facts." It involved no interpretations. William Harvey (1653) added: "For in every Science . . . a diligent observation is required." Bacon said it most strongly: "All depends on keeping the eye steadily fixed upon the fact of nature and so receiving their images simply as they are." The split was complete. Observations provided direct access to the given; theory and interpretation was the work of the imagination. Bacon again: "God forbid that we give out a dream of our imagination for a pattern in the world." They not only said it, they acted on it. Galileo and Newton are replete with denials of the relevance of purposes, goals and causes in the explanation of motion and machines – they sought factual description, not theoretical interpretation.

So, reading the book of nature, that is, science, was simply applied hermeneutics. The distinctions worked up for reading and interpreting Scripture could be applied, without revision, to reading and interpreting the book of nature. In science, the distinction takes the form of that between an observation and inference, fact and theory, claim and evidence, and a whole set of related concepts such as hypothesis, assumption, conclusion, conjecture, which are so important to systematic thought. Yet, children have little idea of the difference between an observation and an inference, or between a fact and a theory, or between a claim and evidence. If my argument is correct, these are sophisticated, literate concepts that, while important to "educated" activities, are not often honored in ordinary discourse. Tests of critical thinking such as the Watson-Glaser appear to be based on just these distinctions and we have begun to observe children's acquisition of them in some of our recent work (Olson & Astington, 1987).

Subjectivity

There is a third prong to the argument which I shall discuss here only in passing. It is that if interpretations are not given in the text, where do they come from? In the seventeenth century, interpretations came to be seen, increasingly, as subjective, that is, made up by the reader of texts or the observer of nature. It was this new recognition of interpretations as mind-made that provided the basis for the new, seventeenth century subjectivity expressed in Descartes' famous, "*Cogito, ergo sum*" ("I think, therefore I am"). Descartes, Locke, Hume, and Berkeley, I suggest, were as much a product of Reformation hermeneutics as Bacon and Galileo were. While Galileo and Bacon were concerned with descriptions of reality stripped clean of the "dream of the imagination," Descartes, Locke, Hume and Berkeley were concerned with the interpretive and imaginative processes themselves. The rise of subjectivity was given by the world. Subjectivity, like objectivity, was the product of hermeneutical distinctions between that given in the text and that invented by the reader.

Children's Distinctions Between What Is Given and What Is Interpretation

The account I have given of the relation between hermeneutics, epistemology and subjectivity has some of the properties of *Just so Stories* (e.g., *How the Tiger got His Spots*). One begins with a modern conclusion and looks back to see if the story can be told in such a way as to make the modern conclusion appear inevitable without doing violence to the historical record. But the record was usually made for quite a different purpose than the one the historian of ideas is subjecting it to. However, the exactly appropriate questions have rarely been asked and it is too late to ask the informants the critical ones. It is here that the psychologist can make a unique contribution to our understanding of these issues. The experimental psychologist can systematically examine subjects, can ask precisely the right questions, and thereby determine the relations between the phenomena in question-interpretation, objectivity, and subjectivity. In the remainder of this paper I will provide evidence indicating that these distinctions are, in fact, achieved by children in the early school years and that they are closely related, indeed that children succeed in recognizing the role of interpretation in what they hear at precisely the same time that they succeed in recognizing the role of interpretation in what they see. The claim is that children come to see interpretations as interpretations at the same time that they come to see inferences from perception as inferences. Let me report two experiments which my colleagues, Nancy Torrance and Janet Astington, and I have performed to examine these relations.

The Say–Mean Task

Children's acquisition of the distinction between what is said and what is meant by it can be examined by looking at their reactions to ambiguous utterances. Nancy Torrance reads stories which include referentially ambiguous utterances to young children ranging in age from 5 to 10 years. A sample story will make this clear. In this case, the child is first shown a picture of Charlie Brown, Lucy, and Linus, and also one showing three pair of shoes in a closet. The shoes are described as Lucy's new red party shoes, her old red running shoes, and her ordinary blue shoes. The following story is then told.

> One Saturday night, Lucy and Charlie Brown were going to a party. Lucy was all dressed in her brand new red party dress, but she didn't have her shoes on. She wanted to wear her *new* red shoes to go with her party dress. Linus was upstairs so she called up to him, "Linus, bring me my red shoes."
> Linus went to Lucy's closet where she kept her shoes. Now Linus picked up the *old* red shoes and rushed down the stairs with them. He said, "Here are your red shoes" and he gave the shoes to Lucy.
> "Good grief", said Lucy, "how can you be so stupid?" and she gave him a whack on the head.

Following the story the children are asked a series of questions. Younger children's (5-year-olds') responses are illustrated by the following exchange:

Q. Did Linus bring the shoes that Lucy wanted?
A. No.
Q. Did he do what Lucy said to do?
A. No.
Q. What did Lucy tell him to bring?
A. The red party shoes.
Q. What were the exact words that Lucy said? She said "Linus, bring me . . ."
A. My new red shoes.

Note that the child assumes an identity between what is said and what is meant by it, claiming that she had asked for her new red shoes. Robinson and Robinson (1977) have characterized this kind of response as "listener blaming" because when asked, "Whose fault was it?" younger children fail to note that the speaker is actually responsible for the failure because he/she provided an ambiguous message. Older children tend to blame the speaker and his message.

In our study, Grade 2 (8-year-olds), children's answers tend to run as follows:

Q. Did Linus bring the shoes that Lucy wanted?
A. No.
Q. Did Linus do what Lucy said to do?
A. No.
Q. What did Lucy tell him to bring?
A. The new red shoes.
Q. What were the exact words that Lucy said? She said "Linus, bring me . . ."
A. My red shoes.

Notice that even the second grade child answered the second and third questions in ways that are technically incorrect. In fact, Linus did do what Lucy *said* to do; he just did not do what she *wanted* him to do. It is only in the last question that this child acknowledges what was actually said. By Grade 4 (10-year-olds), however, the majority of children (75%) that have been tested respond accurately to all four questions. The data for the say-mean task are summarized in Table 1. We interpret such results as indicating that with age and

Table 1. Say–mean
Number of Subjects Responding Correctly

Grade	16–18 correct	0–15 correct
SK	3	13
2	8	8
4	12	4

$$\chi^2_{(2)} = 10.18, \ p < .01$$

experience children come to distinguish what a person or a text "says" from what is "meant" by it. It is not a distinction directly tied to age but rather, here we just suspect, to the language and literacy practices of parents.

The critical part of my hypothesis is the following. It is the child's *conceptual* distinction between the given, namely, the text, and its possible interpretation that provides the basis for the child's epistemological distinction between what he *sees* and what he *knows*. That hypothesis is examined in a second experiment.

The See–Know Task

To examine children's knowledge of the see-know distinction, Janet Astington prepared a series of cut-out animals, some of which were unambiguous in their coloring and some of which were ambiguous in a way analogous to the ambiguous sentences in the preceding experiment. Children were shown the collection of animals shown at the bottom of Fig. 2. The cat was red, the horse was green, the dog and the pig were both blue.

They were asked to identify these and to name their colors. When it was clear they knew them well, they were told that the animals would be hidden in the barn and they would be asked to find them. Copies of the animals remained in front of the child to ensure that the animals and their colors would not be forgotten.

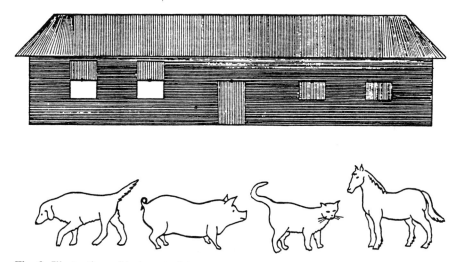

Fig. 2. Illustration of task materials

The barn and the visible parts of two animals were shown at the top of Fig. 2. Only a sample of the color of the animal is visible in the window. In the case of the unambiguously colored animals, the child has grounds for identifying the animals; when the ambiguous pair is revealed in the other two windows, the child, of course, does not have grounds for identifying them. The question is, will young children recognize the ambiguity of the second pair and acknowledge that they do not know which animals they see?

The contrast is even more clearly drawn in the second half of the experiment. All of the materials except for a new barn are removed and a doll named Katie is produced. The child is told that Katie has not seen the animals and is now asked to answer the same questions about what Katie would see. This part of the experiment is similar, in principle, to that conducted by Chandler and Helm (1984) and Taylor and Flavell (1985) on children's ability to take the role of the other person. The question sequence for both self and other is shown in Fig. 3. Consider first children's responses when asked which they, themselves, see. A typical pattern of responding by a younger child is the following:

E: (Pointing to the window revealing a red animal) What do you see?
S: Cat.
E: Do you know it's a cat?
S: Yes.
E: How do you know it's a cat?
S: Red.

Older children do much the same thing on the unambiguous stimuli. More interesting is the younger child's response to the ambiguously colored animals. Here is a sample:

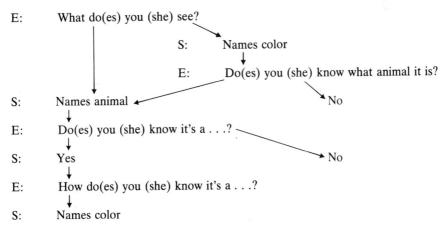

Fig. 3. See–know question sequence for self and other

E: (Pointing to one of the two windows revealing blue animals) What do you
    see?
S: Dog.
E: Do you know it's a dog?
S: Yes.
E: How do you know it's a dog?
S: 'Cause it's blue.

It is not that the child is blind to the ambiguity; rather it is that the child has
no conceptual means for dealing with it. Thus, the child may continue as
follows:

E: (Pointing to the other window revealing the other blue animal) What do you see
    here?
S: Pig.
E: Do you know it's a pig?
S: Yes.
E: How do you know it's a pig?
S: 'Cause it's blue too.

The child marks the similarity with "too" but the child fails to acknowledge
the ambiguity and its role in the fact that one may see something but not know
what it is. The child fails, we say, to distinguish what one sees from what one
knows.

A similar pattern, but delayed by a year or two, occurs when the child is
asked what the doll, Katie, sees. Here is a sample transcript:

E: (Pointing to the window revealing the red animal) What will Katie see?
S: Cat.
E: Will she know it's a cat?
S: Yes.
E: How will she know?
S: 'Cause it's red.

As Table 2 indicates, this pattern shifts with age, although age is not, I
suggest, the major factor, as older children acknowledge that Katie would see

Table 2. See–know
Number of Subjects Responding Correctly

Grade	SELF		OTHER	
	4 correct	0–3 correct	4 correct	0–3 correct
SK	9	7	3	13
2	11	5	2	14
4	14	2	8	8
	$\chi^2_{(2)} = 3.83$, $p{<}.10$		$\chi^2_{(2)} = 6.54$, $p{<}.05$	

the red but that she would not know what it was. Similarly, older children acknowledge that they themselves do not know what animal they see when the colors are ambiguous. We have conducted this study twice with somewhat different questions. In the first study (Olson & Astington, 1986) the children who could handle the ambiguous stimuli for themselves were the very children who could recognize that the doll would not know either. In the present study, conducted by Nancy Torrance and me, the children were considerably better at acknowledging that they did not know, in the ambiguous case, than they were at acknowledging that the doll, Katie, would not know what animal she was seeing. We are currently attempting to resolve these small differences. In general, older children appear to recognize the role of belief and knowledge in their own and others' interpretation of their observations and perceptions while younger children appear to have no devices for differentiating what they see from the prior beliefs and knowledge that they use to interpret what they see. Consequently, they are unable to withhold ascribing their beliefs to the naive observer, the doll Katie. They fail to acknowledge that Katie, operating on knowledge different from their own, would see things differently.

The clinching part of the argument connecting notions of interpretation of texts to interpretation of perceptions would be provided by showing that precisely those children capable of solving the say-mean task also solve the see-know task. That evidence shows that, for subjects just acquiring the distinction, the Grade 2 children, the two tasks are quite highly correlated ($r = .53$) but not identical. That evidence is presented in Table 3.

For the youngest children, the majority of whom have not yet acquired the distinction, and for the oldest subjects, the majority of whom have already acquired the distinction, the relations between the two tasks are negligible. But for the subjects just acquiring the distinction, the Grade 2 children, the performance on the tasks is highly correlated ($r = .53$ for self and $r = .34$ for other). Even then, the relation is not perfect. However, it must be noted that the tasks are quite different in format, and perhaps difficulty, so a perfect correlation would be unlikely. In fact, Robinson and Robinson (1980) have provided just the data we need. They gave their subjects two listener-blamer tasks which were identical in every way except that in one case the message was a set of words which was ambiguous while in the other it was the picture that was ambiguous. In this study, the responses were exactly as expected: children who solved the verbal task were the ones who solved the pictorial task. This

Table 3. Say–mean and See–know Correlations

Grade	Self	Other
SK	.38	−.11
2	.53	.34
4	−.03	.28

suggests that the same sets of categories were used in interpreting language as were used in interpreting observed events. Conversely, when children worked up the appropriate conceptual distinctions for interpreting text, they could readily be applied to interpreting nature. The achievement in both cases depended upon the recognition of the existence of subjective mental states in themselves and others. Their hermeneutics, epistemology, and notions of subjectivity are all reflections of the given-interpretation distinction.

We must note that the relation of these literal distinctions to the actual process of learning to read and write is indirect. One could begin to sort them out in oral discourse with literate parents prior to learning to read and one could sharpen those distinctions in learning to review one's writing to make what is said correspond more clearly to what is meant.

Conclusions

We began with the well-documented inference relating literacy to the social and psychological changes that occurred with the invention of alphabetic literacy in Greece and, more particularly, with the growth of literacy in the late Middle Ages and the early Renaissance. I argued that while the relation is well known, there was no theory connecting the Reformation with the rise of modern science or with Cartesian mentalism. I advanced the notion that the three were by-products of literacy and offered, as a mechanism for the change, the new conceptual distinction between what was given in a text and the interpretations a reader brought to or assigned to a text. I called it the "given-interpretation distinction." I could as well have called it the "reading-interpretation distinction" (cf. Havelock, 1976). It was the hypothesis that something was given, invariant, and autonomous about a text, and that givenness could be contrasted with the interpretations of that text which were subjective, fallible, and the product of the imagination. That distinction, I say, was invited by literacy because writing, in fact, split the comprehension process into two parts, that part preserved by text, the given, and that part, the interpretation, provided by the reader. Printing sharpened just this distinction. With the exact duplication of the original text, free from copyist errors, that part given in the text was more readily distinguished from the interpretation brought to the text by the reader. In a single move the layers of meaning of Scripture which Aquinas had claimed to be in the text were suddenly taken by Luther to be mere additions, accretions, and interpolations. Galileo followed the lead, taking Aristotle's notions of "final causes" as mere interpretation of motion, quite independent of the properties of motion itself. The distinction between the given and the interpreted, then, invented for reading and interpreting texts, was simply borrowed for "reading" the book of nature. The product of the distinction was modern science, science built on the notion of a discontinuity between observation and inference, facts and theory, claims and evidence. Furthermore, when scientific epistemology succeeded in exorcising interpretations from the world, the source of such interpretations came to be recognized as products of the mind. This new awareness of mind and of the autonomy of ideas was the basis for Cartesian mentalism and the beginning of modern notions of subjectivity. Modern scientific epistemology, like modern notions of subjectivity, was, therefore, a by-product of the hermeneutics of written texts.

And finally, to show how language and the world appear to someone who did not make these distinctions, I showed you how young children conflate what is said with what is meant and what they see with what they know. And I showed that at about the time that they "solve" the interpretation problem they solve the "observation" problem; their epistemology reflects their hermeneutics. And I suggested that the related distinctions such as *say, mean, intend, interpret*, as well as *observe, infer, claim, evidence, fact, theory* which are both fundamental to education and to Western thought generally, are the cognitive consequences of literacy.

References

Aquinas, St. Thomas (1968–70). *Summa theologia* (Latin/English ed.). London: Black-friars/McGraw-Hill.

Bacon, F. (1857–64a). The great instauration. In J. Spedding, R. Ellis, & D. Heath (Eds.), *The works of Francis Bacon* (Vols. 1–14). London. (Original work published 1605.)

Bacon, F. (1857–64b). The advancement of learning. In J. Spedding, R. Ellis, & D. Heath (Eds.), *The works of Francis Bacon* (Vols. 1–14). London. (Original work published 1605.)

Beal, C., & Flavell, J. (1984). Development of the ability to distinguish communicative intention and literal message meaning. *Child Development*, 55, 920–928.

Chandler, M. J., & Helm, D. (1984). Developmental changes in the contribution of shared experience to social role-taking competence. *International Journal of Behavioral Development*, 7, 145–156.

Evans-Pritchard, E. (1937). *Witchcraft, oracles and magic among the Azande*. Oxford: Oxford University Press.

Goody, J. (1985, March). *Writing and religion*. Paper presented at the McLuhan Centre for Culture and Technology, University of Toronto.

Goody, J., & Watt, I. (1968). The consequences of literacy. In J. Goody (Ed.), *Literacy in traditional societies* (2nd ed., pp. 27–68). Cambridge: Cambridge University Press. (Original work published 1963.)

Harvey, W. (1653). *Anatomical exercitations concerning the generation of living creatures*. London.

Havelock, E. (1963). *Preface to Plato*. Cambridge, Ma: Harvard University Press.

Havelock, E. (1976). *Origins of western literacy*. Toronto, Ont.: The Ontario Institute for Studies in Education.

Innis, H. (1951). *The bias of communication.* Toronto, Ont.: University of Toronto Press.

Leach, E. R. (1966). Ritualization in man in relation to conceptual and social development. *Philosophical Transactions of the Royal Society of London, 251,* 403–408.

McLuhan, M. (1962). *The Gutenberg galaxy.* Toronto, Ont.: University of Toronto Press.

Olson, D. (1986). Mining the human sciences: Some relations between hermeneutics and epistemology. *Interchange, 17,* 159–171.

Olson, D., & Astington, J. (1986). Children's acquisition of metalinguistic and meta-cognitive verbs. In W. Demopoulas & A. Marras (Eds.), *Language learning and concept acquisition: Foundational issues.* Norwood: Ablex.

Olson, D., & Astington, J. (1986). Children's acquisition of metalinguistic and meta-cognitive verbs. In W. Demopoulas & A. Marras (Eds.), *Language learning and concept acquisition: Foundational issues* (184–199). Norwood: Ablex.

Olson, D., & Astington, J. (1987). Seeing and knowing: On the ascription of mental states to young children. *Canadian Journal of Psychology, 41, 399-411.*

Robinson, E., & Robinson, W. (1977). Children's explanations of failure and the inadequacy of the misunderstood message. *Developmental Psychology, 13,* 151–161.

Robinson, E., & Robinson, W. (1980). *Understanding about ambiguous messages: A symptom of learning to distinguish message from meaning.* Report written for Bishop Road Infant School. University of Bristol School of Education.

Rousseau, J. (1966). *Essay on the origin of language.* (J. Moran, Trans.). New York: Fredric Ungar. (Original work published 1749).

Stock, B. (1983). *The implications of literacy.* Princeton: Princeton University Press.

Taylor, M., & Flavell, J. (1985, May). *The development of children's ability to distinguish what they know from what they see.* Paper presented at the annual meeting of the Society for Philosophy and Psychology, Toronto, Canada.

CHAPTER 8

Learning to Read –
Some Possible Consequences for Thinking

Hazel Francis

The importance of children's literacy for formal education is almost universally accepted, and its significance for the individual in exercising and claiming political and social rights and dues is widely recognised; hence the vast extent of national and international resource and concern attached to its development. However, there are other possible consequences of the experience of learning to read, and in this paper I shall outline some of these as they bear on the nature of children's thinking. In particular I shall consider conceptions of language, of learning and of authority.

Hitherto research into learning to read has generally explored conditions for literacy rather than its consequences for the learner. I shall therefore tend to raise issues worth further consideration rather than to offer any firm conclusions. I shall also be raising questions about appropriacy of research meth--od for investigating consequences of a development which is by its nature imbued with personal and socio-cultural significance.

Literacy and Thinking

While it is generally believed that the intellectual resources of mankind have not changed in historical time, it is also held that environmental conditions affect the exercise of those resources. Written language has been seen to aid memory and to extend the nature and content of thought in whole societies.

Psychologists have asked whether the tools of a culture might extend intelligence, recently with particular reference to computer technology, but also with respect to literacy. Scribner and Cole (1981) made it a central question in a cross-cultural study of cognitive abilities in which they attempted to differentiate the effects of literacy from those of schooling. Whilst they found substantial schooling effects, they were unable to show any effect of literacy without schooling on the particular kinds of mental operations investigated. However, since they did find small cognitive consequences particularly related to the functions of literacy, and since the conditions of literacy without schooling amongst the Vai people were so restricted, the findings should invite further work rather than close the question.

Thinking may be extended in other ways than by the development of mental operations. In a recent article Olson (1985) distinguishes between such operations and the knowledge base to which they may be applied. This may also be enlarged in particular ways by particular cultural experiences. Olson suggests that children, in reflecting on written language as an object of interest, may come to know that beyond the task of identifying what is written is that of dealing with the resolution of the writer's intentions. Literacy may thus extend pragmatic knowledge, developing a capacity to deal with ambiguity and with reference to the hitherto unknown. According to Olson it encourages a "theoretical stance towards nature" (p. 6).

Observations of young children suggest that such an enlargement of knowledge may have its roots in the very beginnings of learning to read. Söderbergh (1971) quoted her three-year-old daughter as refusing to accept a written sentence referring to her father because the event concerned did not in fact come to pass. I have found infant school children surprised on rereading a passage not to find words their comprehension led them to expect. One little boy who had read about the disappearance of a snowman under a warm sun was convinced the word "melted" was in the text until his searches satisfied him that it had come from his own thinking about it. It is not easy to give the same attention and reflection to ephemeral conversational speech in such a fashion, nor even to more formal or ritualised speech; though it is not, of course, impossible.

But literacy may not only influence thinking and ways of knowing, it may also affect the mental organisation of knowledge. It seems most unlikely that the words of speech as it is encountered in everyday life are mentally organised in accordance with the dictionaries, thesauri, and cataloguing systems of literate adults; but the curious salience of first letter identification in word reading and of first letter similarity (combined with semantic appropriacy) in the errors of beginning readers (Biemiller, 1970; Weber, 1970; Gibson & Levin, 1975; Francis, 1984) suggests a very early literacy-influenced move in that direction. If an alphabetic script does have some such organising effect on the mental lexicon, then what happens with other scripts?

This and other questions are suggested by the notion that literacy may extend thinking capacities in ways other than the development of logical reasoning. Such an idea is a specific development of the long established argument about the relationship between language and thought, but, by separating experience of the spoken and written forms, it prompts further consideration of the effects of the latter on thinking about language.

Children's Conceptions of Language

One possible effect of literacy on children's thinking has to do with their conceptions of its structure. When investigating the linguistic competence of five- to seven-year-olds I found (Francis, 1973) that they spoke of spaces between words in speech and commented on sound similarities and differences between spoken words in terms of the spelling of their written correlates. Moreover their ability to use the terminology of reading instruction, terms such as "sound", "letter", "word", and "sentence", grew with their reading ability rather than preceding it. In a further paper (Francis, 1975a) I argued that children's reflections on language, influenced by the written form, promoted some kind of awareness of linguistic structure.

Generally speaking, other studies of linguistic awareness have found correlations between reading ability and indices of awareness such as understanding of the above-mentioned terminology (Downing, 1970; Liberman, 1973; Ehri, 1975). Bradley and Bryant (1978, 1983) claimed to show that one aspect of such awareness, namely the ability to detect rhyme and alliteration precedes the ability to read, and promotes it if taught. Mattingly (1972, 1984) has argued the case, from a Chomskyan perspective, for linguistic awareness as a prerequisite for reading. Ehri (1976), however, found that in age-matched kindergarten children, those with experience of reading were better able than those without to deal with a task requiring word awareness. She argued (Ehri, 1979) that linguistic awareness might promote learning to read but could not be a necessary condition for it, and in a further paper (Ehri, 1984) summarised evidence to suggest that learning to read and spell may promote some aspects of awareness, particularly of the phonemic structure of language. This accords with my own earlier argument and with a further paper (Francis, 1984) which showed how knowledge of spelling acquired in learning to read preceded explicit linguistic awareness at the level of relating sounds with letters or letter groups. It seems likely that there is no simple causal relationship involved, but that whatever practices and whatever prior knowledge facilitate learning to read, the experience itself promotes further knowledge of linguistic structure. Whilst in actual reading such knowledge is mostly deployed below some threshold of consciousness, it also remains available for conscious use if some problem or reflection calls on it.

One of the difficulties with the above reports is that different indices of linguistic awareness are not of equivalent theoretical status. Some imply the processing of linguistic units without it being evident that children consciously treat them as entities, whilst others require children's explicit recognition of units; and it does scant justice to linguistic theory not to recognise important distinctions between physical and abstract units and between levels such as morphemic and phonemic. Nevertheless there is sufficient substance in the reports to suggest that some systematic effort to deal with these inadequacies would be worthwhile if we are to understand better the effects of acquaintance with the written form on children's conceptions of language. Such improved knowledge might help us to understand better how children deal with the ways we try to help them learn to read.

There are arguments that any relationship between reading experience and linguistic knowledge is a function of developing reasoning capacities (Watson,

1984) but, although correlations may be found between operational thought in Piaget's sense (Lunzer, Dolan & Wilkinson; 1976), it is difficult to claim that more is necessary than such reasoning abilities as are available to intelligent three-year-olds, since appreciable numbers of children learn to read from such an age. Such abilities are the basic capacities to utilise similarities and differences which lie behind the growth of perception and cognition. I have elsewhere referred to them as "analytic competence" (Francis, 1975b). On the basis of such competence, conceptions of linguistic structure are in principle derivable from speech (as was the case with the inventors of writing systems and is the case with children who try to write before they can read) but in practice they are probably more easily derivable by young children as they reflect on more permanent representations in the written form.

Literacy and Learning

How and what children think about written language is likely to depend in part on the conditions under which they encounter it. Instruction which emphasises a decoding approach to reading is likely to draw attention to units within the word whereas an emphasis on whole word learning and dependence on context is likely to leave such units to incidental learning (Barr, 1978). Experience, however, is also likely to affect conceptions of learning itself – both of learning to read and of learning more generally. It cannot, therefore, be assumed that literacy has only favourable consequences for learning.

Insights into children's conceptions of learning can be gleaned from observational studies and structured interviews. These have been obtained with both pre-school and school children, but accounts of children learning before schooling tend to be of successful learners and to emphasise conditions where they are highly motivated and either receive or demand appropriate support for their efforts. Söderbergh (1971) and Clark (1976) have supplied reports of pre-school children learning to read successfully in literate homes in literate societies. Others, notably Ferreiro and Teberosky (1982), Heath (1983) and Schieffelin and Cochran-Smith (1984), have extended our knowledge by describing the experiences and meanings of literacy for pre-school children in other cultures. Daily episodes involving written language occur, sometimes very frequently, in such rituals as shopping, meal-times, story-reading, attending church, and other family activities embedded in the local culture. Other literacy episodes occur spontaneously in the children's activities. Where this happens children grow to understand that learning to read is personal, meaningful and a 'life resource'. They learn that written language is a medium for gaining and remembering information, for expressing and finding out about feelings and happenings. It is less easy, however, to identify their conceptions of their learning, since none of the studies was directly addressed to this end. However, it seems that, while certain episodes might be identified by the children as entailing learning, the overall experience of literacy is so embedded in daily life as to be a very elusive object for thought. Since the experience of learning in school is more disembedded and is open to all children in receipt of schooling, including less successful readers, studies of children beginning school are of particular interest.

Reid (1966) and Downing (1970), amongst others, have shown that children beginning school may have very limited conceptions of reading, but these studies have not focused particularly on the child's conceptions of learning to read.

In my own structured interviews with children (Francis, 1975b, 1982) I have included two questions which have given particularly illuminating replies, one concerned with motive and the other with practice. To the question "Why are you learning to read?" children have responded in terms of either self or other – on the one hand saying that they want to be able to read certain books, or to be able to read to their own children, and on the other explaining that their parents or their teachers want them to. These differently based motives seemed to correlate to some extent with understanding of the nature of reading, the other-related motives being linked with poorer understanding. The possible further relationship between self-motivation and active learning and between other-motivation and passive learning is obvious and worth checking.

My further question was "What do you do when you can't read a word?". Replies to this also divided between self-reference and other-reference. In the former case children said they "think" or "try to say it", reflecting a self-demanding problem-solving approach, whilst in the latter they said they asked the teacher or a friend. One significant feature was that children who were least successful were least likely to ask an adult and most likely to consult an equally unsuccessful friend. That this wide spread of replies was obtained both within and between school classes suggested that they were not solely adult prompted, but were children's own preferred strategies.

Observation of children carrying out literacy-related activities in their classrooms enlarged the picture of different approaches to learning. These activities were part of the micro-culture established by the teacher within the school for the purpose of teaching. This, for the children was very different from their home-based literacy experiences, and the meanings of activities were often unclear. What was obviously a literacy-related activity to the teacher was not necessarily so for the child. And even if, by some act of faith, it was accepted, the scope for incomprehension or misunderstanding was considerable. Imagine the difficulty for the child who had not realised that each written word had a unique spoken counterpart! And why was writing sometimes a linear repetitive pattern and sometimes strings of strange shapes called "letters"? These and other insights into children's difficulties threw light on the way learning to read could degenerate into doing what they were told, to try to please the teacher who wanted them to learn. How can children adopt an active, problem-solving approach to learning if they cannot get hold of the problem?

It may be answered that what is needed is more or better prior explanation by teachers, but once the nature of such explanation is grasped it becomes clear that this is no mean feat. What is required is not so much a set of separate explanations for each classroom task, as a coherent policy for making sense with children of a classroom culture in which *school-based* learning to read is so important. Included in such coherent teaching would be the kind of practices which are evident in all meaningful learning – practices to do with conversation about the how and why of new skills. "Let's talk about what doing this is like and what it means to be able to do it" – and *this* might be anything from pattern copying and word recognition to fluent writing and reading.

One of the great difficulties of conducting a learning conversation is that of understanding what the other is trying to say, and this is particularly so with children. In their various home micro-cultures parents have the advantage of a history of conversation with their children within shared familiar experiences. Teachers and pupils have to start from scratch. As an observer in an infant classroom I have been struck by the difficulties of conducting interviews with children and the ease with which an adult can misunderstand. To adults in schooled societies the worlds of home and school are part of the same world and the significance of both is understood. To children they are worlds apart, so how can they use the materials of the classroom to demonstrate and explain what they and their parents can do at home, particularly to a stranger to their home environment? The adult's lack of comprehension of the child's world can match the child's incomprehension of the ways teachers talk about reading. It should come as no surprise then to find that many children treat reading in school as to do with learning a vocabulary of school-defined words and teacher-selected texts and with operating on them according to teacher requirements. As far as reading is concerned school can seem a strange, perhaps artificial and somewhat irrelevant, part of an otherwise interesting and active life, whether this be in a literate society or not.

What then do children learn about learning as they become more literate? Apart from realising the advantages of an additional source of information, as in five-year-olds who claimed to be learning to read so that they could read certain books about such matters as history, castles and dinosaurs, children also learn different ways of learning and develop various conceptions of the process. Pramling (1983, 1988) has studied in some detail the development of general concepts of learning to do, to know and to understand, showing how children tend at first not to discriminate between learning and doing or wanting to do, but then speak of gaining competence with age and later of learning from experience. It would be interesting to know in what ways such development relates to the experience of learning to read. Dahlgren and Olsson (1985) made a more specific study of children's conceptions of reading, including aspects of their thoughts about learning. An interesting distinction emerged between children who saw reading as a possibility for themselves and those who felt it to be a demand made on them by others.

Both from my own studies and theirs I conclude that much thinking about learning depends on experiences of learning to read. Reading is so central to teachers' conceptions of learning in school, and learning to read so prominent an experience in primary school, that the various ways children learn to read may permeate the whole of their school learning both in the early years and throughout their formal education. What is learned as school behaviour may continue as school behaviour. In my own work I have contrasted active, self-directed and other-supported learning with passive and other-directed, as have Dahlgren and Olsson, whereas others have distinguished between deep and surface approaches (Marton & Säljö, 1976), meaningful and rote learning (Ausubel, 1968) and comprehension and operation learning (Pask, 1976). Whilst they seem to cluster in a comprehensible way, these distinctions are different and each is important. Of particular interest is any explicit statement of a relationship between learner and teacher, or novice and expert. In my thinking I have been indebted to Pask and I tend to see approaches to learning as characterised by varying degrees of fulfilment of necessary criteria for judging that learning is achieved with competence and comprehension. My argument has been that children's experiences of learning to read, particularly in school, do not always match the simple criteria of being able to demonstrate to the self and to others how to do something, and why that particular way of doing it is in some sense a better way than other possible ways. Insofar as the experiences fall short and yet are thought to be school learning, so may a less than adequate approach to formal education be established.

Literacy and Authority

Meanings in ordinary speech are contingent on the context of its use, thus children learn spoken language within the experience of joint perspectives on events, and of understandings held in common with adults or more expert children. They learn that some usage is deemed inappropriate, but not that words and longer utterances have invariant meanings. Determining authority lies with the speaker, not with speech. Children believe the particular things they are told if they think the speaker is knowledgeable and is not lying or teasing; they do not believe a saying because it can be treated as a general statement which is open to verification. Such abstraction serves other functions than communication in daily life, and is difficult, if not impossible for pre-school children to grasp. To some extent, outside formal education, written language is similarly treated. It serves personal and temporary functions rather than abstract and general. But within schools, and indeed within other institutions such as churches, the bias may shift considerably as the introduction to literacy is expected to give better access to publicly agreed knowledge. Unfortunately this may carry an inappropriate investing of authority in the written word.

Prominence is often given in school instruction to the individual word or sentence, and children have to make some sort of sense of learning individual words, but they bring to this a propensity for not regarding meaning as invariant, a learning which can be seen in circumstances such as vocabulary testing. They give such varied responses to the question of what a word means that tests have to be highly selective, using words which yield minimal variation, or scoring has to allow explicitly for several most probable anwers. Moreover, until they have learned to look for synonyms or related concepts, children find it hard to "give a meaning" without contextualising the word in some usage that they try to explain. Such replies might be perfectly adequate to the question if the tester is prepared to allow for a child's perspective, but may nevertheless be too far from the precision being sought. Yet such precision is often asked for in the way children are taught to read.

The notion of precise or literal meaning for words or sentences taken out of context is one to which educators are particularly vulnerable. The educated person's sense of language is often influenced by the feeling that behind the work of linguists and philosophers of language lies an ideal account of word meaning, an ideal dictionary and an invariant language. It is as though the immensely useful tools of reference, derived from common expert understandings, are separated from their crafting and come to usurp the authority of the speaker and writer. To the extent that this happens for teachers, children may be introduced through learning to read and write to the idea or sense of authority in the written word itself.

Even if their teachers are not so influenced, children still have to face the power of print whose very machine quality removes it from the hand of the author, and whose permanence obscures its temporal origins. Children often lack the experience or knowledge to imagine the writing of what they read and thus are vulnerable to the notion of literal as distinct from writer's truth. Moreover, in school they share the same texts. Instead of a reading being a forging of what is felt to be at the time and in that particular context of reading a personal common understanding with an author, it may become the means of establishing a replicable, common understanding amongst readers, with the teacher as final arbiter of text meaning. Again the text rather than the author can be given authority, and a context-free literal meaning ascribed to it.

Given the different literacy experiences of home and school, with the broader spread of functional value in the former, such hazards are more likely to be associated with learning to read under conditions of formal education. This is particularly unfortunate since so much of what children have to learn in school is experienced through reading and writing. Early experiences which incline children not to question the authority of the written word, particularly if reinforced by the perception of adults' reliance on it or by the realisation that at least some texts are not to be questioned, may dispose towards not exploiting written language to the full. Too much deference to the notion of literal meaning will incline pupils to accept rather than search a text, and to memorise 'fact' rather than forge an understanding. Such different tendencies have been noticed, even in students in higher education; and there teachers, too, cannot be entirely absolved from blame, especially if arguments seem to rest more on quotations from respected sources than on reasoned cases.

Literacy within formal education may thus partially defeat its own ends. Instead of liberating learners into Olson's (1985) "theoretical stance towards nature", it may, with a bias towards misplaced authority, restrict the range of such a stance, so inhibiting curiosity and cramping intellectual growth. If an open attitude to knowledge is desired and literacy is to include writing to construct possible as well as actual, and transient as well as more permanent, worlds, then the relationship between author, reader and authority has to be explored and understood. Even young children, if they distinguish writing from copying, can realise that text is a product of both truth and imagination and as such ought to be thought about and tested. If such a realisation can be fostered and maintained throughout schooling then a proper realisation of the nature of authority behind the written language may allow a real appreciation of its role in scientific and poetic thinking as well as in the more prosaic political, social and economic business of everyday life.

The intention behind this paper was to explore some possible consequences of literacy for children's thinking, but it effectively concludes that the conditions of learning may be as significant as actually becoming literate in any technical sense of the word. The effects of learning within schooling may not always be conducive to children making the most of their reading and writing ability within the general context of school learning, and even further within the broader framework of the uses of schooling in society. This possibility has been explored with respect to several aspects of children's thinking and a number of research questions have been highlighted. If insights gained from pursuing them can lead to useful modifications of learning conditions in schools, then such an enterprise must surely be worthwhile – the more so if it addresses schooling for literacy in a variety of cultures and educational systems.

Research Issues

The above comments abound with suggestions that ask for research substantiation, rebuttal or clarification. The nature of literacy, implying command of a writing code and a form of language with its own personal and social significance for the individual, demands that such research questions be addressed by a variety of methods and with different philosophical perspectives.

There is a place for experiment, particularly with the more technical aspects of mastering written language and of making judgement about the physical aspects of text. Varying the conditions of instruction for their systematic evaluation may also be possible, whether by planned intervention or by taking advantage of variation within a system. Such evaluation, must however, address the identification and description of learning processes, taking account of the intentions and understandings of participants, as well as assessing out-comes in terms of acquired skills. The strategies learners adopt with text may be more significant for their thinking than whether they read a word correctly or not. Further, if the experimental approach can be adapted to lead to a construction of a developmental or historical account of children's learning, thus illuminating thinking in the process of change, so much the better.

However, at every point the researcher who uses experimental design ought to evaluate its validity, not only in terms of threats to control, but also in terms of faithfulness to the phenomenon concerned. There comes a point when, in order to do this, different research perspectives may have to be entertained. If the meaning of literacy to the learner has to be explored, whatever aspect is at issue, then this requires an ethnographic approach. In my own research I have tried to use both a developmental/experimental and an ethnographic approach, not because I have any prior philosophical commit-ment, but because trying to write a history of children's learning has seemed to me to require some effort to understand what the experience means to the child. Entailed in it, however, has been a tension between viewing print and meaning objectively, seeing literacy as related to public knowledge, and taking a subjective approach, seeing it as related to personal thinking and know-ing.

My final comment then, is that since the understanding of literacy expe-rience raises issues about the nature of knowing and knowledge, the research questions asked and the methods used may well depend on the researcher's own experiences of literacy and consequent personal views as to the nature and authority of the written word. This could well provide a topic for "learning conversations" within the research community.

References

Ausubel, D. (1968). *Educational psychology: A cognitive view.* New York: Holt, Rinehart & Winston.

Barr, R. (1978). Influence of instruction on early reading. In L. J. Chapman & P. Czerniewska (Eds.), *Reading: From process to practice* (pp. 210–229). London: Routledge & Kegan Paul.

Biemiller, A. (1970). The development of the use of graphic and contextual informa-tion as children learn to read. *Reading Research Quarterly, 6,* 75–96.

Bradley, L., & Bryant, P. E. (1978). Difficulties in auditory organisation as a possible cause of reading backwardness. *Nature, 271,* 746–747.

Bradley, L., & Bryant, P. E. (1983). Categorising sounds and learning to read: A causal connexion. *Nature, 301,* 419–21.

Clark, M. M. (1976). *Young fluent readers.* London: Heinemann Educational Press.

Dahlgren, G., & Olsson, L. E. (1985). *Läsning i barnperspektiv* [Reading in the child's perspective]. Göteborg: Acta Universitatis Gothoburgensis.

Downing, J. (1970). Children's concepts of language in learning to read. *Educational Research*, *12*, 106–112.

Ehri, L. C. (1975). Word consciousness in readers and pre-readers. *Journal of Educational Psychology*, *67*, 204–212.

Ehri, L. C. (1976). Word learning in beginning readers and pre-readers: Effects of form class and defining contexts. *Journal of Educational Psychology*, *68*, 832–842.

Ehri, L. C. (1979). Linguistic insight: Threshold of reading acquisition. In T. G. Waller & G. E. MacKinnon (Eds.), *Reading research: Advances in theory and practice* (Vol.1, pp. 63–114). New York: Academic Press.

Ehri, L. C. (1984). How orthography alters spoken language competencies in children learning to read and spell. In J. Downing & R. Valtin (Eds.), *Language awareness and learning to read* (pp. 119–147). Berlin, Heidelberg, New York: Springer-Verlag.

Ferreiro, E., & Teberosky, A. (1982). *Literacy before schooling*. Exeter, N. H.: Heinemann Educational Press.

Francis, H. (1973). Children's experience of reading and notions of units in language. *British Journal of Educational Psychology*, *43*, 17–23.

Francis, H. (1975a, September). *Reading and language learning*. Paper presented at the Third International Child Language Symposium, London.

Francis, H. (1975b). *Language in childhood*. London: Paul Elek.

Francis, H. (1982). *Learning to read*. London: Allen & Unwin.

Francis, H. (1984). Children's knowledge of orthography in learning to read. *British Journal of Educational Psychology*, *54*, 8–23.

Gibson, E. J., & Levin, H. (1975). *The psychology of reading*. Cambridge, Ma.: M.I.T. Press.

Heath, S. B. (1983). *Ways with words*. Cambridge: Cambridge University Press.

Liberman, I. Y. (1973). Segmentation of the spoken word and reading acquisition. *Bulletin of the Orton Society*, *23*, 65–77.

Lunzer, E., Dolan, T., & Wilkinson, E. (1976). The effectiveness of measures of operativity, language and short term memory in the prediction of reading and mathematical understanding. *British Journal of Educational Psychology*, *46*, 295–305.

Marton, F., & Säljö, R. (1976). On qualitative differences in learning: I. Outcome and process. *British Journal of Educational Psychology*, *46*, 4–11.

Mattingly, I. G. (1972). Reading, the linguistic process, and linguistic awareness. In J. F. Kavanagh & I. G. Mattingly (Eds.), *Language by ear and by eye* (pp. 133–147). Cambridge, Ma: M.I.T. Press.

Mattingly, I. G. (1984). Reading, linguistic awareness and language acquisition. In J. Downing & R. Valtin (Eds.), *Language awareness and learning to read* (pp. 9–25). Berlin, Heidelberg, New York: Springer-Verlag.

Olson, D. R. (1985). Computers as tools of the intellect. *Educational Researcher*, *14*, 5, 5–8.

Pask, G. (1976). Styles and strategies of learning. *British Journal of Educational Psychology*, *46*, 128–148.

Pramling, I. (1983). *The child's conception of learning*. Göteborg: Acta Universitatis Gothoburgensis.

Pramling, I. (1988). Entrance into the "world of learning". In this volume.

Reid, J. (1966). Learning to think about reading. *Educational Research*, *9*, 56–62.

Schieffelin, B. B., & Cochran-Smith, M. (1984). Learning to read culturally: literacy before schooling. In H. Goelman, A. Oberg, & F. Smith (Eds.), *Awakening to literacy* (pp. 3–23). Exeter, N.H.; Heinemann Educational Press.

Scribner, S., & Cole M. (1981). *The psychology of literacy*. Cambridge, Mass.; Harvard University Press.

Söderbergh, R. (1971). *Reading in early childhood*. Stockholm: Almqvist & Wiksell.

Watson, A. J. (1984). Cognitive development and units of print in early reading. In J. Downing & R. Valtin (Eds.), *Language awareness and learning to read* (pp. 93–118). Berlin, Heidelberg, New York: Springer-Verlag.

Weber, R. (1970). A linguistic analysis of first-grade reading errors. *Reading Research Quarterly*, 5, 427–451.

CHAPTER 9

Entrance into the "World of Knowledge" – Pre-school Children's Conceptions of Learning

Ingrid Pramling

For adults, knowledge and learning are two concepts which are closely related. But what about young children? What are their views of acquiring knowledge? The child's conception of learning has been described earlier by Pramling (1983a) in terms of its two related aspects: *what* we learn and *how* we learn. Concerning the first aspect – the *what* of learning – there seems to be a progression from conceiving learning as *to do* via conceiving learning as *to know*, towards conceiving learning as *to understand*. To each of these answers to the question 'what', there is a corresponding set of qualitatively different answers to the question of the 'how' of learning. Development in this respect goes from an inability to distinguish between *to do* (to know and to understand) and *to learn to do* (to know and to understand), to seeing a transition between a state of *being able*, simply as a function of *getting older*. At the third level, the child realizes that learning (i.e. becoming (more) able) comes about by *experience*. Experience, again, may have three distinctly different forms, namely, learning by *doing*, *perceiving*, and *thinking*. There are also developmental differences as to the awareness of the various forms learning may take.

The basis of the brief description above is about 300 interviews with children ranging from 3 to 8 years of age. The interview method was the clinical one developed by Piaget (1926/1975), where the two main criteria are to have an idea about what kind of information is required and to follow up the child's answers as far as possible (Doverborg-Österberg & Pramling, 1985). Encouraging children to share their thoughts is to a large extent a question of getting them to talk about topics which represent their world. This means allowing them to suggest areas to talk about which they consider important. The interviews in this collection of data were taped and later transcribed. They were then analysed in order to delimit and describe qualitatively different conceptions of the phenomena talked about. The results are developed and described in terms of categories indicating different *conceptions of reality*. This means that a second-order perspective is applied, i.e. the aim is one of understanding how children conceptualize the world around them (Marton, 1981). Marton has called this research approach "phenomenography". Phenomenography might be regarded as a methodological standpoint for describing the variation of conceptions to be found about a particular concept, principle or phenomenon in a group of subjects.

Table 1. Percentage of children conceiving of learning as *to know*.

Age (years)[a]	3	4	5	6	7	8
To learn *to know* (%)	–	4	11	15	11	28

[a] In Sweden children start primary school at 7 years of age.

In the study reported here on children's awareness of their own learning (Pramling, 1983a), there was also a quantitative part, and Table 1 shows the developmental trend in the percentage of answers in which children suggest something they have learnt *to know*. Questions were asked in various ways:

– Tell me something you have learnt.
– Tell me something you learned at pre-school.
– What are you going to learn in primary school? etc.

There was also another kind of question where the way to learn was implied:

– Have you ever learnt anything from watching television?
– Have you learnt anything from reading books? (or)
– Have you learnt anything when someone has read a book to you?

In spite of all the different ways of putting the question to the child, no more than 28% of the children who had already spent 1 year in primary school (i.e. who were 8 years of age) suggested something they had learnt which could be interpreted as understanding learning in terms of knowledge. As is also evident, children rarely suggest during pre-school years that they learn in terms of acquiring knowledge. Since children suggested this so seldom, the interviewer asked a large number of questions which implied that one can learn to know. These were question like:

– How would you go about finding out how a radio works?
– How would you go about finding out why a boat floats in spite of it being so heavy?
– What would you do if you wanted to find out how far away the moon is? (later called the 'moon question')

From these and similar questions Table 2 summarizes the structure of the qualitatively different categories for children's thinking about how to acquire knowledge.

Quite a few children at these age levels suggest that they will *do* something themselves to gain knowledge. Very few children, on the other hand, suggest finding out something by *thinking*. As finding out by *perceiving* is the logical way to deal with knowledge as well as the most extended conception, we will

Table 2. The structure of the child's conception of how to get *to know* something

		By *being there*
	By *doing*	By *asking someone who does*
How to acquire	By *perceiving*	By *asking someone who knows*
knowledge	By *thinking*	Through *media* (reading or watching TV)

develop these conceptions and illustrate them by excerpts from the interviews. Table 2 also shows that the acquisition of knowledge by *perceiving* is differentiated into four categories of description: by *being there*, by *asking someone who does*, by *asking someone who knows*, by *media* (books or TV).

To Acquire Knowledge by Being There

Conceptions of knowing as related to *being there* refer to the child's talking about his exposure to a situation or setting. This means that the child has to be involved in a situation which creates knowledge. Although s/he is a passive spectator, s/he will nevertheless acquire knowledge. Reality is represented in the world of the child as s/he perceives it.

> Christian 7:1 (in a long dialogue about how aeroplanes function):
> E: How do you know?
> S: I know because I've seen it . . . flew in a plane once.

> Fredrik 6:4 (in an interview about experiments with plants and coloured water):
> E: Aha . . . why do you think that theirs became another colour?
> S: I don't know.
> E: Can you find out in some way? How is it that theirs is a different colour from yours?
> S: I'll maybe try to do it.
> E: How do you go about finding out?
> S: I'll look very carefully one time at what they have in it.

To Acquire Knowledge by Asking Someone Who Does

Conceptions of gaining knowledge in this category mean that the child is able to acquire knowledge from someone who tells him. This someone is, however, a particular person who has experienced a situation or been involved in an action or setting. In a sense one could say that this is a kind of expert conception, where the best answers are found by asking people who are involved in a particular domain. Knowledge is personified by people who illustrate the possession of knowledge in a tangible way. With regard to the moon question, the child says he has to ask an astronaut, someone who has been to the moon, or who works at a satellite base.

> Stig 7:3:
> E: If he wants to know how far it is, how will he find this out?
> S: He can ask . . . someone who travels in a space rocket.
> E: But do you think this boy Orvar can find out in another way?
> S: He can ask the astronaut.

> Jenny 6:7 (in a discussion about how a radio works):
> E: If mummy and daddy don't know, how could you find out?
> S: You can ask the people who work on the radio.

> Michael 7:0:
> E: Have you any idea about how to find out about it?
> S: I would ask someone who works on the radio.

To Acquire Knowledge by Asking Someone Who Knows

Conceptions of learning *to know* now begin to reflect the idea of general knowledge. Grown-ups know a lot and if you want to find out something you can ask someone who knows. Knowledge begins to be understood as universal, but it is still connected with people. The oral way of transmitting knowledge is most important to the child, so that someone in possession of knowledge can transfer this by talking about it. With regard to the moon question, the child says s/he can ask his/her teacher, parents, etc.

> Susanna 5:9:
> E: How would you go about getting to know?
> S: I'd ask mummy or daddy and if they didn't know I'd think of something else.
> E: Wouldn't you be able to find out in any other way?
> S: No, I'd have to wait until they know.

> Marie 7:7:
> E: If you want to know how music comes from a radio, what would you do to find out?
> S: I'd ask daddy.
> E: Do you think he knows?
> S: Yes.

To Acquire Knowledge Through Media

In this category, knowledge has become impersonal. The source of knowledge is information from the medium (a book or TV). Knowledge can be transferred without a person; it is something in itself. With regard to the moon question, the child suggests that the distance to the moon can be found out by reading a book or watching TV.

Li 5:9:
E: How have you learnt?
S: From TV.
E: What kind of programme was it?
S: That a bird lay dead in oil.

Johan 7:4:
S: Ask others if they know, or look at books. Perhaps it is in pictures
E: What can you get to know from reading books?
S: You can learn to read . . . and learn as much as you want, and if you don't know
 you can do it if you read a lot in books . . . you get clever then.
E: How are you when you are clever?
S: You know a lot.

In one sense children seem in this case to possess a more universal conception of learning, though this is not always the case. Although children have expressed the conceptions categorized here, these conceptions represent specific answers to specific questions. Here, we must stress the relation to the content of the dialogue. Thus, children very often refer to a particular programme in which this information has been given. The child says, for example, "We have a book about this topic in pre-school" or "I saw a programme about that the other day".

Even if children understand how to acquire knowledge via media, this does not mean that they understand that there is a vast amount of knowledge in existence. Table 3 shows the extent to which children suggest ways of finding out knowledge in a large variety of areas. As is apparent from this table, approximately one quarter of the 6- 7- and 8-year-old children have grasped that one can acquire knowledge by *being there* in a concrete situation. The child not only knows that he has "been there", but also what this "being there" leads to in terms of knowledge. There is a gradual increase with age in the frequency of conceptions of learning *to know* by *asking someone who does* something or by *asking someone who knows*. The children's answers indicate that they mention more often that parents are asked rather than other people around them. The acquisition of knowledge from books or TV is mainly mentioned in children's responses to that particular question. Thus the child has grasped, for example, that there is a message in a book. The dramatic increase

Table 3. The child's conception of how to acquire knowledge

Age (years)	3	4	5	6	7	8
By *being there* (%)	–	–	11	22	21	24
By *asking someone who does* (%)	–	–	7	33	50	60
By *asking someone who knows* (%)	–	4	33	52	68	76
Through *media* (%)	–	11	15	33	39	76

in children's awareness of learning about the content of a book or TV programme comes after one year of schooling.

On the whole, however, we could summarize this section of the study on
children's conceptions of how to acquire knowledge by saying that, at the age
levels investigated, knowledge is very much personified. We could also say that
learning in terms of gaining knowledge (in a more general sense) is a conception which very few children suggest spontaneously. This means that there is
not a very obvious connection between learning and knowledge for children,
even when the interviewer relates learning to books or TV programmes.
Dahlgren and Olsson (1985) have shown that there is a difference between
children who see learning to read as an *opportunity* or as a *demand*. Among
children who see reading as a demand, none see the content in the text as a
reason for learning to read. But even among the children who saw learning to
read as an opportunity, only 17% thought they could gain knowledge from a
text. Why is it then that knowledge is so invisible to children, and how do they
come to have such a personified conceptualization of knowledge?

In a longitudinal study Francis (1982) has thoroughly described the development of ten children's conceptions about school–related activities during
their first 3 years in primary school. She distinguishes three categories of
readers: the skilled readers, the slow readers and the late beginners. Each of
these groups of children set about the task of learning to read and write in
different ways. The skilled readers had grasped some understanding of the act
of reading and writing for themselves in their daily life. The slow readers were
characterized by connecting reading and writing with school. Finally, the late
beginners were characterized by copying patterns without understanding.
These children also shared the situation that they had no support from home.
We know that children grow up in different families with different prerequisites, but what of the role of the pre-school, the child's first encounter with
society, and his/her socialization in becoming a member of society?

Teaching and Learning in Pre-school

In Swedish pre-school, teaching is mainly related to working with themes over
a shorter or longer period of time. Themes in pre-school involve working with
a specific content, e.g. the autumn, the cat, shape and colour, the farm. The
theme is treated through class discussions, singing, playing, reading stories,
working with arts and crafts, visiting different places outside the pre-school
etc. Thus the teacher plans for the theme to include all these activities, because
together they constitute for her the theme about which the children are to
learn. And since teachers think that children's learning takes place by their
working concretely, activities play an important role.

In a study by Pramling (1986), ten children between 3 and 7 years of age
were investigated during their work with one such theme, 'the horse'. They

were interviewed individually once before the theme began and a second time after 3 months, in the week during which the work was to be completed. Tape recording of the interaction in the whole group of children was carried out during class discussions. The main purpose of this study was to find out how children perceived the different activities which the teacher defined as learning about the theme 'the horse'. For this purpose the children were asked to say what they themselves would do if asked to teach children in another pre-school what they had learnt during 'the horse' theme. The results indicate that all those who could answer the question said: *they would tell the children about it.* None suggested any of the other activities which they had been involved in themselves in learning about the horse. What children instead said was that visiting the riding school, modelling or drawing horses was all for fun, i.e. these activities had nothing to do with learning. Thus these young children are – I suggest – on their way to becoming socialized into a school-like attitude to learning, i.e. that knowledge is dependent on what the teacher tells you and nothing else.

The transmission of knowledge by oral tradition has deep roots in history, but children's thinking can also be seen as an artifact of culture, of their experience. Children believe in experts and teachers and not in their own active search for knowledge. Since none of the ten children read fluently, it is fully understandable that they did not suggest reading as a possible way to teach other children. But we can see in Table 3 how children also suggest that *they could acquire knowledge by observing reality.* It seems that our organization of the child's learning from our way of thinking as adults is counterproductive, i.e. it blocks the insight that knowledge is equal to the child's results of learning about reality.

Some Concluding Remarks

The directions for pre-school (Socialstyrelsen, 1983) as well as elementary school (Lgr 80) argue for the construction of knowledge through being an active individual. In spite of this, it seems as if children become socialized instead into a role as passive spectators, where learning becomes connected with what the teacher says.

Teaching in pre-school is to a large extent equal to denominating, defining or answering questions. Children's experiences derive from teachers' behaviour. Interacting with children in this traditional way of teaching means that they are socialized to become passive consumers, who are only required to give answers and never pose questions. The teacher talks about different subjects, which she tries to ask questions about later. This is a situation which has very little in common with the 'normal' communication to which the child is used. The child now tries to discover his/her role. "What does the teacher expect of me here?" Of course s/he expects the right answer. Why should s/he otherwise raise these questions which the child knows s/he knows the answer to? What is the metacontract between the child and the teacher, i.e. what is taken for granted as the basis for communication (Hundeide, 1987)? The teacher distributes not only knowledge, but also what learning is all about. And, as it would appear from this small study, the passive role as pupil is already grounded in pre-school, by trying to "play school" when teaching children about reality.

If children learn nothing else in pre-school, they do at least learn their roles as pupils. To learn, or to acquire knowledge, is defined in terms of particular periods during the day when the teacher behaves in a certain way. Children are requested to copy what the teacher relates to them in order to acquire knowledge, instead of developing their own active creation of knowledge about reality. Reality is outside pre-school, and to understand this reality, children create their own conceptions to express reality in a satisfactory way. These everyday conceptions, which can be seen at an early age with reference to, for example, strategies in mathematics (Doverborg-Österberg, 1985) have also been found in Grade 6 in elementary school (Unenge, 1984). Thus conceptions about counting established in the pre-school years have not been altered by teaching in school.

Brumby (1979) has shown that post-'A'-level students of biology have a very advanced conception of the main concepts in their field from a disciplinary perspective, but very naive conceptions of the same concepts when confronted with everyday life situations.

It has been shown earlier (Säljö, 1982; Dahlgren & Pramling, 1981; Pramling, 1983b) that many adult students perceive knowledge as separate from reality. Säljö (1982) has shown how students perceive knowledge as arising from memorizing a text. In other words, it is the text as such that has to be learnt. On the other hand, students who perceive knowledge as constructed by themselves from the text are students who focus on reality and on bridging the gap between what exists in the written text and what is "out there".

In a combined observation and interview study by Pramling (1983a), the same phenomenon could be found in relation to the teaching of a theme with pre-school children. The text was translated into the pedagogical setting in which teaching took place. We could then see that some children only grasped the situation as such, i.e. the play or activity they had been involved in. Other children, however, grasped what was behind the situation, what it was intended to convey.

It seems as if teaching as early as at the lowest levels of the educational system forces children to distinguish between knowledge and reality instead of opening up their conceptions of reality. It is, according to Vygotsky (1934/1972), the meeting between everyday life conceptions and more scientific meanings from which possibilities can emerge to develop an understanding of the surrounding world. Why do we then find this lack of integration between everyday life conceptions and academic conceptions? Perhaps because children, from their first meeting with the educational system, define the situation and their own roles as something apart from what takes place in everyday life. Children interpret their experiences as something separate from reality. How do children, for example, perceive the frames, the interaction; or what is their understanding or insight into what takes place in the teaching situation?

As we have seen from the empirical studies, very few children below the age of 8 years spontaneously connect learning and the possession of knowledge. The idea of acquiring knowledge is, in other words, rather an invisible part of reality for younger children. In spite of this, they have ideas about how to find out about things in qualitatively different ways when asked directly about finding something out. These conceptions are not elaborated further in pre-school, but narrowed down instead to school-like questioning-answering conceptions about how to gain knowledge. The way to help children in their struggle to understand reality should be to widen rather than narrow their view.

By studying the learning process in relation to the results of its content, we gain an idea of what remains from teaching in the children's way of thinking. What they perceive in pre-school as learning and knowledge becomes a conception which they later bring to elementary school. But how do these conceptions help the child to enter into the 'world of knowledge'? It is self-evident that children need guidance to attain modern society's way of thinking. Piaget (1948/1980) says:

> Considering that it took centuries to arrive at the so called new mathematics and modern, even microscopic, physics it would be ridiculous to think that without guidance toward awareness of the central problems the child could ever succeed in formulating them himself (p. 16).

According to Piaget, knowledge is not a reproduction of reality, but an active transformation of the categories of experience a person uses in his interaction with the world. Piaget does not mean that children should reproduce what other generations have done, but that they need guidance from earlier experience.

Children meet modern society's way of thinking in the form of textbooks in school. The function of textbooks is to distribute experience. The system of writing signs is designed by man to distribute as well as collect this experience. The nature of the text is based on experience, a fact which does not seem to be obvious to all students (Säljö, 1982). What then should the role of pre-school be in this case?

The first connection children must make in this respect seems to be to link experience with learning. When this link is clear they have a basis for making the link between text and reality. Thus if pre-school succeeds in making children aware about the close relation between experiences and learning, the ground is prepared for later text learning in school.

References

Brumby, M. N. (1979). *Students' perceptions and learning styles associated with the concept of evolution by natural selection.* Unpublished doctoral dissertation, University of Surrey.

Dahlgren, G.,˙& Olsson, L-E. (1985). *Läsning ur barnperspektiv* [Reading in children's perspective]. Göteborg: Acta Universitatis Gothoburgensis.

Dahlgren, L. O. & Pramling, I. (1981). *Högskolestudier och omvärldsuppfattning* [University studies and conceptions of reality]. Rapporter från Pedagogiska Institutionen, Göteborgs universitet, no. 1981:1.

Doverborg-Österberg, E. (1985). *Barns uppfattningar av matematik* [Children's conceptions of mathematics]. Pedagogiska Institutionen, Göteborgs universitet (manus).

Doverborg-Österberg, E., & Pramling, I. (1985). *Att förstå barns tankar* [To understand children's thoughts]. Stockholm: Liber.

Francis, H. (1982). *Learning to read.* London: Allen & Unwin.

Hundeide, K. (1987). *Barns livsverden* [The life-world of children]. Oslo: Cappelen.

Lgr 80. (1980) *Läroplanen i arbete* [The curriculum at work]. Stockholm: Liber.

Marton, F. (1981). Phenomenography – describing conceptions of the world around us. *Instructional Science, 10,* 177–200.

Piaget, J. (1975). *The child's conception of the world.* New Jersey: Litterfield, Adams & Co. (Original work published 1926)

Piaget, J. (1980). *To understand is to invent.* New York: Penguin. (Original work published 1948)

Pramling, I. (1983a). *The child's conception of learning.* Göteborg: Acta Universitatis Gothoburgensis.

Pramling, I. (1983b). *Möte med arbetslivet* [Meeting working life]. Rapport från Pedagogiska Institutionen, Göteborgs universitet, no. 1983:01.

Pramling, I. (1986). *Inlärning ur barnperspektiv* [Learning in children's perspective]. Lund: Studentlitteratur.

Säljö, R. (1982). *Learning and understanding.* Göteborg: Acta Universitatis Gothoburgensis.

Socialstyrelsen. (1983). *Förslag till pedagogiskt program för förskolan* [Proposal for a pedagogical programme for the pre-school]. Stockholm: Liber.

Unenge, J. (1984). *Matematikdidaktik för klasslärare* [Didactics of mathematics for teachers]. Jönköping: Mapro-Matematikprodukter.

Vygotsky, L. S. (1972). *Taenkning og sprog I og II* [Thought and language. Vols. 1–2]. Köpenhamn: Mezhdunarodnaja Kniga og Hans Reitzels Forlag. (Original work published 1934)

CHAPTER 10

Towards an Anatomy of Academic Discourse: Meaning and Context in the Undergraduate Essay

Dai Hounsell

Introduction

First Class Answers in History (Bennett, 1974) is a collection of reflections by seven Cambridge tutors on the characteristics of outstanding essay answers in the University's final examinations. In his editorial introduction to the volume, Bennett demolishes the notion that there is any "hidden mystery about good history writing" (p. 6). He contends:

> Excellence in historical writing consists of simple and solid virtues, not of facile tricks and gaudy gadgets. It can therefore be appreciated by all who have the wit and the diligence to seek it; it is no monopoly of those who possess superior talents (1974, p. 2).

The logic of this stance leads Bennett inevitably to the question of precisely what does constitute a 'first-class answer', but here boldness seems to shade into equivocation:

> To examine in history is to use one's experience and discrimination to record the *impression* that this answer of this candidate is better than that . . . Of course the impressionistic element in marking is rigorously controlled through careful scrutiny of the evidence cited or overlooked by the candidate and by close attention to his ability to argue a case with logic and prudence; but the nature of historical study itself determines that at the crucial moments of an examiners' meeting decisions turn upon one man's impression that a particular answer deserves alpha and another's that it is worth no more than beta. But since an impression is not a totally rational thing, susceptible of proof or disproof after the fashion of a theorem in Euclidean geometry, there can be no precise definition of it and no exact guide to ways of creating any particular impression in another's mind (1974, pp. 2–3).

To many aspiring students of history, this statement must seem puzzling, especially when contrasted with the directness of Bennett's opening remarks. The issue is less that of *how far* a particular piece of historical writing might embody excellence – that judgement is clearly the province of professional historians – than of the criteria upon which any judgement made would be based. If the touchstones of excellence are, in Bennett's words, "simple and solid virtues", why cannot they be stated? From a different standpoint, however, Bennett's statement need not be considered perfunctory. Instead, we could take the view that qualitative judgements of this kind of writing turn upon what Polanyi (1967) has called a "tacit form of knowing": we attend *from* something (a collection of proximal particulars) *to* something else (a distal entity), but we are unable to specify what these particulars are, even though we are totally reliant upon them as the means by which we attend to the entity. From this perspective, then, Bennett's failure to be specific is neither perverse nor remiss, exemplifying instead the dilemma that in many domains, we "know more than we can tell" (Polanyi, 1967, p. 18). Yet we are still left with the question: must the tacit remain unfathomable, or can we attempt to particularise it?[1]

My personal answer would be a tentative 'yes', and my aim in this paper is to make explicit some hitherto tacit aspects of the undergraduate essay, against the wider background of a discussion of writing in educational settings. As, for example, many historians have done (Bennett, 1974; Elton, 1969; Hyam, 1974), I shall assume that in certain fundamental respects the undergraduate essay mirrors academic writing in the larger discipline, and thus constitutes one form of academic discourse. Academic discourse is, then, a particular kind of written world, with a tacit set of conventions, or 'code', of its own. It is a code, nonetheless, which is crackable.

Over the last decade, and after a long and unjustified period of neglect, writing has begun to blossom as a research topic, attracting the attention of researchers from a wide range of disciplinary backgrounds, including English (Britton, Burgess, Martin, McLeod, & Rosen, 1975; Martin, D'Arcy, Newton, & Parker, 1976), philosophy (Hirsch, 1977), psychology (Gregg & Steinberg, 1980; Hartley, 1980; Wason, 1980) and various socio-cultural perspectives (Whiteman, 1981).

Yet the relevance of this burgeoning literature to the study of writing in educational settings is constrained in a number of ways. In part, this is for the familiar reason that some research on writing is not centrally concerned with the activity of writing per se: the chief focus lies elsewhere in, for example, writing as a means of examining cognitive processes or of exploring the differences between the spoken and the written word, and so extending an understanding of the nature of language. The study of writing has also frequently been governed by an assumption which is parallelled in research on learning (see for example Säljö, 1984): it has been all too readily taken for granted – particularly in the archetypal publication in this field, the compendium of research papers – that writing is a relatively discrete and homogeneous

---

1 The view could be taken that Bennett's observations are far from tacit, since he refers to three facets of the history essay – arguing a case, logical coherence, and the use of evidence – which are also characteristic of the 'argument' conception examined in a later section of this paper. My own position is that, paradoxically perhaps, these references *reinforce* a tacit view, since Bennett seems to take it for granted that the character of the essay is immediately recognisable and that it is not incumbent upon him to help the reader to grasp its central features.

activity. Tasks such as drafting essays, composing letters or designing forms (see for example Gregg & Steinberg, 1980; Hartley, 1980) are made to huddle under the common umbrella of writing, but without any serious attempt to demonstrate a material affinity or to pinpoint fundamental differences between ostensibly similar tasks. In this respect, such dimensions seem prey to a mythology of writing which has its source in the great array of student guides to 'effective' writing. Such guides generally display not only a preoccupation with the trappings of academic writing – a mastery of bibliographic conventions, accuracy in syntax and punctuation, a high degree of self-organisation – but a tendency to treat form in isolation from substance. Activities such as planning and drafting are considered hermetically, without reference to the content of what is to be conveyed or to the mode of discourse to which the writer is expected to conform. Research on writing has often followed a similar path, as two very different examples can illustrate.

First, from a cognitive perspective which emphasises the relations between writing and thinking, Flower and Hayes (1980) have undertaken a series of studies of planning, which they see as "the writer's defence against the very nature of writing and its deluge of constraints" (p. 83). However the model of the planning process which they sketch out is drawn from observational experiments involving synthetic writing tasks. Flower and Hayes do not appear to regard the subject matter of the task as crucial in itself nor to consider the array of constraints and demands characteristic of a natural – as opposed to an experimental – setting. Thus the question of what might constitute authentic or appropriate planning in a given situation, or of the extent to which planning activities might be coloured by what the writer apprehends his or her planning activities to be directed towards, are overlooked or obscured. My own research (Hounsell, 1984a), on the other hand, suggests that, at least as far as essay-writing is concerned, planning strategies cannot be properly understood in isolation from students' conceptions of what an essay is and what essay-writing involves – a point to which I shall return later.

A second example is Hirsch's elegant dissection of the characteristics of composition (Hirsch, 1977) in which he argues that communicative efficiency rests upon a principle of relative readability: one prose style is qualitatively better than another "when it communicates the same meanings as the other does but requires less effort from the reader" (p. 9). We can applaud this attempt to articulate a single overarching principle under which a set of specific practical prescriptions can be subsumed, but still feel bound to ask: is it reasonable to regard stylistic accomplishment as if it were content-neutral (cf. Marton, 1981) and untouched by considerations of form? Galbraith (1980) would not think so, for he has argued that tensions between form and content, expression and presentation, and topic and goal are endemic to certain kinds of writing. Galbraith's case analysis of a doctoral student suggests that the lack of clarity and structural cohesion apparent in the student's writing did not stem from a lack of accomplishment in writing as such but was instead a symptom of her inability to reconcile her conception of what others demanded of her with her private conception of the research topic – i.e. her personal and innermost thoughts about the nature of the topic and how she might best pursue it. When Galbraith succeeded in finding ways of nourishing her private conception of her work, her writing took on the coherence and fluency which it had earlier lacked. The point can be further illustrated with an example taken from my own experience as an academic adviser. "Margot", a mature student, had been told that her psychology essays betrayed an inadequate grasp of written English, and that she should therefore seek help in learning to write more fluently. Yet as interviews with Margot indicated, and her essays confirmed (see Appendix for a typical instance), to a significant degree Margot's attempts to write fluently were inhibited by an inappropriate understanding of tutors' expectations. Having interpreted her objective as that of producing an exhaustive menu of all the points which might be made (rather than as a searching scrutiny of one or two central issues) she had set herself the near-impossible task of coherently itemising a list within a form – the short essay – to which this was patently ill-suited.

Neither this example nor Galbraith's case study, of course, constitute hard evidence, yet they do powerfully exemplify ways in which form and expression can be interwoven. If only as a counterpoint to the long tradition of treating these twin facets of writing separately, it is worthwhile recalling the Latin dictum cited by Eco (1985, p. 24). *Rem tene, verba sequentur*; grasp the theme and the words will follow.

There is also the problem of context which, despite evidence of its pervasive influence upon learning (Ramsden, 1984), has tended to be given insufficient attention in studies of writing. Indeed, in cases where the focus of research has been specifically directed upon writing in the school setting, context has been a significant influence both on the nature of writing activities undertaken and on the conditions under which these activities are assigned and pursued. Thus, in a study of the development of writing abilities in secondary schools, Britton et al. (1975) found that as pupils moved through successive years of secondary schooling, the range of functional categories of writing in which they were engaged narrowed considerably, while at the same time a steadily increasing proportion of written work was addressed to a particular category of audience: that of the teacher-as-examiner. Later research in Scotland (Spencer, 1983) broadly confirmed this picture. Such studies, Bereiter has observed, tell us more about schools than about students as writers (Bereiter, 1980; see also Newkirk, 1982). But while this observation springs from the developmental perspective which Bereiter adopts, it is suggestive of a more general danger: that researchers can somehow approach writing and schools as if they were two separate phenomena and yet yield findings which are pedagogically significant. Fortunately, research on writing has shown a marked shift away from the still-dominant research tradition of the controlled laboratory experiment, which cannot easily accommodate a context-sensitive approach nor easily come to terms with the limits to generalisation which such approaches serve to underline.

Up to this point in the discussion, I have tried to show that writing in educational settings has a distinctive character which sets specific limits on the relevance of a fast-growing body of research on writing. These observations are therefore a necessary preliminary to what follows, in which the questions I have raised are pursued through an examination of findings from my own research. The study I shall be concerned with is an investigation of undergraduate essay-writing in the social sciences (Hounsell, 1984a, 1984c). This was essentially a qualitative study undertaken within the framework of an emergent phenomenographic approach to research on student learning (see, for example, Marton, Hounsell, & Entwistle, 1984). The main source of data comprised semi-structured interviews with 16 psychology and 17 history students in their second year at university. This data was supplemented by information on students' essay marks and final degree results, a selective analysis of the students' essays, and scores on the Lancaster Approaches to Studying Inventory (Entwistle & Ramsden, 1983). Here I shall concentrate upon three issues: the context within which essay-writing took place; the students' conceptions of essay-writing as a form of discourse; and disciplinary frames for discourse.

The Context of Essay-Writing

In this study, the outward requirements of essay-writing followed a pattern typical of many higher education institutions in Britain. Students were offered a choice of questions and were required to submit their essays by a given date. Broadly speaking, while students could draw upon lecture and seminar notes and follow up recommended reading material in preparing their essays, there was no direct match between lecture and seminar topics and essay questions, and students were expected to go beyond what notes they had and track down further material in the library which might be germane to the specific questions set. Essays were typically 2500–3000 words in length, and the marks awarded contributed to students' overall grade for a course unit. The reported median time spent on an essay in each subject group was 13–15 hours, but the range from one student to another was very wide: from a low of 6 hours to a high of 30 hours in history and from a low of 9–10 hours to a high also of 30 hours in psychology. A small number of students took hardly any notes, while others took as many as 30 or 40 sides.

The context within which essay-writing took place was not altogether the same for each subject group. For history students, as many as 18–20 coursework essays had to be completed over the course of their second year. Writing essays therefore took up the bulk of their private study time and while most found this demanding, many students found essays a distraction from wider reading or, in some cases, an unwelcome chore. In psychology, on the other hand, there were considerably fewer essay assignments, and writing essays took up substantially less than half students' overall working time. In many respects, however, the context was broadly similar for both subject groups. Essay-writing was essentially a private and solitary activity: there was no substantive discussion between students of essay content or of essay-writing strategies, and the traffic of comment from tutors to students was very largely formal, post hoc, product orientated and limited in scope (Hounsell, 1985). In general, then, it would be misleading to regard essay-writing in these course units as an untrammelled opportunity for learning, in the sense of apprehending and making sense of a topic and communicating one's findings to a tutor.

Conceptions of Essays as Discourse

Germane though it is to an understanding of the study's findings, this resumé of the outward requirements of essays tells us virtually nothing of the kind of discourse in which an essay writer is expected to engage in undergraduate settings. Nor should we assume that what constitutes an "essay" is necessarily self-evident or culturally invariant. In France, for example, written examinations have traditionally favoured a Hegelian ideal of form which follows the pattern of thesis-antithesis-synthesis (Clignet, 1974, p. 335). And in China – at least until early in the present century – access to high-level administrative positions was dependent upon prowess in the Confucian "eight-legged" essay, in which the prescribed eight paragraphs each had to conform to a particular mode and sequence (Rowntree, 1977; cf. Hyam, 1974). Indeed, beyond cultural differences in writing conventions and the treatment of ideas, Kaplan (1966) has suggested, lie more deep-seated cultural variations in thought patterns. But the Anglo-Saxon tradition of the essay, if in certain respects culturally distinctive, is essentially tacit rather than explicit, as I suggested at the beginning of this paper. Those attempts which have been made to define the essay answer have not been signally successful. The result tends either towards circumlocution, as in Sim's definition of the essay:

> A relatively free and extended written response to a problematic situation or situations (question or questions), which intentionally or unintentionally reveals information regarding the structure, dynamics and functioning of the student's mental life as it has been modified by a particular set of learning experiences (1948, p. 15).

Or it tends towards an all-embracing blandness, as in Harris and McDougall's specification of the three universal characteristics of undergraduate essays:

> They are of a certain length (1000–2000 words); they require that evidence be presented to support the judgements given; and they are ultimately judged on the success with which the student is able to demonstrate his knowledge of the subject (1959, p. vii).

Acknowledging this tacit dimension to the undergraduate essay is an important preliminary to exploring the central finding of my own study, which was that fundamental qualitative differences could be identified in the students' conceptions of what an essay was and what essay-writing involved. And although the various conceptions identified differed between as well as within each of the two subject groups, for the moment I want to consider them as constituting two cross-disciplinary groupings.

In the first group, essay-writing is conceived of as a question of *argument*, coherently presented and well-substantiated (in history), or (in psychology) as a matter of *cogency*, where substantive discussion is rooted in a solid core of empirical findings. The two conceptions in this group are essentially *interpretive* in character, since they share a concern with the disciplined pursuit of meaning. In essay-writing, one attempts to make sense of a problem or issue in a way which is individually distinctive yet conforms to an accepted mode of discourse. For a fuller grasp of the nature of these conceptions, however, it is necessary to dissect them into three interlocked facets or sub-components: a referential or *interpretive* sub-component: an *organisational* or structural sub-component; and an evidential or *data* sub-component.[2]

The interpretive sub-component is the superordinate one. It crystallises the sense one has made of a topic or problem in the form of the distinctive position or consolidated view one presents:

Will (history):
In an essay you really have to think about something, and then . . . well, just keep thinking about it as regards to all the reading and the evidence you're going to use. You have to follow a coherent argument, basically, and that's the only time you have to – like in a lecture you don't and in a seminar you just usually state your point of view on a certain point. You don't form an actual, coherent argument, along a broad theme, really.

Barry (psychology):
An essay develops your ability to grasp a particular aspect of a subject and sort of work out . . . look at the different arguments that people have put forward, and decide where your own feelings lie.

But this interpretive core which an essay must convey is underpinned by the two other sub-components. The organisational sub-component evinces a concern with essays as coherent, integrated wholes:

Vicky (psychology):
The points you're making or whatever you're trying to write about should follow logically, and clearly. You shouldn't jump about from one theme to another.

Edward (history):
Conclusions are just, you've really got to just tie everything together then, you've got all your strands of argument. But then conclusions, since I've come to univer-

---

2   See Svensson (1984) for a more general examination of the referential and organisational aspects of skill in learning.

sity they've become less important, I think, 'cos your argument should be developing all the way through the essay anyway.

The data sub-component expresses a concern that one's chosen interpretive stance can be firmly substantiated and therefore carries conviction:

Barry (psychology):
You need to know as many accounts as possible, and then sort of point out which you think are the useful ones, or which ones you can bring in to make the point that you intend to make in the end. I think they want you to have your own views, but as I say, you need to sort of know everybody else's first before you can make your own, for sure.

Kate (history):
I think what (the tutor's) looking for is a very clear argument, with quite a lot of facts to back it up. Because I have given essays for this course where the argument's been, sort of, fairly clear but I haven't really backed up – given enough detailed facts to support it. But I think – I hope – it was a fairly sort of tight argument in this essay. I don't think I got too sort of sloppy.

In marked contrast, the *non-interpretive* conceptions do not share an orientation towards meaning-making. Essay-writing is conceived of as the *arrangement* of facts and ideas (in history) or as *relevance* (in psychology), in the sense of an ordered arrangement of material pertaining to a topic or problem. Dissecting this pair of conceptions into their sub-components is again illuminating. As far as interpretation is concerned, there is a recognition that tutors "want your own opinions" (Ellie, psychology) or that for an essay topic you find particularly engaging you might "put more of your own views in" (Frank, history) but such thoughts and ideas have an almost incidental or value-added status. They are not drawn together and honed into a distinctive and explicit position or point of view, nor is the sub-component of interpretation superordinate, as it is in the two interpretive conceptions. Instead the sub-components of organisation and data are considered as if self-contained. Organisationally, therefore, introductions and conclusions tend to be viewed as conventions to be adhered to rather than structural devices through which essays can achieve a unity of theme and content:

Pattie (history):
I usually start off with a quote, and then finish with a quote. I find that's the easiest way to start it. But I think the worst thing is starting an essay. Once you get halfway through you're alright. The first few pages...

Holly (psychology):
Well, the summary I don't usually bother with too much. I just, sort of, put in all the facts I've put in the essay. That bit I never plan. I just write, I don't even write it out in rough. I just add it on to the end of the essay.

Similarly, the sub-component of data is treated quantitatively, as a matter of trying to cover one's sources exhaustively rather than selecting out material which could substantiate or refute a given interpretive stance:

Donna (history):
It just seems to me as though you're reading about a period, and trying to fit your reading into an essay. It just seems like a lot of facts more than anything else.

Ellie (psychology):
I tried to cover all the different areas. But one of the tutor's criticisms of the essay was why did I just keep going from one to the other. But I thought that's what I was supposed to do.

Disciplines as Frames for Discourse

Thus far I have sketched an anatomy of two groups of conceptions: an *interpretive* group, geared towards making meaning in a form which is ordered and offers substantiation and thus reflects accepted norms for academic discourse; and a *non-interpretive* group, in which this constructive orientation is lacking and in which interpretation, organisation and data are treated discretely, disjunctively and uncertainly. These fundamental differences in the two groups of conceptions are in fact evident not only in those parts of the interview accounts where students offer definitions of the activity of essay-writing, but also in students' accounts of essay-writing procedures and essay content, and are reflected too in the students' essays (see Hounsell, 1984b, 1984c for a much fuller treatment). However, to focus upon characteristics of conceptions common to the two subject groups is to risk obscuring those features which are discipline–specific, and I shall now move on to consider the latter.

That different subjects make different writing demands is self-evident – and not just to teachers and lecturers. As Britton et al. have noted, there is:

> . . . scarcely a secondary school pupil who cannot (or does not) say that what he writes for History is different from Science and different again from English; or alternatively that he has to be more personal here and more impersonal there; here he must use his imagination, there he mustn't and so on (1975, p. 138)

Undergraduate students are of course no less acutely sensitive to such differences, as is illustrated in two examples from the present study, where contrasts are made between expectations in English literature[3] and expectations in the students' major discipline:

Edward (history):
You've got to look for arguments, and prove yourself. I wrote an essay last term in English, and I didn't even use a textbook for it, I just used a text. And I got as good a mark for that, or as good comments, as I would for any history essay. And yet for

---

3   It is the perception that there are contrasting demands across disciplines which is my concern here. Whether, therefore, these two students' perceptions of the English literature essay are valid or not is an open question, and one which clearly would merit further investigation.

me it was just reading a text and putting my own opinion forward. Whereas in history, I mean, you've got to take other people's ideas, and mould them into your own argument.

Mike (psychology):
It's difficult to make a transition from writing a psychology essay to writing an English essay, because the things that are wanted are totally different ... So as I say, with a psychology essay, stick to facts first, and work round them, examine those facts and employ them in your essay. But in English, you do the reverse really; you can't really write with any facts, unless you refer to biographies where you can artistically interpret ... novels or poems, in relation to the artist's life. But with, uh, with that sort of essay you speculate more, it's more your own creative powers. This is not a creative essay ... to an extent that an English essay would be. So I would say be wary of waffling in a psychology essay, but I wouldn't actually say beware of citing too much fact in an English essay, but certainly that way definitely.

But we can also take the anatomy of conceptions further and examine the distinctive features of the two focal subjects of history and psychology. Table 1 summarises the core characteristics of the four conceptions, but since my concern here is with what constitutes valid academic discourse, I shall deal only with the two interpretive conceptions, exploring the two sub-components which differ – namely those of interpretation and data. These two sub-component differences are linked. While both conceptions acknowledge the importance of evidential substantiation, the cogency conception entails an interpretive stance which places relatively less emphasis on the distinctiveness of the position or point of view adopted and relatively more emphasis on the bedrock of the literature of the discipline in which the essay is grounded. Put another way, the history student has comparatively greater freedom both to articulate an argument which represents his or her own interpretation of an historical problem and to focus the essay discussion around evidence relevant to this argument. In short, the history student has more scope for interpretive manoeuvre. This difference can be regarded as bound up with the nature of the two disciplines, insofar as these two course settings are concerned.

The knowledge base of psychology derives from empirical enquiry and experimentation which proceed from particular principles, conceptual frameworks or theoretical perspectives. Thus although the literature of psychology offers an accumulated body of established knowledge, what we might call the "data" of psychology (in the sense of empirical findings) are for the most part inseparable from their conceptual or theoretical underpinnings. This means that in attempting to ground his or her essay firmly in the literature of the discipline the psychology student cannot make free play with empirical findings but must anchor the discussion in whatever conceptual frameworks gave rise to those findings. In presenting a "consolidated view", then, the student must do justice to the differing (and often competing and contrasting) schools of thought from which particular findings stem, and so come to a considered judgement.

Table 1. Interpretive and non-interpretive conceptions of essay-writing in history and psychology: global definitions and sub-components

1.1 Interpretive conceptions

	Psychology	History
Conception of essay-writing	"Cogency"	"Argument"
Global definition	Define an essay as a well-integrated and firmly grounded discussion of a topic or problem	Define an essay as the ordered presentation of an argument well-supported by evidence
Sub-Components		
a. Interpretation	A concern to present a consolidated view of a topic or problem within which your own ideas and thoughts have been integrated	A concern to take up a distinctive position or point of view on a problem or issue
b. Organisation	A concern with an essay as an integrated whole	A concern with an essay as an integrated whole
c. Data	A concern to build an essay upon a firm empirical foundation	A concern with data as evidence, substantiating or refuting a particular position or viewpoint

1.2 Non-interpretive conceptions

	Psychology	History
	"Relevance"	"Arrangement"
Global definition	Define an essay as an ordered discussion of relevant material on a topic or problem	Define an essay as an ordered presentation embracing facts and ideas
Sub-components		
a. Interpretation	An acknowledgement that essays entail the expression of any ideas, thoughts and opinions you may have	An acknowledgement that it is useful or important to express any ideas or opinions you may have
b. Organisation	A concern with organisation in the sense of linking parts to one another rather than structuring a whole	A concern with organisation as such, but without reference to the aptness of organising principles
c. Data	A concern with coverage of relevant material, where relevance is viewed as if it were an inherent characteristic of the psychological literature	A concern with data, but quantitatively, with no explicit criteria of selection

By contrast, the data which form the raw material for the history student's essay do not have that same conceptual anchorage. While historical knowledge consists in part of the accumulated interpretations by historians of issues, events and people, an equally substantial part of the data which the history student confronts has its source in historical records such as public documents, diaries, manuscripts, and so on. And while the accuracy or veracity of some historical records may sometimes be open to challenge, there is likely to be a large corpus of data on, say, the Tudor and Stuart sovereigns which can be accepted as reliable. To a significant degree, therefore, the raw material of history exists independently of the historian, in a way that the empirical data of psychology do not. And this means that the historian has comparatively greater scope to invest the available data with whatever interpretation might reasonably be held to be plausible.

Some Concluding Comments

In their central features, the two interpretive conceptions I have examined constitute what Raaheim (1981) broadly refers to as "academic discourse" – that is, they reflect and embody accepted norms for reasoned intellectual debate in higher education institutions. In the humanities and social sciences, the term "argument" is often lecturers' shorthand for "academic discourse", but the use of this term is problematic because it can refer either to the interpretive stance adopted (one's argument) or to the accepted mode of discourse within which an interpretive stance is presented and conveyed. "Argumentation" would therefore be a more precise if more ungainly term since it can stand for the wider meaning expressed in the interpretive conceptions: a distinctive interpretive stance presented in a form which aspires towards logical coherence and evidential substantiation.

The cultural roots of contemporary notions of abstract rational thought (of which academic discourse as articulated here would form part) have been traced by Olson (1976). Olson suggests that the "essayist technique" – his term for logically connected prose statements of an abstract kind from which "series of true implications could be drawn" (p. 196) – is of relatively recent origin, its emergence stimulated at least in part by the invention of printing. Apparently taking a similar view, Gouldner (1976) locates what he calls "modern rational discourse" both in enlightenment assumptions and revolutionary experience (p. 43) and in the introduction of the technology of printing, which has had the effect of decontextualising argument by enabling a writer to address a variety of possible audiences and to seek, in his or her writing, to anticipate their responses:

> Given the (relative) decontextualisations of printing, a writer cannot rely on the seen – but – unnoticed premisses, or seen and noticed reactions, of a face-to-face audience. The printed expression of arguments requires (and allows) a writer to

make *explicit* the chain of his assumptions and articulate the grounds of his arguments.

Thus, Gouldner argues, with the spread of printing "the structure of what is regarded as a convincing argument begins to assume a specific character" (p. 42), the linchpin of which is the ideal of *self-groundedness*:

> ... that the speaker be able to state articulately all the premises required by his argument, and ... show that his conclusions do not require premises other than those he has articulated.

Nonetheless, while there is an obvious affinity between academic discourse and what Gouldner calls "the grammar of rational discourse", the former, as we have seen, has features which are variant as well as universal. Specific disciplines – each with their own distinctive sets of concepts, approaches and analytical procedures – establish particular frames of reference which determine the precise form which academic discourse is to follow within their own domain.

From a student perspective, however, learning to engage in academic discourse entails not merely a sensitivity to particular disciplinary frames, but apprehending a mode of discourse which is essentially tacit in character. The implications of this for teaching-learning transactions are considerable, especially as far as feedback to students is concerned. In the present study (not untypically, I would contend), such feedback was predominantly in the form of general guidelines, circulated at the beginning of a course of study, or written comments on individual essays. As I have argued elsewhere (Hounsell, 1985), we should not assume that feedback of this kind has a meaning which is self-evident. The comments made are more than simply particularised observations; they *allude* to a tacit mode of written academic discourse, and may thus remain opaque to students whose premises for discourse are fundamentally at variance with those of their tutors. The consequences of this communicative gulf may therefore be that students fail to grasp what academic discourse entails and, beyond that, what is entailed in the socially even more important conventions of everyday rational discourse.

From a pedagogical standpoint, one important step forward would thus be to attempt to lay bare the anatomy of academic discourse, and so to explicate as fully as possible what is at present largely tacit. My own research can be seen as a possible contribution towards that goal, and many others can be found in recent research on student learning, which offers compelling evidence that many students do not perceive texts as purveying messages (Säljö, 1982) or "horizontalise" the hierarchical discourse structure of texts patterned in accordance with such widely used forms as "facts-conclusion" or "principle-examples" (Dahlgren, 1984; Marton & Säljö, 1984; Svensson, 1984; Wenestam, 1980). But although an anatomy of academic discourse can be considered a necessary condition for pedagogical advance, it is not a sufficient one. Firstly, an examination of the context of undergraduate essay-writing pinpoints other features which seem educationally dysfunctional. Some of those identified in the present study, such as a virtual absence of peer discussion and a predominantly formal traffic of comment from tutors to students, may be amenable to improvement. Others, such as the tensions between learning and studying, and learning and assessment, may be much more difficult to address given the obduracy of institutional custom and tradition. Secondly, whilst a more sharply differentiated anatomy of academic discourse may help to narrow the communicative gap between tutors and at least some of their students, the very process of grasping what is meant by academic discourse may represent the kind of personal intellectual revolution charted by Perry (1970), and so can perhaps be facilitated but not ensured. In fact, Polanyi himself has argued that tacit thinking depends on "indwelling", an empathetic interiorisation of particulars, for "it is not by looking at things, but by dwelling in them, that we understand their joint meaning" (Polanyi, 1967, p. 18).

Beyond dissection, then, the most formidable pedagogical challenge may be to create a learning environment in which indwelling in academic discourse is vigorously fostered.

Acknowledgements. I am particularly grateful to Professor Noel Entwistle for his helpful comments on an earlier draft of this chapter.

Appendix

Margot's Essay

How and Why Do Children's Drawings Differ from the Drawings of Adults?

How and why do childrens drawings differ from adults? This question can be split into two parts, what are the differences and similarities between them. Firstly the differences will be dealt with and some reasons for these differences. Secondly some general similarities will be given again with some kind of reasons for them.

Firstly, the level of physical skill between the child and the adult is very different. The child has to learn how to use the materials, he has to experiment with different materials available. The second difference is that a child will draw what he knows rather than what he sees. Luquet (1927) termed this stage the intellectual realism as opposed to visual realism in adults and older children. Freeman and Janison (1972) demonstrated this with the cup experiment. The crucial age being 8 years old.

A third difference is that children seem unable to grasp that principles can change and are not constant. Rather than alter a sequence they will omit a part. They see each unit in a drawing as having its own space and boundaries (Booth). Children have to learn that parts are inter-related not seperate before they are able to significantly alter their drawings. A fourth difference is that young children do not have a title for their picture. For them it is the process of drawing that is important not the end product. Older children and adults often name their drawings and they are recognisable by their title. Another difference is that children tend to use symbols to represent things and slightly alter these symbols to represent different objects. Adults tend to draw each object seperately as an individual item not a representation.

Moving onto the similarities between the two kinds of drawings. The drawings are an illustration of self-expression, a kind of visual thinking. Even though the drawings might differ they represent the same thing. Another similarity is that they also represent a means of communication between people. It is a way of expressing feelings to others. The production of drawings by adults and children demonstrates the skills of organisation and sequence. The levels of these skills increase with the child's development.

Other skills that are used are perception, feeling and making. A drawing is a combination of these put together. A childs perception develops before his pysical skill has developed. Another kind of similarity between the two types of drawing is the inclusion of some method of problem solving. They adapted their knowledge to try and include different information. In children it is not always successful but they do try.

I took the definition of an adult as in the 'western culture' as the reading seemed to indicate so. I would expect the drawings of adults in different cultures to differ according to their customs. e.g. the different method of writing would influence how people would draw, writing from right to left could make the drawings anti-clock-wise.

In concluding it can be said that there are differences and similarities between children and adult drawing. The differences diminish with the childs development. The similarities that I have mentioned are of a very general type. If they are taken individually and examined further I feel that then they become differences between the drawings rather than similarities.

Reading:

J.Goodnow. Children's Drawings.
H. Gardner. Developmental Psychology.

References

Bennett, R. (Ed.) (1974). *First class answers in history*. London: Weidenfeld & Nicholson.
Bereiter, C. (1980). Development in writing. In L. W. Gregg & E. R. Steinberg. *Cognitive processes in writing* (pp. 79–93). Hillsdale, N.J.: Lawrence Erlbaum.

Britton, J., Burgess, T., Martin, N., McLeod, A., & Rosen, H. (1975). *The develop-
   ment of writing abilities, 11–18*. London: Macmillan Education.
Clignet, R. (1974). *Liberty and equality in the educational process*. New York: Wi-
   ley.
Dahlgren, L. O. (1984). Outcomes of learning. In F. Marton, D. Hounsell, & N.
   Entwistle (Eds.), *The experience of learning* (pp. 19–35). Edinburgh: Scottish Ac-
   ademic Press.
Eco, U. (1985). *Reflections on 'The name of the rose'* London: Secker & Warburg.
Elton, G. R. (1969). *The practice of history*. London: Collins/Fontana.
Entwistle, N., & Ramsden, P. (1983). *Understanding student learning*. London: Croom
   Helm.
Flower, L. S., & Hayes, J. R. (1980). The dynamics of composing: making plans and
   juggling constraints. In L. W. Gregg & E. R. Steinberg (Eds.), *Cognitive processes
   in writing* (pp. 31–50). Hillsdale, N.J.: Lawrence Erlbaum.
Galbraith, D. (1980). The effect of conflicting goals on writing: A case study. *Visible
   Language, 14*, 364–375.
Gouldner, A. W. (1976). *The dialectic of ideology and technology*. London: Macmil-
   lan.
Gregg, L. W., & Steinberg, E. R. (Eds.). (1980). *Cognitive processes in writing*.
   Hillsdale, N.J.: Lawrence Erlbaum.
Harris, R. S., & McDougall, R. L. (1959). *The undergraduate essay*. Toronto: Toronto
   UP.
Hartley, J. (Ed.). (1980). *The psychology of written communication*. London: Kogan
   Page.
Hirsch, E. D. Jr. (1977). *The philosophy of composition*. Chicago: Chicago UP.
Hounsell, D. (1984a). Essay planning and essay writing. *Higher Education Research
   and Development, 3*, 13–31.
Hounsell, D. (1984b). Learning and essay-writing. In F. Marton, D. Hounsell, & N.
   Entwistle (Eds.), *The experience of learning* (pp. 103–123). Edinburgh: Scottish
   Academic Press.
Hounsell, D. (1984c). *Students' conceptions of essay-writing*. Unpublished doctoral
   thesis, University of Lancaster.
Hounsell, D. (1985, July). *Writing, learning and teaching: The quality of feedback*.
   Invited address, Society for Research into Higher Education and British Psycho-
   logical Society Cognitive Section international conference, "Cognitive Processes in
   Student Learning", University of Lancaster.
Hyam, R. (1974). The expansion of Europe: "Imperial", African and Asian history
   since c. 1800. In R. Bennett (Ed.), *First class answers in history* (pp. 135–165).
   London: Weidenfeld & Nicholson.
Kaplan, R. (1966). Cultural thought patterns in inter-cultural education. *Language
   Learning, 16*, 1–20.
Martin, N., D'Arcy, P., Newton, B., & Parker, R. (1976). *Writing and learning across
   the curriculum, 11–16*. London: Ward Lock Educational.
Marton, F. (1981). Phenomenography – describing conceptions of the world around us.
   Instructional Science, 10, 177–200.
Marton, F., & Säljö, R. (1984). Approaches to learning. In F. Marton, D. Hounsell, &
   N. Entwistle (Eds.), *The experience of learning* (pp. 36–55). Edinburgh: Scottish
   Academic Press.
Marton, F., Hounsell, D., & Entwistle, N., (Eds.). (1984). *The experience of learning*.
   Edinburgh: Scottish Academic Press.

Newkirk, T. (1982). Cognition and writing. *Harvard Educational Review*, *52*, 84–89.

Olson, D. (1976). Culture, technology and intellect. In L.B. Resnick (Ed.), *The nature of intelligence* (pp. 189–202). Hillsdale, N.J.: Lawrence Erlbaum.

Perry, W. G. (1970). *Forms of intellectual and ethical development in the college years: A scheme*. New York: Holt, Rinehart & Winston.

Polanyi, M. (1967). *The tacit dimension*. London: Routledge & Kegan Paul.

Raaheim, K. (1981). The first examinations at university. In K. Raaheim & J. Wankowski. *Helping students to learn at university*. Bergen: Sigma Forlag.

Ramsden, P. (1984). The context of learning. In F. Marton, D. Hounsell, & N. Entwistle (Eds.), *The experience of learning* (pp. 144–164). Edinburgh: Scottish Academic Press.

Rowntree, D. (1977). *Assessing students. How shall we know them?* London: Harper & Row.

Säljö, R. (1982). *Learning and understanding: A study of differences in constructing meaning from a text*. Göteborg: Acta Universitatis Gothoburgensis.

Säljö, R. (1984). Learning from reading. In F. Marton, D. Hounsell, & N. Entwistle (Eds.), *The experience of learning* (pp. 71–89). Edinburgh: Scottish Academic Press.

Sim, V. M. (1948). The essay examination as a projective technique *Educational and Psychological Measurement*, *8*, 15–31.

Spencer, E. (1983). *Writing matters across the curriculum*. Edinburgh: Scottish Council for Research in Education/Hodder & Stoughton.

Svensson, L. (1984). Skill in learning. In F. Marton, D. Hounsell, & N. Entwistle (Eds.), *The experience of learning* (pp. 56–70). Edinburgh: Scottish Academic Press.

Wason, P. (Ed.) (1980). Dynamics of writing. (Special issue). *Visible Language*, *14*(4).

Wenestam, C-G. (1980). *Qualitative differences in retention*. Göteborg: Acta Universitatis Gothoburgensis.

Whiteman, M. F. (Ed.). (1981). *Writing: The nature, development and teaching of written communication. Vol. I. Variation in writing: functional and linguistic cultural differences*. Hillsdale, N.J.: Lawrence Erlbaum.

CHAPTER 11

A Text and Its Meanings: Observations on How Readers Construe What Is Meant from What Is Written

Roger Säljö

In his fascinating book *Sound and Sentiment*, the musical anthropologist Steven Feld (1982) reports on a study of the ethnography of sound of the Kaluli of Papua New Guinea. In Kaluli culture and folklore, birds play a prominent role, and to understand the expressive modalities of weeping, song, poetics, Feld felt the need to devote considerable energy to delineating the existing folk ornithology. After being exposed to extensive questioning on bird taxonomy, one of Feld's informants obviously grew tired of the inquisitive Westerner. With the statement, "Listen – to you they are birds, to me they are voices in the forest" (p. 48), the informant expressed his disapproval of the premises of the questioning and, at the same time, effectively demonstrated the ethnocentric nature of the undertaking of establishing a bird taxonomy according to the customary reductionistic strategy of Western analytical thinking. What Feld learned was that what we regard as distinctive characteristics by means of which species can be identified, do not form the most significant basis for distinguishing birds in the Kaluli "version of the world", to borrow Goodman's (1978) suggestive terminology. Instead of a static, taxonomic classification of birds, the expression "to me they are voices in the forest" implies both that "Kaluli recognize and acknowledge their existence primarily through sound" and that "there are many ways to think about birds, depending on the context in which knowledge is activated and social needs that are served" (loc. cit.).

The fact that the Kaluli possess an efficient, descriptive language for discriminating among birds on sight, then, only hides the socially more profound knowledge, which derives its prestige from the fact that birds "are the spirit reflections . . . of deceased men and women" (ibid. p. 45). To "know" something significant about birds in the Kaluli sense, then, is to have access to a knowledge system about sound of utmost importance to their way of life, but which is based on a different principle of division. It was questions recognizing this alternative point of departure that the informant – we may hypothesize – felt was lacking.

What Feld's experiences illustrate is the pluralism of knowledge bases or "conceptions of reality" (Marton, 1981) in terms of which human thinking can develop. Neither of the two knowledge systems – the one taken for granted by the initially naive representative of Western social science and the one defended by the informant – is, of course, reducible to the other in the sense of being less precise or less efficient in a general sense. Rather, they form part of two different ways of rendering the world intelligible and they have evolved as aspects of the social needs and traditions of different societies. With respect to the phenomenon in focus in the present article, i.e. human learning, it thus seems probable that one can develop and become increasingly knowledgeable within both systems.

In scientific contexts, the notion that "different social realities provide different experiences" (Marková, 1982, p. 2) is normally, in my view, relatively easy to communicate when we are referring to comparisons across what can be readily recognized as differing cultural spheres, such as between European and non-European societies. An epistemologically similar perspective has been adopted in research on children in recent decades. The insights into children's thinking provided by the rapid expansion of developmental psychology have made it obvious that it is insensitive – if not pointless – to view children's thinking simply as inferior versions of adult cognition. Rather, it has been shown to be a much more rewarding strategy to refrain from imposing standards of correctness and logicality 'from without' before we have some grasp of possible inner consistencies that deviate from what we assume to be "natural" or "evident".

When stepping over to other, but neighbouring, academic specialities, such as learning, memory, intelligence and related areas devoted to the study of human cognition, the assumptions change and the world becomes – as it were – unidimensional. The questions posed are addressed and explained in terms of more or less, as differences in intellectual capacities accessible as variations in points achieved on standardized tests, latencies, etc.

There are deep scientific and extra-scientific motives why "main-stream" research into learning and related cognitive phenomena has taken this route. In fact, the very beginning of empirical research, in the modern sense, on cognition can be identified with the ingenious contribution by Hermann Ebbinghaus (1885/1964): the nonsense syllable. This invention, to which many cognitive theorists pay their respects as forming a platform for a rational study of man (cf. e.g. Hilgard, 1964), solved the easily recognized obstacle to studying learning and memory as such, namely the annoying problems of variations in previous knowledge that were beyond rigorous control. Thus, since Ebbinghaus "could not control language or the past history of the subject", Giorgi (1985, p. 53) argues, he "introduced material as devoid of meaning as possible". Phrased differently, a clear conception of what it meant to be scientific according to the *Zeitgeist* of the era, determined the aspects of human cognition that could be considered as forming a legitimate object of inquiry.

In this process, the research subject became an ahistorical and asocial being whose ways of interpreting the world were consciously disregarded. In the laboratory setting, s/he was condemned to temporary ignorance, stripped of the intellectual tools and "meaning-giving attributes" (Giorgi, 1985) in terms of language and previous experiences through which one normally makes sense of the world. In the laboratory version of thinking, knowledge was conceived of as a fixed entity and defined as discrete units of information. At this point, it is, however, important to remember that this view is not the sudden invention of behavioural scientists. As Douglas (1971) and Svensson (1979) have argued, there is a strong tradition in everyday thinking to construe knowledge in an absolutistic and reified way. Thus, it seems likely that cognitive research has inherited and maybe enforced this conception of knowledge rather than invented it.

In the perspective advocated here, everyday learning of the kind taking place in formal educational situations and elsewhere should be dealt with within a cultural conception of man. In complex societies, assumptions about homogeneity that allow cognitive phenomena to be explained as the unfolding of either biologically or socially given qualities of the mind are clearly untenable. *Acts of learning* take place in a social world, and are bound to differ in accordance with the needs and traditions of groups and with the technologies that dominate knowledge production and reproduction.

This view is, of course, in conflict with the basic tenets of established traditions. Indeed, with respect to the phenomenon of learning, the very starting point for theorizing and knowledge accumulation has been the belief that one has to overcome the problems of finding "an entirely satisfactory definition of learning" (Hilgard & Bower, 1966, p. 2). The problem of our failure to arrive at a clear-cut definition is, however, not necessarily to be conceived of as possible to solve through increasing the endeavours to achieve analytical clarity at a general, conceptual level. The reason for this is, as Neisser (1982, p. 12) remarks in his discussion of the development of cognitive research, that "unfortunately, it turned out that 'learning' in general does not exist". In establishing the object of inquiry in empirical research, it seems as if we have been deceived by the combined efforts of our using the everyday word 'learning' to refer to a very wide class of phenomena and the wish to establish abstract knowledge generalizable to all contexts and situations. The limitations of this approach are obvious. There is a critical trade-off between generality and specificity in the sense that the tendency to strive for abstract formulations about phenomena may lead to a result where we are "holding a fistful of propositions that are largely or exclusively banal" (Hudson, 1978, p. 36). Even restricting the object of inquiry to encompass human learning and thinking, "we will grow old learning little and deserving to do so" if we "allow our analytic assumptions to limit us to what is true of whole populations of people, to people irrespective of their contexts, to what is true about a person in general" (loc. cit.).

Learning from Reading

In modern, complex societies, the understanding of learning processes is intimately related to the understanding of the cognitive consequences of the domination of the written word as a means of instruction and knowledge production. The cultural and social consequences of literacy have received growing attention among researchers in different fields. According to strong statements, the differences between "Western" knowledge systems (and thinking) and other traditions have been claimed to be "reducible to contrasts between deeply interiorized literacy and more or less residually oral states of consciousness" (Ong, 1982, p. 29). Avoiding the intricacies of the issues surrounding the debate of the 'great divide', it is obvious that even within literate societies, cultural groups differ with respect to the role which communication through writing and reading plays in daily life (cf. e.g. Heath, 1983). Indeed, even in "fully literate" societies, written discourse seems to be such a marginal aspect of life to certain groups that the task of learning to read for some children starts from very vague notions of the usefulness and communicative functions of written text. This problem of children not realizing that written and spoken language constitute alternative means of communication, and that, consequently, written words have meanings that are translatable into spoken language, was discovered by the Swedish primary school teacher Ulrika Leimar (1974; cf. Edfeldt, 1982). She used this insight to design a much-debated method of learning to read based on the notion that from the very start of the process of learning to read, this parallel between the spoken (and familiar) way of using language and the written (and unfamiliar) technique for communicating should be emphasized. The means for achieving this end was to start learning to read on the basis of children's everyday language and, at the same time, always preserve the genuinely communicative function of written text, even in the process of acquiring the ability to read (cf. also Francis, 1982, p. 3, in-depth analysis of learning to read and children's "not grasping that script is a medium of communication").

This realization that – as Olson (1977) put it – the written code is not a mother tongue, highlights the problems for educational systems that have accepted the definition of knowledge as "prose statements known to be true" (Olson, 1977, p. 86). The heavy reliance on written language has led to an emphasis on abstract and formal knowledge in schooling. Although the gap between "academic" and "practical", "everyday" knowledge, or whatever term is used, has been discussed in recent years, this problem is by no means new. Indeed, "an inability to accept learned ideas and techniques as having much to do with ongoing real life" (Calhoun, 1973, p. 130) seems from the beginning to have characterized formal and decontextualised learning processes of the kind characteristic of formal schooling. As Calhoun observes in his analyses of protocols and reports on teaching in American schools in the nineteenth century, this gap between everyday life and schooling could be

observed most clearly in "reading, where lack of expression in oral performance indicated children's refusal to adopt even the fiction of assimilating
material to their own personalities" (loc. cit.). This compartmentalization of
the mind and the widespread acceptance of the separation between what
constitutes valid knowledge in everyday life on the one hand and in schools on
the other is understandable only against the background of the social prestige
associated with the mastery of the literate type of knowledge.

The view of associating knowledge with "prose statements known to be
true", which Olson ascribes to education, has a wide underpinning and can, in
fact, also be said to characterize research into 'discourse processing' and
related phenomena. Most of the results in these areas are formulated in terms
of text processing models (e.g. Meyer, 1975; Kintsch, 1974; cf. Kintsch & van
Dijk, 1983) and provide analyses of texts per se in terms of propositions and
relationships between these. Understanding of written documents is then
conceived of as a result of the individual processing the text at different levels
of generality. In this sense, "prose analysis procedures reduce the surface form
of a prose passage into an ordered list of semantic elements . . . which represents the author's meaning" (Bieger & Dunn, 1984, p. 258). These elements
are then assumed to be "processed" by individuals in order to ascertain
"meaning". In spite of frequent use of variables referring to characteristics of
individuals and groups, and, in recent years, also to contextual factors, the
underlying image of man is firmly within the philosophical tenets of Cartesian
dualism. In defining one's object of inquiry as "the mental machinery" which,
when appropriately applied, sees to it that the reader "ends up with something
in his mind which captures the gist of what has been written" (Sanford &
Garrod, 1981, p. 3), and in ascribing meanings to texts without a reading
subject, understanding is conceived as essentially passive and as resulting from
the application of algorithmic procedures in an ordered and stepwise fashion.

The knowledge interest underlying the research from which the following
observations derive is one of focusing on the reader's (or learner's) contribution to the act of decoding written text. Essential issues concerning intersubjectivity, communicative success and failure are not restricted to research into
oral communication, but can also be raised – we would argue – with respect to
how people read (and learn from reading). Conceiving reading and learning
from written discourse as *acts* and focusing for the moment on how people
construe meaning without necessarily immediately judging what is said according to prespecified criteria of correctness, we may – if we are lucky – begin
to approach an understanding of distinctive features of how people make sense
of what they read.

The observations to be reported here concern how people interpret an
expository text of the kind which is so common in educational contexts. The
general idea is to illustrate the diverse ways in which a text can be made
meaningful. More specifically, the intention is to highlight the difficulties even
highly literate and educated readers have in identifying relationships between

general statements (abstract scientific principles) and concrete illustrations of these general formulations. The research reported here is to be understood as taking place in what Reichenbach (1932) referred to as the 'context of discovery' (rather than 'verification') (cf. Glaser & Strauss, 1967, for an elaboration of this distinction).

The Study

As said, the observations to be reported derive from a study of how "fully literate" people read and interpret an expository text. Various aspects of the outcomes of this study have been reported elsewhere (see e.g. Säljö, 1982, 1984). The study was of a "naturalistic" as opposed to "natural" kind in the sense that the act of reading was not the result of a voluntary and self-induced decision to engage in that particular activity, but rather took place as part of an empirical investigation which the participants knew had something to do with 'how people read scientific texts'.

The text (3757 words in length) was taken from an introductory reader in psychology intended to be used in the Swedish upper secondary school (i.e. when students are 16–19 years of age). It contained a presentation of the fundamentals of the psychology of learning and was divided into three sections dealing with classical conditioning, instrumental conditioning and verbal learning, respectively. Participants varied widely with respect to their age (from 15 years up to over 73) and formal education. However, the observations reported below are limited to three distinctive groups comprising 15 participants each. The first group consisted of students, 16 years of age, who had just finished the Swedish comprehensive school. The second group contained individuals who were 19 years of age, and who had just finished the Swedish upper secondary school (gymnasium). The third group, finally, was slightly more heterogeneous with respect to the educational background of its members. It consisted of students, aged 22–23, with at least two years of successful academic studies behind them (although none of them had studied any of the behavioural sciences). The data source from which the following observations derive were the recalls of the text that the participants were requested to give shortly after reading the text.

Construing Meaning from Written Discourse:
Some Observations

Texts, even though they are often referred to as an externalized memory, do not store knowledge. "Unless a human mind knows the code for interpreting writing", as Ong (1981, p. 20) points out, "letters on a page are no more knowledge than random scratchings would be". Knowing the code in this context cannot be equated with being able to decipher the strings of letters that appear on the page to establish the "literal meaning", but has to be understood as the interaction between the form of knowledge characteristic of expository prose, the conception of the particular aspect of reality that the person holds, and the "premises for communication" (Rommetveit, 1974) which the actor assumes to be valid for the situation which s/he is in. Incidentally, a decisive difference between individuals in this study, causing clearly different 'variants of reading' the text could be related to whether they interpreted the reading situation as taking place in a school context or not (cf. Säljö, 1982).

The observations to be reported here will focus on illustrating how the participants construed certain parts of the text. In other words, the "unit of analysis", to use the language of Vygotsky (1962), is *meaning* and the ways in which readers reconstrue what is meant from what is written. By means of a microanalysis of how readers make sense of passages of written text, we shall attempt to illustrate that "the activity of 'getting meaning'" is "problematic practice, however transparent and natural it may seem" (Morley, 1983, p. 107).

Example 1

The first illustration of 'variants of reading' concerns what was said in the text about the *difference between classical and instrumental conditioning*. Apart from the fact that this difference can be derived from the descriptions of the various procedures used to study these two forms of learning (presented through brief accounts of the approaches used by Pavlov and Skinner, re-spectively, and some additional examples), it was specifically touched upon in the following passage in the text.

> Through the principles of classical conditioning, one can explain certain types of changes in behaviour, especially how specific responses can be elicited by other stimuli than those initially having this consequence. Through conditioning one can, at least in theory, make the organism react in specific ways as responses to almost any kind of stimuli. The limitation lies in the fact that classical conditioning is only possible to use when we are dealing with responses of a reflex character, i.e. when there exist unconditioned stimuli (for example, food – salivation).

> Instrumental Conditioning

> The principles, which have been most thoroughly studied by the American psy-chologist B. F. Skinner, have to do with the issue of how the probability that a response of any kind will be repeated is affected by the consequences of this response (i.e. how what follows a response affects the chances of it being repeated). Thus, instrumental conditioning has to do with the responses that are controlled by the will, and of which there are more kinds than the reflex reactions that are studied in classical conditioning.

Example 1   185

As can be seen, a central aspect of what the author wants to communicate, or "make known" (Rommetveit, 1974), is that the two forms of conditioning apply to different types of reactions, and that the principles of instrumental conditioning apply to a wider range of more advanced behaviours. In scrutinizing how participants retold this passage, it becomes clear that many of them interpreted this distinction between two forms of conditioning along the lines suggested by the author. The following is an excerpt from one participant in the group of university students.

> The classical conditioning is the simplest type of learning, learning that is based on things that can be learned on the basis of reflexes, like this experiment here, salivation ... [goes on describing conditioning through one of the examples in the text] ... there were some different kinds, but it's mostly on this reflex type of thing ... Then we have Skinner. He has a different ..., a bit more advanced form of learning. They took an example, for instance, with a rat. Here they showed how one ... [continues by describing the mechanisms of instrumental conditioning by using of an example].

This student, then, construes the difference between the two forms of conditioning as having to do with different kinds of responses that, for analytical purposes, can be distinguished on the basis of how complex or 'advanced' they are. The second person, belonging to the group of those students who just had finished comprehensive school, used more directly the distinction between reflex responses and responses controlled by the will that is emphasized by the author when accounting for the difference between the two forms of conditioning.

> [Describes initial example of conditioning in the text] ... That was classical conditioning. And then there was a story about a researcher, a Russian researcher who had been working on this quite a lot ... And then there was instrumental conditioning, and that had to do with this here that one should not create ... The classical conditioning had to do with reflexes and such, but the instrumental had to do with, sort of, things that were controlled by the will ... [goes on to give an account of the principles of instrumental conditioning by using example from text] ...

As we have already pointed out, a complex text of the kind used here is semantically open and can be interpreted in numerous ways. However, viewed in the perspective of presenting a certain distinction between, in this case, two types of conditioning, there are certain restrictions with respect to which interpretations maintain critical aspects of the meaning suggested in the text. Our point is, then, that one can not argue that there is one literal or most basic meaning in expository texts of this kind. At the same time, it is obvious that as we look at other recalls, the interpretations of the nature of the difference between the two forms of conditioning begin to take on a different meaning, and they also begin to deviate from what is suggested in the text.

In the empirical material, i.e. in the recalls, one way of dealing with this topic was simply to state that there were two types of conditioning but to leave out any attempts at specifying what constituted the difference. Other 'variants of reading', however, illustrate how the general point of there being two types of conditioning has been grasped, but at the same time that *the meaning of this distinction becomes different from the one suggested in the text*. The following excerpt begins after the participant had given an account of the initial example in the text at some length.

> In other words, there are, sort of, different kinds of conditioning. Besides classical conditioning there ... there is instrumental conditioning and ... I don't know. I saw it as a form of ... I would translate it into methods where you use ... well, quite simply unpleasant and pleasant things to ... Like this study where they let a dog do something, learn something. And if they do, they either get praise or an unpleasant feeling through punishment ...

As can be seen, the distinction between two types of conditioning is recognized but is given a different meaning compared to the one used by the author. What distinguishes the two types, according to this participant, is whether the consequences are positive or negative. In looking at the text, it is not difficult to see how this, in certain respects creative, reinterpretation of the meaning of the differences between the two forms of conditioning has arisen. Some of the examples used to convey the meaning of the distinction illustrate consequences that are positive for the organism while some are negative. However, this particular difference, although present in the text and its examples, is not the one in terms of which the two forms of conditioning are distinguished in the text. Yet another way of making sense of the distinction is given by the following participant.

> [Gives account of initial example of conditioning in text illustrating how such procedures appear in a torture situation in a prison] ... These two first passages, classical and instrumental ... Classical is, sort of, if you look at it in broader terms ... it is about how you can sort of destroy a human being by physical terror or yes, well ... Yes, that's about it. The second one, it has to do with ... the instrumental it has to do with the hearing, sort of. It was an experiment ... [goes on to describe a Pavlovian experiment with a dog that is conditioned to salivate at the sound of a bell].

Again, we see how the reader gives meaning to the distinction between the two forms of conditioning in a way that is different from the one used by the author. Also, in this case, it is understandable how it is possible to construe the meaning as having to do with unpleasant experiences on the one hand and with hearing on the other. One extensive example in the text illustrated conditioning in the context of physical pain caused by torture with electricity, and in Pavlov's experiment, hearing is clearly a critical aspect, although it is not the association between sounds/hearing and subsequent responses that is the characteristic feature that defines the phenomenon of conditioning.

In sum, what this brief account illustrates is how the readers interpret what is said about different types of conditioning as meaningful, and even interesting, and yet construe it quite differently. What appears critical for developing our understanding of how people construe meaning from what they

Example 1   187

read is the issue of how people bridge the gap between abstract formulations and terms (such as "conditioning"), and the concrete instances of these that are used in the text as means of conveying meaning. The contextual specification of meaning made by the author, with respect to what distinguishes the two forms of conditioning, is clearly not adopted by all, in spite of it in some sense being there 'in the text'. What seems to pose problems, even for these groups of advanced readers, is the abstract nature of the distinction outlined in the text. A common feature in the recalls that gives a different meaning to this distinction is that subjects base their abstraction on a number of more concrete and immediate aspects of the illustrations. Some of these new, abstract formulations of what constitutes the difference between the types of conditioning were, as has been said, quite creative. Yet, learning from text – in the sense of changing one's conceptions of reality – relies on the establishment of a "commonality of meaning" (Rommetveit, 1974), and if it is to build on the *"sprachlich verallgemeinerte Erfahrungen der Gesellschaft"* ("linguistically generalized experiences of society") (Fichtner, 1980), it also requires a subordination on the part of the reader to the contextual combination of "parts" and "wholes" that the text suggests. However, we will comment on this below after yet another illustration of similar differences in construing meaning.

Among the group of 45 participants, 41 include in their recalls comments on the nature of the distinction between the two forms of conditioning. The significant issue here is to what extent the distinction employed by participants parallels the one presented in the text (i.e. considering classical conditioning as applying to a limited class of reactions of a reflex character and instrumental conditioning to a wider class of responses that are controlled by the will). In the analysis, 15 of these 41 participants were judged as basing their distinction between the two forms of conditioning on the same criteria as those used by the author.[1] A consequence of this is that nearly all of these particular groups of readers/learners, 91%, noticed the difference between the two forms of conditioning, but that a clear majority construed this difference in terms of a different set of features, or did not specify the difference. Looking at the

---

1   The methodological procedure employed here (as well as in the case of Example 2 below) consisted of using judgement instructions in two steps. First, a co-judge read through all the transcribed recalls to see whether this (and several other) issue(s) was commented on. Secondly, following the specification of the nature of the distinction between the two forms of conditioning, the co-judge, with the assistance of judgement instructions, had to judge whether the participant based his distinction on the one suggested in the text (i.e. the difference between the two forms of conditioning was construed in terms of the difference between reflex behaviour and behaviour that is controlled by the will), or if another meaning was ascribed to this difference. With respect to the second issue, which is the one of interest us here, the two judges agreed in more than 80% of the cases on the two examples used in this study. This, then, is to be seen as an indication that the differences which, according to the present text, characterized the recalls could be communicated.

Table 1. Recall of passage about differences between classical and instrumental conditioning (number of participants)

		Level of formal education		
		Low	Intermediate	High
Distinction construed	As applicable to reflex behaviour vs. behaviour controlled by the will	1	7	7
	On the basis of other features of description given in text	10	8	8

distribution over the three educational groups, we see from Table 1 that there is a clear tendency for the group with the lowest level of formal education to base the distinction on the more concrete aspects of the account. Only one of the 11 participants in this group was judged to base her distinction on the division between reflex behaviour and behaviour controlled by the will. As can be seen, in the two groups with an average and a high level of formal education, respectively, almost half of the participants were judged as identifying the distinction between the two forms of conditioning along the lines suggested in the text. The lesson to be learned from this specific example is thus that the participants notice the distinction, but that they render it meaningful in clearly different ways.

Example 2

As an introduction to a presentation of research findings on the topic of verbal learning, the following passage appeared in the text.

Learning Through Language

This "normal" type of learning has strangely enough been given rather little attention in research up to now. Instead, there has been a tendency to follow the ideas presented in the nineteenth century by the German psychologist Ebbinghaus. Ebbinghaus wanted to study learning in its "pure" form, i.e. he attempted to eliminate the significance of previous knowledge and experience that people have. As a consequence, he used nonsense syllables and in his studies people would have to learn e.g. to respond with *buf* when the experimenter showed them *lox*, and to say *kas* when *fim* was presented. Learning was thus understood as the establishing of connections between things appearing together in time.

Furthermore it can be pointed out that to the extent that one succeeds in elimi-

Example 2   189

nating the role of previous knowledge, one also loses what is most characteristic for everyday learning, namely that we interpret new experiences in terms of earlier ones and relate new information to previously acquired knowledge.

Clearly, this passage is also complex enough to be given many possible interpretations, and, since a written document lives its life independently of its originator, we cannot hope to establish any 'true' meaning. However, it is obvious that the author argues that the approach of Ebbinghaus is a technique for doing away with the confounding influences of previous knowledge. It is also claimed that this approach, in certain respects, is artificial since it deprives human learning of its most typical feature, namely that new knowledge is always based on what we previously know. To achieve the aim of illustrating how the role of previous experiences can be eliminated in research, the learning materials of such studies are exemplified in the text.

In this case, 22 of the 45 participants, evenly distributed over the three groups, comment on this passage in their recalls. Again, there are obvious differences in the contextual determination of what is meant. Consider first this excerpt from the recalls of one of the university students.

> This final bit here, that was about learning through language. And obviously they didn't start doing research on that until the end of the nineteenth century. There was a man by the name of Ebbinghaus who started doing this kind of thing. And he sort of understood that learning through language ... it depends very much on what you've learned before ... your previous knowledge and such. So he tried to get rid of such factors by having his research subjects work with completely meaningless syllables ...

The point about introducing a certain learning material to balance the influence of previous knowledge is preserved in the recall, and it is also obvious that it has been understood that this procedure was adopted in scientific studies of learning. However, in looking at the total group of recalls of this passage, other ways of interpreting what is said can be discerned. In the following excerpt, another, and quite common, version of what was said in this passage emerges.

> After this there is something about ... learning via language, where they mention a German psychologist, Ebbinghaus or something like that ... He tried to say that ... one should not learn new things by associating to previous knowledge. They start with ... He would take new letters, completely different letters in certain combinations, for instance, he'd write *bus*, then he'd say it should be *tlx* instead, and so one should learn everything from the beginning, whatever is the ... But this is questioned somewhat here in the text, if this really is the right way to learn things ...

This interpretation of the passage as dealing with how *one should learn* instead of *how one does research into learning* was very common in the group as a whole. This, in turn, exemplifies a tendency that could be noted in many instances in this study, namely to extract 'recipe knowledge' (Berger & Luckmann, 1966), i.e. knowledge that relates to a pragmatic issue (how one should learn) instead of interpreting what was said as referring to more abstract, and philosophical, issues (how one designs scientific studies on learning).

A final quotation will be given to illustrate yet another way of interpreting this passage that points in a slightly different direction. The excerpt is taken from a member of the group of participants who had just finished upper secondary school.

> And then it was about this learning of letters, this German, Ebbinghaus. And he wanted to show from the beginning that . . . a person can really learn . . . I mean, even if it doesn't have any meaning to him, he can learn, for example, combinations of letters that don't have any meaning whatsoever. . . .

According to this version, the passage is about Ebbinghaus wanting to prove that people *can* learn meaningless things. This is, of course, not what Ebbinghaus wanted to do, or what the author was trying to say that Ebbinghaus wanted to prove. Yet it is a perfectly reasonable way of making sense of what one has read if we conceive of learning as a process of construing meaning. The person in question uses the information in the text, and she construes a coherent 'whole', although one that in critical respects deviates from the one suggested in the text.

Looking at the total group of participants, it is also evident in this case that the tendency to follow the reasoning suggested in the text is not randomly distributed over the three groups, as can be seen from Table 2. As can be seen, the tendency to interpret the use of nonsense syllables as a means of reducing the influence of previous experiences, when studying the phenomenon of learning, becomes clearer the higher the level of formal education of the reader. This means that the tendency to identify the particular relationship between the "whole" (the phenomenon of learning) and the "part" (the use of nonsense syllables) that was suggested in the text, and thus the tendency to subordinate one's interpretation to the one outlined in the text, becomes clearer the higher the level of formal education of the participant. At one level, this can be seen as an indication of the existence of different "interpretative

Table 2. Recall of passage about use of nonsense syllables in research into human learning (number of participants)

	Level of formal education		
	Low	Intermediate	High
Technique of using nonsense syllables interpreted as a method for reducing influence of previous experiences when studying learning	2	4	5
Other interpretation of use of nonsense syllables	5	4	2

communities" containing different explicit and implicit rules as to how written texts should be interpreted in order to arrive at coherent messages. At the same time, it is obvious that half the group of participants who include this passage in their recalls, construe a slightly different configuration of "wholes" and "parts" that gives a different sense to the use of nonsense syllables in this specific context.

Meaning in Context

The basic point of these limited empirical observations has been to illustrate some of the subtle but, in our view, significant differences in how people construe meaning from a text that deals with a complex phenomenon. Learning from a written text is thus not to be equated with the memorization of discrete units of information, nor can the activity of extracting meaning from written discourse be understood as an algorithmic process. In this perspective, it is doubtful if "learning (from linguistic inputs or otherwise) can be analysed conceptually into a series of stages during which particular mechanisms perform some elementary operation", or if a "likely hypothesis about comprehension is that the sensory input (words) is first organised into STM into surface constituents, then underlying propositions are extracted, then referents are looked up, then semantic interpretation of the sentence occurs" (Bower & Cirilo, 1985, p. 73 and 81) prove to be reasonable points of departure for understanding how readers/learners extract meaning from what they read, or how they manage to relate what they read to what they previously assumed to be true about that aspect of reality that they are attending to.

What we have attempted to exemplify is how the "effort after meaning" seems to be a fundamental aspect in learning of the kind studied here. The reader/learner is to be conceived of as making a genuinely semiotic contribution in his/her encounter with the text in the sense of actively suggesting ways of interpreting what is written that make sense. The epistemological perspective suitable for the study of such processes of communication and cognitive growth seems, therefore, to be more in line with the one suggested by Goodman (1978, p. 96) when stating; "never mind mind, essence is not essential, and matter doesn't matter", and consequently, "we do better to focus on versions rather than worlds". Learning problems of the kind encountered in real life are thus not necessarily to be conceived of as capacity problems; they seem to be better construed as communication difficulties that have to do with the diversification of knowledge and the rapid growth in ways of understanding and explaining the world.

The "effort after meaning" did not, in our case, result in homogeneous interpretations of the text, but rather in distinctive variations in terms of the messages that were identified. In particular, what caused variation was the nature of the relationship between general and abstract statements (in this case, about phenomena such as conditioning and verbal learning) and the specific illustrations used in the text to give meaning to these general statements. At one level, it is obvious that the readers in general had no difficulties in comprehending, for example, how the various experiments on conditioning were designed. Viewed in isolation, the logic of this experimentation was obviously quite accessible. However, the communicative variations seem to arise when abstract aspects of these stories are singled out as a basis for distinguishing different forms of learning. At this level of combining descriptions of certain, rather concrete events with an abstract concept, variations in meaning become more obvious. It is also in this context that we found that the particular "variants of reading" imposed by the participants with a high level of formal eduction were more sensitive to the framework suggested in the text and the relationships between "parts" and "wholes" specified. In this case, this means that one relies on the more exclusive linguistic context used in the text for interpreting the phenomena described (classical conditioning and verbal learning) and at the same time refrains from imposing direct connections with everyday life that create alternative contexts for these phenomena and the examples used to illustrate them.

Recently, the issues addressed here have been discussed by Marton (1984) in terms of the distinction between organizational and referential meaning. As pointed out by Marton, the critical issue with respect to the meaning that people extract when learning from reading seems to be related to the problem of how the reader chooses to organize the relationship between "parts" and "wholes" in the text, or to use the language of Gestalt psychology, what figure-ground relationships are perceived. As our few examples have shown, it is possible to construe different figure-ground relationships and still conceive what one has read as a meaningful and coherent whole. This perspective may be the obvious one for the researcher engaged in studies of how other forms of written discourse, e.g. literature, is understood. When reading expository text, presenting "cultural sediments" in the form of concepts and ways of construing the world that are accepted as valid knowledge, and that often contain considerable intellectual investments from earlier generations, the situation becomes slightly different. In this sense, pedagogical processes are restricted by the nature and meaning of the conceptual knowledge accumulated in society. This, of course, is true of not only the literate type of knowledge, but applies to other forms as well. However, the problems of mediating knowledge in the form of abstract categories that do not rely on direct experience in social encounters, but which have been derived as a consequence of the availability of the reflective capacities of the "technology of the intellect" (Olson, 1977), become much more apparent in cultures which produce and communicate knowledge through writing. As Heath (1983) puts it in her in-depth analysis of what distinguishes "literacy events" and reading practices in various communities, "academic success . . . depends on becoming a contextualist who can predict and maneuver the scenes and situations by understanding the relatedness of parts to the outcome or the identity of the whole"

(p. 352). The activity of extracting meaning when reading relies on the special skill that involves focusing on identifying a specific kind of coherent wholes, the nature of which are determined by the abstract type of knowledge characteristic of a literate tradition. The extension of the knowledge base to encompass such "categorical thinking" that is neither organically related to everyday experience, nor confirmed in more than a specific class of communicative situations where the literate, academic type of knowledge is the valid currency, separates private knowledge from those forms that have their background in "the shared experience of society" (Luria, 1976). The bridging of such gaps between forms of knowledge valid in lay perspectives on the one hand and valid within the various "provinces of meaning" (Berger Luckman, 1966) in which knowledge is accumulating at a rapid pace on the other, is a growing problem in communication in educational contexts in complex societies. An important contribution of a genuinely social interpretation of learning would perhaps be to communicate this conception of the dilemma.

Acknowledgement. The research reported here has been financed by the Swedish Council for Research in the Humanities and Social Sciences.

References

Berger, P., & Luckmann, T. (1966). *The social construction of reality*. New York: Anchor.

Bieger, G. R., & Dunn, B. R. (1984). A comparison of the sensitivity of two prose analysis models to developmental differences in free recall of text. *Discourse Processes, 7,* 257–274.

Bower, G., & Cirilo, R. (1985). Cognitive psychology and text processing. In T. A. van Dijk (Ed.), *Handbook of discourse analysis* (Vol. 1) (pp. 71–105). London: Academic Press.

Calhoun, D. (1973). *The intelligence of a people*. Princeton N. J.: Princeton University Press.

Douglas, J. (1971). *Understanding everyday life*. London: Routledge & Kegan Paul.

Ebbinghaus, H. (1964). *Memory*. (H. A. Ruger & C. E. Bussenius, Trans.) New York: Dover. (Original work published 1885)

Edfeldt, Å. (1982). *Läsprocessen* [The process of reading]. Stockholm: Liber.

Feld, S. (1982). *Sound and sentiment*. Philadelphia: University of Pennsylvania Press.

Fichtner, B. (1980). *Lerninhalte in Bildungstheorie und Unterrichtsprozess* [Contents of learning in educational theory and teaching process]. Cologne: Pahl-Rugenstein.

Francis, M. (1982). *Learning to read*. London: Allen & Unwin.

Giorgi, A. (1985). The phenomenological pshychology of learning and the verbal learning tradition. In A. Giorgi (Ed.), *Phenomenology and psychological research*. Pittsburgh: Duquesne University Press.

Glaser, B. G., & Strauss, A. L. (1967). *The discovery of grounded theory. Strategies for qualitative research*. New York: Aldine.

Goodman, N. (1978). *Ways of worldmaking*. Hassocks, Sussex: The Harvester Press.

Heath, S. B. (1983). *Ways with words*. Cambridge: Cambridge University Press.

Hilgard, E. (1964). Introduction. In H. Ebbinghaus *Memory*. New York: Dover.

Hilgard, E. R., & Bower, G. H. (1966). *Theories of learning*. New Jersey: Prentice-Hall.

Hudson, L. (1978). *Human beings*. London: Triad Press.

Kintsch, W. (1974). *The representation of meaning in memory*. Hillsdale, N.J.: Erlbaum.

Kintsch, W., & van Dijk, T. A. (1983). *Strategies of discourse comprehension*. New York: Academic Press.

Leimar, U. (1974). *Läsning på talets grund* [Reading on the basis of speech]. Lund: Gleerups.

Luria, A. R. (1976). *Cognitive development. Its cultural and social foundations*. Cambridge, Mass.: Harvard University Press.

Marková, I. (1982). *Paradigms, thought, and language*. Chichester: Wiley.

Marton, F. (1981). Phenomenography – Describing conceptions of the world around us. *Instructional Science, 10*, 177–200.

Marton, F. (1984, September). *Exploring the means through which learners arrive at differing meanings*. Paper presented at the XXIIIrd International Congress of Psychology, Acapulco, Mexico.

Meyer, B. (1975). *The organization of prose and its effects on recall*. Amsterdam: North-Holland.

Morley, D. (1983). Cultural transformations: The politics of resistance. In H. Davis & P. Walton (Eds.), *Language, image, media*. Oxford: Blackwell.

Neisser, U. (1982). Memory: What are the important questions? In U. Neisser (Ed.), *Memory observed* (pp. 3–19). San Francisco: Freeman.

Olson, D. (1977). The languages of instruction: On the literate bias of schooling. In R. C. Anderson, R. J. Spiro, & W. E. Montague (Eds.), *Schooling and the acquistion of knowledge* (pp. 65–89). Hillsdale, N. J.: Erlbaum.

Ong, W. J. (1981). Oral remembering and narrative structures. In D. Tannen (Ed.), *Analyzing discourse: Text and talk* (pp. 12–24). Washington: Georgetown University Press.

Ong, W. J. (1982). *Orality and literacy. The technologizing of the word*. London: Methuen.

Reichenbach, H. (1932). *Experience and prediction*. Chicago: University of Chicago Press.

Rommetveit, R. (1974). *On message structure*. London: Wiley.

Säljö, R. (1982). *Learning and understanding*. Göteborg: Acta Universitatis Gothoburgensis.

Säljö, R. (1984). Learning from reading. In F. Marton, D. Hounsell, & N. Entwistle (Eds.), *The experience of learning* (pp. 71–89). Edinburgh: Scottish University Press.

Sanford, A. J., & Garrod, S. C. (1981). *Understanding written language*. New York: Wiley.

Svensson, L. (1979). *The context dependent meaning of learning*. Reports from the Institute of Education, University of Göteborg, no. 2.

Vygotsky, L. S. (1962). *Thought and language*. Cambridge, Ma.: MIT Press.

CHAPTER 12
Insight into Understanding

Erik Jan van Rossum

The reading and understanding of texts is probably the most important learning activity in higher education. Doblaev (1984, p. 12) feels it is obvious that "... the cultivation of skills to handle study texts and to understand them, is of great importance to the development of the creative activity in opposition to merely acquiring an amount of knowledge". He states, as does Brudnyi (cf. Doblaev, 1984, p. 19), that the problem of understanding texts reveals two basic, allied aspects:

- A psychological analysis of the object of the activity (the text)
- The study of the psychic activity itself (the process of understanding the text)

Although we agree with this statement, in this article, the emphasis will be on one of the aspects; to be precise, the various ways in which students conceive of the process of understanding.

An Example

Doblaev (1984, p. 13) justifiably asks himself what understanding a text really covers. In the following anecdote, he sketches a striking picture of the different levels at which, in his opinion, the process of understanding can manifest itself.

> In the group it was decided to read *Das Kapital* by Marx.... And the torment began. However not because Marx immediately defeated us with complicated constructions or other difficult things. No, on the contrary, already in the first chapter we succumbed to very evident issues, of which he made ridiculously elaborate points. "The commodity is primarily an external article, a thing that can satisfy every human desire through its properties..." So what? That I understood very well indeed. "20 yards linen = 1 long coat, or 20 yards of linen is enough for one long coat." That too I understood perfectly. What then is it really about? The case was that we understood every separate word very well. The words made sentences which we also understood. But when we wanted to integrate these

sentences to a whole, everything came tumbling down and we remained – not understanding it at all – amidst the rubble after which, agonized, we started all over again.

Supported by research, Brudnyi also discerns a number of levels of understanding texts (Doblaev, 1984, p. 19). At the first level, the process of understanding is one where "one subsequently moves from one meaningful part of the text to the next meaningful part". At the next level, the strategy changes as follows: "the focus of the mind does shift from one element to another, but this shift need not always concur with the actual sequence of elements in the text, because there are also leaps backwards". At the third level, "the basic thought, the overall meaning of the text is formed, which mostly is of an extra textual nature (meaning to say it isn't precisely phrased)". It may be noted that in the past such subsequent levels of understanding texts have also been discerned (van Rossum & Schenk, 1984). Further on in this article, it will become clear that the understanding of texts is indeed interpreted differently by students and that these different interpretations are linked with subsequent stages in the development of thinking about the nature of the learning process itself.

Understanding Magnified

Before going into this last point, we would like to put the concept of understanding under the magnifying glass, by analysing answers given by several subjects participating in the 1984 study. The fact that new students in tertiary education experience this concept as troublesome may become evident in the following answer to the question: What do *you* mean by *learning*? (with regard to this notion of *conceptions of learning*, see also Säljö, 1979; van Rossum & Schenk, 1984):

> In practice learning means to me studying the subject matter a few days before a test and then filling in a small questionnaire (= test). Learning things by heart in a short time, which, however, you forget rather easily. Preferably I would like to learn by understanding the subject matter, and by studying the material actively through which you understand it better and remember and learn much more.

The problems around this concept are probably connected to the nature of the preceding, secondary education. From research involving teachers in secondary education (van Rossum, 1984) it becomes clear that they emphasize reproduction of knowledge, especially in the case of teaching languages. The importance of understanding and insight is brought forward almost exclusively by the teachers of subjects such as physics and chemistry, a phenomenon that can also be found in many (33 %) of the students' answers (third grade of secondary education) although in most answers (42 %), learning is merely seen as a process involving memorizing and reproducing:

Learning: knowing it by heart, but this is with English etc., the languages you can learn by heart, but with physics and mathematics you have to get to understand it and this they also call learning.

Moreover, as Doblaev (1984) states, understanding texts actually is not being taught at school:

> Some teachers even find the question about teaching understanding and insight into the meaning of texts odd. For instance we heard the following reaction: "You can teach children to solve math, physics and chemistry sums. But to understand a text? I wouldn't know how". (Doblaev, 1984, p. 14).

To us, it seems plausible that (good) teaching of text understanding can be stimulated when more data about the nature of the process of understanding become known by means of research. An immediate side effect of this would be that also students' thinking about learning would be furthered in a more insight-aimed way. In our studies, first year students in higher education differ very little from students halfway through secondary education with regard to their thoughts about learning and understanding. The next two answers display how little students' thinking sometimes develops in secondary education (the time gap between the answers is nearly four years):

> First answer: third grade, secondary education:
> "Learning: that you understand it and in most cases also know it a bit".

> Second answer: first year, tertiary education:
> "Learning means to me especially: understanding. Because I believe that you, when you understand something well, you also *know* it".

From the examples above, in our opinion, an image of the process of understanding emerges that is somewhat atomistic, detail aimed (as is also brought out in the quote about reading *Das Kapital* by Marx). These students evidently interpret understanding texts as understanding *everything* that is said (every word, every sentence). To show the importance and the implications of different interpretations of the process of understanding, we shall first expand on a number of protocols we have collected in the past.

A Reproductive View

In the learning conception of the next student, the process of understanding is viewed in an essentially reproductive way as in the previous instances:

> When I try to memorize subject matter, I try to make connections and learn with understanding as much as possible. I feel that simply drumming things into my head is pointless.

In our opinion, this subject merely distinguishes between memorizing with and without understanding; in short, the basic conception is reproductive.

The study strategy used by this student, when reading a text, supports this reproductive interpretation (the same text was used in van Rossum & Schenk, 1984):[1]

> I read the text as attentively as possible and underlined the most important things. After this I tried to memorize the underlined parts twice.

When this student is asked to construct from memory a table of contents for this text, we get the following type of table of contents (abbreviated as table):

Introduction
Punishment
Causes
Review

It will soon become clear how qualitatively poorly this answer compares to another type of table. The quality of the learning outcome often used in this type of research (the answer to the question on the essence of a text) also credits a reproductive interpretation of the process of understanding:

- Around 1734 the Bokkerijders (goat riders), roaming gangs of thieves, were very active in Southern Limburg. It was said that they conspired with the devil and flew through the air on the backs of their goats.
- They chiefly stole from churches and rectories, so that especially the authorities saw them as a revolutionary movement.
- Two periods are discerned in which they were particularly active: 1735–1755 and 1760–1775.
- Often they were tortured without any evidence to such an extent that they had to confess willy-nilly.
- In retrospect the Bokkerijders stole very little; they carried off little in many raids.
- The cause of their tendency to crime is sought in external influences: foreign tramps, like gypsies.
- The case being that they were there long before 1734, the author feels the cause must lie with poverty, dipsomania, unemployment, climatic influences, war circumstances, roaming about.
- Because of harvest failures the prices went up; poor farmers had to steal to stay alive and began scouring the countryside.

The dashes in the margin were put there to indicate that this answer is best characterized as an *enumeration* of main *and* side issues in the text. The

---

1 This text is a historical treatise on an alleged gang of robbers that roamed Southern Limburg in the eighteenth century. The author unravels the legends by pointing to social circumstances and judicial persecution. The empirical material presented here comes from a study of the relationship between conceptions of learning and study strategies in which this text was used. In this study, first-year psychology students were asked to read the text as if it were a regular study text.

intention of the author is mentioned, but not used as *relating concept* to forge the answer into a coherent and correct whole.

A Constructive View

A more constructive attitude with regard to the process of understanding is found in the learning conception of another student:

> By learning I would mean, for as far as the material permits mastering a text or theory (mostly) in the course of which it is especially desirable that the main line is understood, and consequently that there are relations, because of which details are also better retained.

Here, in contrast with the corresponding answer given by the former student, the process of understanding is seen as a very much holistic, main-line directed activity. Such an interpretation is also supported by the description of the way in which the same student studied the previously mentioned text:

> First, I quietly read the whole text through. Then I made some notes in the form of underlinings, arrows, etc., after which I worked through the whole thing again with main points and essence marked.

The type of table this student constructed for the text looks qualitatively better than the former type:

1. Introduction
2. The legend of the Bokkerijders
3. Time and place of the Bokkerijders phenomenon
4. Cause of historiography and notoriety: the legal practice
5. The soco-economic cause of the phenomenon: pauperism

Lastly, the quality of the learning outcome (the answer to the question on the essence of the text) also shows that this student has a more holistic view of the process of understanding:

> The phenomenon of the "Bokkerijders" appeared in the eighteenth century. It consisted of groups of agricultural labourers, small farmers and craftsmen, who were forced into stealing and plundering by rapidly spreading pauperism. They got their name from the widespread rumour that they moved through the air on the backs of goats. Their notoriety is due more to judicial practice than to actual criminal activity.

This answer is, in our opinion, a coherent whole that is "only" based on the main issues of the text. When one compares these answers with those of the first student, two, evidently different, interpretations of the process of under-standing emerge. Doblaev (1984, p. 82) also discerns two levels of understand-ing which seem to overlap with the distinction described above. He describes the lowest level of understanding (see the answers of the first student) as incomplete and deceptive:

> When the pupil reads texts as part of the study material and he doesn't use strategies to seek out the meaning of them, then he is unaware whether he understands the text or not, or he will experience a deceptive feeling: he thinks he has understood something, while at the same time it remains incomprehensible (pp. 81–82).

Doblaev briefly indicates the consequences of such an attitude towards understanding (p. 82):

> The child can't answer questions about the deeper lying meaning of the subject-matter. The pupil becomes confused. He has prepared himself so carefully for this lesson and at home, while learning, he understood everything. How else should you learn then?

Understanding: An Integrative View

The question is, for that matter, whether the two interpretations of the process of understanding treated cover all possible levels of understanding. A third student who remarks that "learning to me is learning to understand" obviously interprets the process of understanding in an even deeper way:

> Learning in a broad sense is the acquiring of insight and knowledge about what takes place on the interface between myself and the outside world. The aim of learning is to be able to organize the outside world, through an interactive process between the outside world and myself, in such a way that I have a grip on this outside world. Having a grip on the outside world has as goal to bring myself in harmony with the environment.

The strategy this student uses when studying a text shows that at this level, holistic and atomistic learning activities are integrated to arrive at an optimal understanding of the text (as another student with such a learning conception phrased it: "..knowledge and insight are two sides of the same coin. The one cannot be without the other"):

> First I read through the text and try to form a picture of the content. The second time I read more accurately and try through the structure of the text to make the small connections in and between the paragraphs. The third or fourth time I try to repeat to myself, without looking at the text, the main lines of the argument, emphasizing the reasoning.

The type of table found at this level belongs, in a qualitative sense, to the category of the best answers (a completely correct table):

1. Legend of the Bokkerijders
2. Causes of legend generation
3. Organization of the persecution and method of interrogation

4. Causes of the gang appearing
5. Conclusion

One must note that only a remarkably small number of students in this study were able to produce a complete and correct table for the text. In a number of cases, it was evident that the students did not even know what was meant by this assignment: the concept table of contents was, for instance, confused with the making of a reference list or a summary. Anyway, this result shows once more (cf. van Rossum & Schenk, 1984) that many first-year students do not possess the (study) skills their teachers take for granted.

In his somewhat abstract answer to the question on the essence of the text, this student explicitly discusses the author's intent:

> In a legend about a gang of robbers in the eighteenth century there is talk of thefts and robberies which mostly took place within two intervals of time. These robbers were supposed to move through the air on the backs of goats, that's why they were called Bokkerijders. The author says that this gang was no exception at that time and that during the whole of the eighteenth century such gangs existed contrary to what the legend wants us to believe.

Lastly, a special characteristic of this level of thinking about learning and the understanding of texts (cf. van Rossum, Deijkers, & Hamer, 1985) is the ability to take a truly critical standpoint of which this student, in contrast to the former two students, clearly gives evidence of in another answer:

> I observe whether the structure is logical and I look into the nature of the arguments supporting a statement, for instance, to what extent are certain causes generalizable, etc. . . .

With regard to this last answer, it is interesting to compare it to what the first student interprets "being critical" to mean, namely, to see whether (or not) what the author says is true: "I have looked at the story critically, but just like witch-hunts these sorts of phenomena were fairly common in earlier days. People were executed without evidence or reason".

From the above, it will have become clear that not only the process of understanding study texts is subject to different interpretations, but that also, for instance, "being critical" can be interpreted in a number of different ways. In another example, taken from the literature on arithmetic and mathematics education (Treffers, ter Heege, & Dekker, 1982; and also van Rossum, 1984, p. 8), in one sentence we come across three different conceptions of "application of knowledge":

What we mean by applications: not only application as *ap-plication-afterwards*, but also application *integrated* in the formal arithmetic, and even preceding it as *pre-plication*, as point of departure for the development of understanding.

In van Rossum et al. (1985) we have described these three conceptions of "application of knowledge" and their corresponding conceptions of learning.

The Impact of Conceptions of Learning on the Interpretation of Understanding

This last example brings us to a theme that we would like to discuss to some extent as we feel it to be an essential part of this article. In our opinion, it is obvious that one should look into the matter of to what extent the various interpretations of the process of understanding are related to the five different conceptions of learning that in the past have been discerned by Säljö (1979; 1982) and by us (in addition to the previously mentioned articles, also in van Rossum & Deijkers, 1984; van Rossum & Hamer, 1985): in these studies, learning is subsequently seen as
- The acquisition of knowledge (vague)
- Memorizing, reproducing knowledge
- The ability to apply knowledge (at a later time)
- The gaining of insight into the subject matter
- The gaining of insight into reality

However, it must be pointed out that we, in contrast to the Göteborg group, see learning conceptions as manifestations of an epistemological development which takes place *within* the university context and *during* the period of university studies. Säljö's (1982) work, for that matter, also provides evidence of a developmental perspective (see also Epilogue).

In a study, in which we (van Rossum et al., 1985) wanted to find out the different ways in which students view various aspects of the teaching-learning process, 42 arts students were asked to define *the understanding of a text*, and *insight into the subject matter*. From the results, it not only became clear that these concepts were interpreted differently by the students, but also that a specific interpretation linked up logically, as well as empirically, with the corresponding learning conception. We shall try to clarify this by means of a few examples.

At the first level of thinking about learning, learning conception 1, learning is interpreted somewhat homogeneously as "getting to know all sorts of things" and a very atomistic and undifferentiated meaning is given to the process of understanding and insight:

> So I have understood a text when for me there are no more difficulties in it and I can explain this text to someone else.

Understanding at this level evidently means that one has understood *everything*. Moreover understanding is not per se necessary:

> Understanding the subject matter and learning the subject matter are very different things. You may well learn something without understanding it.

The second level of thinking about learning, learning conception 2, is characterized by the strong emphasis that is put on the ability to memorize the material, with the goal of being able to reproduce it in an examination. We find this theme again in the answers to the question about the meaning of understanding and insight:

> I have understood a text when I literally understand what is said and when I can apply this in an exam. For me to understand a text and to apply it is something very different from having insight into the subject matter: when I have insight *and* understanding of a text I'll get the best results. But I can also get good marks when I just understand the text – I only repeat what is said. For me, the latter is not satisfying because then I don't see why I do things the way I do. I only have insight into the subject matter when I really stand above it and for instance can put the various texts together.

Even though insight is distinguished from understanding, the difference between these two concepts is not very clear to students at this level. This interpretation is confirmed by the answer of another student in this category:

> I don't find the difference between "understanding" and "having insight" so large. Perhaps that "having insight" goes a little further than the text itself, that then you also understand (?) in which framework you must place the text itself, where it fits into the picture of that subject. Understanding could then, for instance, relate to the structure of the text. But the difference isn't very clear to me.

In our opinion (see also van Rossum et. al., 1985), these students see insight as a more general (but vague) case of understanding. The possibility of later use or application of what is learnt before forms the central theme at the next level of thinking about learning, learning conception 3. This theme is again prominent in the answers to the question about understanding and insight:

> "Understanding", "having insight into the subject matter": by this I don't actually mean the fact that you can literally reproduce all kinds of facts and definitions, etc., but more so that you can follow the continuous thread through the subject matter, that you know what it's about in a broad sense (that you can reproduce it generally in your own words). Besides I think that, if you understand the subject matter, you must then be able to use it, to apply it to other areas or problems, to discuss it.

This student discerns two forms of understanding, namely (a) the overall knowledge of and ability to reproduce the subject matter; and (b) the ability to apply it. Sometimes, these two forms are disconnected from each other and respectively reconnected with understanding and insight:

> Having insight into the subject matter goes in my opinion a lot deeper than understanding. Then you not only understand what it's about, but you also see how it can be used, what can be done with it. You are able to see the applications, or the usefulness of it.

Characteristic of the levels of thinking about learning treated up to now is that understanding and insight are of a fundamentally reproductive nature. Within this reproductive domain, the students discern several variants of understanding and insight which very gradually evolve in the direction of a more constructive interpretation. At the fourth level of thinking about learning, learning conception 4, we encounter for the first time such an interpretation: learning is then, rather technically, seen as the penetration to the main lines, the relations within and between the subjects. The interpretation of understanding "of course" causes no problems at this level:

> *Understanding a text*: knowing what a text is about; knowing what the theme of a text is; what the author of a text has tried to get across to the reader.

> *Insight into the subject matter*: if you can see interrelationships between different texts and perhaps the lecture notes and can then discover the main lines in them (the entire subject matter) and maybe connect them to other subjects.

It will be clear that, in essence, the meaning given to understanding and insight at this level boils down to the comprehension of fundamental relations but that the object in question the text, the subject(s), etc. can be chosen more or less broadly. The latter provides some variation in the students' answers. Moreover, understanding and insight are not always distinguished. The next answer is an example of this:

> By understanding a text and having insight into the subject matter I don't mean that I have to understand every line or every passage precisely. Primarily, I want to discover the general main lines of reasoning in a text. Once I have found them, it frequently happens that a whole lot more becomes clear. But once I've got the main lines of reasoning, I feel I have understood a text.

The fifth and final conception of learning (5) to be described here, is characterized by the fact that learning is viewed as a personal, self-directed activity aimed at gaining insight into reality. Concepts such as understanding and insight are interpreted in a very personal way at this level:

> You have probably understood a text well when you can rephrase the content, purport of a text rather easily in your own words, when you can support or oppose it with your own examples, when you can give a personal opinion about the clearness, the correctness, etc. of a text, when you can include the content, purport in your own arguments.

It is most remarkable that at this level the distinction between understanding and insight made by us seems less relevant; instead, a number of study activities are mentioned where the learner himself is always the focal point. This leads, as we see it, to the idea that the process of understanding texts acquires a very dynamic (creative and critical) character in contrast to the more business-like character to be found at the former level of thinking about learning. Also, (a creative view of) the concept of application, i.e. using knowledge, is incorporated into the whole now formed by understanding and insight:

> You must be able to rephrase, in your own words, what the essence of the text/subject matter is and how it fits together; you must be able to use it as a base for further work.

This student sees this "using" as follows:

Using your knowledge in a way which is not reproducing, but problem-solving.

The answer given by one student suggests the existence of a sixth learning conception which, in the past (van Rossum & Deijkers, 1984), we have already found several times in our data: learning seen as a process of self-actualization. According to this student, learning consists of several levels, namely (in her own words):

1. Pure things-to-know
2. Less tangible things such as co-operating, discussing, being critical, etc.
3. A kind of human being who has 'learnt' to combine these things, 1 and 2, to be creative, who's interested in what he does and is prepared to reflect on this with others.

Her view on the process of understanding texts is clear:

You understand a text when you could have written it yourself.

Epilogue

In this article, we have tried to demonstrate that the activity of understanding study texts is interpreted differently by students and that, moreover, these different interpretations seem to flow from the logically corresponding conceptions of the nature of the learning process in general. In other words, the observations reveal a case of *homogeneous* thought and action patterns. This design is, in our opinion, in keeping with the objectives of a recent study by Säljö (1982) aimed at describing qualitative differences in the view of learning and, in connection with this, in the activity of understanding texts:

When people learn, then, they take certain things for granted. It is precisely this which is our concern in the present study: to reveal the meaning that the act of learning acquires for different people and how this relates to what and how they learn (Säljö, 1982, p. 24).

Säljö not only argues for the existence of homogeneous thought and action patterns with regards to learning and understanding, but also for the proposition that the transition from one pattern to another must be seen from a *developmental perspective*:

The distinction between a "flat" reproductive and a "thematic" constructive conception of learning can in consequence be conceived of as tapping some kind of *developmental dimension*. What is involved is a change in a person's basic assumptions about the critical criteria applicable in considering something as knowledge (Säljö, 1982, p. 192).

In accordance with Säljö, and also Perry (1970), we feel that this sort of study supports the assertion that, within the context of the school or university, there exists a number of qualitatively different thought and action patterns with regard to all sorts of aspects of the teaching-learning process. These patterns are also arranged in time in a certain way, i.e. in order of increasing complexity. Within these patterns of thinking and acting there is a large measure of homogeneity: a certain way of thinking about learning and knowledge is accompanied by a logically corresponding conception of reading texts, the nature of (good) teaching, the process of understanding, etc. Our studies up to now (especially van Rossum & Schenk, 1984; van Rossum & Deijkers, 1984 and van Rossum et al., 1985) have without exception supported such a standpoint. The research into the reading and understanding of study texts should, we feel, take such findings seriously. Instead of the traditional striving for very general conceptualizations, research should adopt a more *contextual* approach within which allowances are made for the underlying individual meaning systems (cf. also Svensson, 1979; Säljö, 1982).

Finally, what has been said so far begs the question of to what extent students' conceptions of learning and understanding can attain a more constructive nature by means of systematic training. Developmental research (Perry, 1970; van Rossum et al., 1985) suggests that changes in the above mentioned patterns of thinking and acting occur very slowly. Doblaev (1984) describes an interesting attempt to teach pupils the *basic strategy for understanding texts*, namely, the (independent) seeking out of the hidden questions in a text and the finding out of the answers to them. Without using this strategy consciously, Doblaev feels pupils cannot really understand a text and, moreover, they will not even notice what they do not understand in the text (see also introduction by van Parreren in Doblaev, 1984, pp. 73–74). Examples of hidden questions are: *What would the author mean by this?*, *Why would that be so?*, etc. and, from the formulation of the basic strategy, it is evident that Doblaev views a text as a collection of *problem situations*. Really understanding a text consequently boils down to solving a number of (open) problem situations which contain a hidden question. On the basis of his studies, Doblaev draws the conclusion that this basic strategy is only to a small measure used consciously by students in secondary and upper-secondary school, an argument that Doblaev considers points to the necessity of systematic training. The effect of such a training (characterized by a diminishing fragmentation of the text and increasing pupil independence with regard to the posing and solving of the hidden questions) is best described as follows:

> A remarkable result of the experiments is, that the subjects not only learn to use the basic strategy, but also discover and start to use independently some of the derivable strategies: the question-with-guess, the expressing of a conjecture, the anticipation and the review. These strategies are mutually interrelated and are partly to be seen as shortening the procedure of the basic strategy (Doblaev, 1984, p. 111).

What is perhaps more interesting is Doblaev's discovery that the process of teaching strategies for understanding texts consists of four stages which can be briefly summarized as follows:

Stage 1. Here, the posing of questions by the pupils mostly takes place after inducement by the experimenter and moreover the questions are often superficial, they contribute little to a real understanding of the text and link up with arbitrary, not essential details (Doblaev, 1984, p. 125).

Stage 2. The pupils begin to work much more independently and their questions are more often aimed at the essentials of the text. But in opposition to this stands the fact that they view the assignment to understand a text as an assignment to memorize this text. Their questions, as it were, run ahead of the (memory) questions which they think that the experimenter might possibly pose later (Doblaev, 1984, p. 127).

Stage 3. This stage shows the break-through to the independent formulating of questions subservient to understanding the text. Beside the basic strategy the pupils make ample use of the derived strategies mentioned above (Doblaev, 1984, p. 129).

Stage 4. The pupils are able to use the acquired strategies in new problem situations. Moreover they give evidence of a critical (argument-supported) attitude towards a text. Lastly in this stage, a dynamic state of *ready mental activity and preparedness to solve problems in texts* is found, which may become clear from expressions as "suddenly it flashed through my head", "suddenly I thought", "it was hardly noticable, but I felt it", etc. (Doblaev, 1984, p. 130–135).

In our opinion, these four stages display a striking resemblance to the levels of thinking of and acting towards learning and understanding described in this article (see also van Rossum & Hamer, 1985; van Rossum et al., 1985). Doblaev's results suggest that text understanding is indeed teachable and, at the same time, that the quality of the process of understanding is closely related to the quality of education. The latter is strongly confirmed by the following danger indicated by Doblaev: "However the largest problem still remains whether the time used for teaching strategies to understand texts in the end will yield more than only 'local' or temporary results" (Doblaev, 1984, p. 136).

References

Doblaev, L. P. (1984). *Studieteksten lezen en begrijpen* [Reading and understanding study texts]. Apeldoorn: van Walreven.

Perry, W. G. (1970). *Forms of intellectual and ethical development in the college years: A scheme.* New York: Holt, Rinehart & Winston.

Säljö, R. (1979). *Learning in the learner's perspective. I. Some common-sense conceptions.* Reports from the Institute of Education, Göteborg University, no. 76.

Säljö, R. (1982). *Learning and understanding.* Göteborg: Acta Universitatis Gothoburgensis.

Svensson, L. (1979). *The context-dependent meaning of learning.* Reports from the Institute of Education, Göteborg University, no. 82.

Treffers, A., ter Heege, H., & Dekker, A. (1982). Het stomste vak van de wereld (deel 2) [The most stupid subject in the world – part 2]. *Willem Bartjens, 1 (2)*, 81–88.

van Rossum, E. J. (1984, August). *Arithmetic and mathematics education – as a phenomenon and/or a problem of communication*. Paper presented at the 8th International Conference on the Psychology of Mathematics Education, Sydney University, Sydney, N.S.W., Australia.

van Rossum, E. J., & Deijkers, R. (1984, July). *Students' conceptions of learning and good teaching*. Paper presented at the 10th International Conference on Improving University Teaching, Maryland, U.S.A.

van Rossum, E. J., & Hamer, R. (1985, July). *Learning: qualitative differences between novices and experts*. Paper presented at the 11th International Conference on Improving University Teaching, Utrecht University, Utrecht, The Netherlands.

van Rossum, E. J., & Schenk, S. M. (1984). The relationship between learning conception, study strategy and learning outcome. *British Journal of Educational Psychology, 54*, 73–83.

van Rossum, E. J., Deijkers, R., & Hamer, R. (1985). Students' learning conceptions and their interpretation of significant educational concepts. *Higher Education, 14*, 617–641.

Author Index

Subject Index